WATCHING SHAKESPEARE

Also by Anthony B. Dawson

INDIRECTIONS: SHAKESPEARE AND THE ART OF ILLUSION

Watching Shakespeare

A Playgoers' Guide

ANTHONY B. DAWSON
Associate Professor of English and Drama
University of British Columbia

St. Martin's Press   New York

First published in the United States of America in 1988

Printed in Hong Kong

ISBN 0–312–01563–1

Library of Congress Cataloging-in-Publication Data
Dawson, Anthony B.
Watching Shakespeare: a playgoers' guide / Anthony B. Dawson.
p.   cm.
Bibliography: p.
Includes index.
ISBN 0–312–01563–1: $30.00 (est.)
1. Shakespeare, William, 1564–1616—Dramatic production.
2. Shakespeare, William, 1564–1616—Stage history. I. Title.
PR3091.D33   1988
822.3'3—dc19   87–24166
                                                      CIP

For Honey

There is a fourth creator in addition to the author, the director and the actor — namely the spectator . . . from the friction between the actor's creativity and the spectator's imagination, a clear flame is kindled.

(Vsevolod Meyerhold)

Contents

List of Plates

Preface

Glancing through the bookstall at a major festival theatre a few years ago, I was surprised to observe that, among the many books about Shakespeare, there did not seem to be one available that would exactly suit the needs of most of the audience members who were at that moment browsing around. Since for many years I have been reading, writing about, teaching and acting in Shakespeare's plays, I set myself the task of filling what I saw as a need. The present book is the result. It has been written specifically with the interests of the playgoer in mind. I have tried to approach each play from the point of view of key decisions about it that actors and director must make in order to put it on the stage. Audiences aware of such issues will, I believe, be better able to understand and assess what they see. Since Shakespeare's plays are so various, and the imaginations of performing artists so fertile, the possibilities for performance are almost limitless. Nevertheless, each play poses particular questions and challenges which performers have to face. In discussing these, I have drawn extensively on recent (and not so recent) production history, giving as many examples as I could to illustrate varying approaches. The range of examples will, I hope, make the book useful for students as well as playgoers, indeed for anyone interested in what happens to Shakespeare's plays on the stage.

Since I wanted to handle the oppositions and balances of each play thoroughly, I could not afford to skimp on my treatment of any one. I have thus had to limit the number of plays covered. Still, I have managed to include just about half of them, concentrating on those most frequently performed. Some very popular plays (*The Taming of the Shrew, Merry Wives, Much Ado about Nothing*) I have unfortunately had to leave out, choosing rather to deal with texts that present more complex problems. Some of my selections and omissions may not meet with universal approval, but I was guided by a sense of the theatrical issues raised by a particular play as well as by personal preference. I have grouped the plays by generic category, comedies, histories, tragedies and romances, and have ordered them chronologically within each category. And I have included an introduction that deals briefly with some important background: the contribution of the audience to the stage event, general trends in twentieth-century production of Shakespeare, the role of the director and the designer, and the crucial place of the actor.

An effective way for a playgoer to use the book would be to read the relevant chapter either shortly before or shortly after going to see a performance. (I have assumed at least vague familiarity with the characters and plot.) For anyone studying the plays or deprived of the opportunity of seeing them performed, I would hope that reading this book would make it easier to imagine them on the stage, where they were meant to be. Television and films help, but they are not the ideal media for Shakespeare. I have therefore not paid them too much attention, although I have discussed some of the most outstanding films and taken a few examples from the widely available BBC series.

I have been at work on this book for some time now and have incurred a number of debts: to the staff at the Harvard Theatre Collection and at the Shakespeare Memorial Library in Stratford-upon-Avon; to Dan Ladell at the Festival archives in Stratford, Ontario; to friends and colleagues who have read and commented on parts of the manuscript, especially Crispin Elsted, Joel Kaplan, Peter Schwenger and Herb Weil; to secretaries Jody Harper and Doreen Todhunter; and to Frances Arnold at the Macmillan Press. My dedication records a different, and much deeper, debt.

Introduction

'Theatre', says Peter Brook, 'is always a self-destructive art and it is always written on the wind.'[1] That is perhaps the chief source of its fascination. Paradoxically, its very transitory quality accounts often for its power, the almost revolutionary force that it sometimes exhibits, when it focuses the aspirations or aggressions of particular groups at particular times. In his own era, Shakespeare himself came face to face with this fact when some followers of the Earl of Essex arranged and paid for a performance of *Richard II* on the eve of their ill-fated (and ill-organized) rebellion. Seeing their leader as a new Bolingbroke ready to assume power from a Richard-like Queen Elizabeth, these men interpreted Shakespeare's play in the light of their own desires and their own sense of the pressure of the times.

They were, however, only an audience, commissioning a performance. Today's directors, some will say, go farther than this, since they impose their interpretations on the productions for which they are responsible, and hence on the audiences which go to see them. Those hopeful followers of the Earl of Essex presumably did not direct the show they witnessed, though who can say what effect their presence and the money they had paid had on the actors who performed it? Did Bolingbroke emerge a trifle less tarnished and Richard a trifle more arbitrary and self-willed than either had appeared in previous presentations on the public stage?

Neither audiences nor directors are likely to see Shakespeare's plays in quite that same way again, but some twentieth-century productions have had profound political effects: for example, the allegedly anti-democratic *Coriolanus* at the Comédie Française in Paris in 1933–4, mounted at a time of acute political crisis, which was wildly applauded by the Right and hissed by the Left, the curtain having to be lowered twenty times during the opening performance; or, again, Orson Welles' vigorously anti-fascist version of *Julius Caesar* in 1937, a production which has led to many another highly politicized interpretation of that play. Currently, at least in the English-speaking world, such overtly political readings of Shakespeare are not much in evidence. But other kinds of interpretations, usually the work of individual directors, are. What we are more likely to get now is a *Henry V* or a *King John* which

1

presents a vision of cynicism or corruption throughout the body politic, a *Macbeth* in which evil is in no way dissipated by the death of the hero, an *As You Like It* or *Twelfth Night* darkened and saddened, or a *Tempest* which emphasizes the cruelty or inner turmoil of its presenter–magician.

All these different versions of Shakespeare reveal the need and the power of the theatre to speak to its own time, in the idiom of its own time, to define or confirm a vision of the life from which it emerges. But the very contemporaneousness of the theatre tends to date it as well. If we look at the photos or a programme from a production of only fifteen or twenty years ago, we may be startled to find that a performance then hailed as brilliant now looks as stiff and 'unnatural' as an old fashion-magazine. Like other aspects of culture, Shakespeare has continually to be renewed.

But this poses a problem, since Shakespeare was also an Elizabethan, writing for *his* time. The most difficult task of the modern director is to reconcile the different, often conflicting, claims of Shakespeare the Elizabethan and Shakespeare 'our contemporary'. Various positions have of course been taken on this question, from the view that Elizabethan stage conditions should as far as possible be adopted, to the opposite view that Shakespeare can easily become 'deadly' (Brook's term) and requires total rethinking with no preconceptions whatever nor any particular allegiance to what Shakespeare wrote or what he might possibly have meant. Fascinating theatre has been made from this latter view, Joseph Papp's 'naked' *Hamlet*, for example, or Welles' voodoo *Macbeth*. But few stage directors will go that far; most will say they seek to make Shakespeare speak to the modern world. On this, it is worth quoting Peter Brook, the most radically innovative and one of the most brilliant of Shakespearean directors: 'When I hear a director speaking glibly of serving the author, of letting a play speak for itself, my suspicions are aroused, because this is the hardest job of all . . . if what you want is for the play to be heard, then you must conjure its sound from it.'[2]

When you go to a play, you are at the mercy of the director. Nowhere is this truer than in productions of Shakespeare, for, throughout the English-speaking world, directors and actors still see Shakespeare as the ultimate test of their mettle. Hence they have to flex their artistic muscles. Furthermore, Shakespeare is so *familiar*. The temptation for the director is to pass the test the easy way, simply by being *different*, even if this means falsifying or ignoring the text. Festivals all over Britain, the United States and Canada, as well as repertory companies in major cities, are proving that Shakespeare is good 'box office'. Although this in itself is heartening, it also means that festivals and repertory theatres have to keep drawing crowds, and, to do so, they may be tempted to novelty for its own sake. One thing, perhaps the most important, that will keep the theatre on its toes is an informed audience. Most audience members are probably unaware of how important they are, of how much actually depends on them to make a theatrical event happen. Audiences are a crucial part of the transitory, magical amalgam that is theatre.

There are really only two essentials in theatre, an actor and an audience. When a street entertainer, a juggler, say, or a magician, gathers a crowd around him, the theatrical event is born. I remember one fascinating theatrical experience that took place unexpectedly in a small, crowded Montreal bar during the spring of 1980. A young American street magician was called in from outside to perform. A few people had noticed him through the window, a spontaneous movement erupted and he was suddenly among us, speaking rapidly and confidently in a hip, entertainer's lingo and dazzling us with the most amazing sleight-of-hand I've ever seen. Cards changed in people's hands without their being aware of it, sevens turned to jacks under our noses and all the while the patter sailed on. What added a special air to the performance was that the clientele was largely French-speaking, the girls asked to 'pick a card' barely able to understand. A large part of the fast talk was thus lost on the crowd, but it held them nevertheless. Furthermore the mood at that time, shortly after the defeat of the Quebec separatist referendum, was hardly receptive to the English language. Even so, for fifteen or twenty minutes a fast-talking, brash, utterly unapologetic American magician kept us all riveted, his language as important as his gesture. And, for me at least, the special piquancy of the event was created as much by the situation and the make-up of the audience as by the skill of the performer.

Any actor will tell you how different a production can be before an audience of critics and academics, for example, or, at the other extreme, before an audience of children (Peter Brook held one of the last dress rehearsals of his famous *Midsummer Night's Dream* before such an audience partly in an attempt to free his actors from traditional constraints). Even small things, a rainy night, a special mood, will play into the actors' response to their audience. The present book has been written with the unique role of the audience in mind. My aim is to inform, to offer ways of thinking about and assessing productions. But I do not seek to turn playgoers into critics – the negative force would scorch the actors. The first prerequisite of the audience is still receptivity, openness. If we come to the theatre on the look-out for faulty interpretation, unjustified cuts or the like, then that's all we'll find – and the experience will get lost. Rather, what I have in mind is to suggest questions about the plays, to discuss important scenes or characters in the light of what might be and has been done, to open up those areas of a play which demand interpretation from actor or director. My hope is that my reader will be better equipped to assess an interpretation, to see its consistency and its relevance, not only to the present but to Shakespeare's text as well. If we look at the choices a director has made and must make about a given play, we can go a long way towards understanding how he has conjured its sound from it.

Before proceeding to talk about individual plays, I need to touch upon some general issues. The historical position of the director (or 'producer', as he has often been called in England) can be put in perspective by a quick survey of Shakespearean production over the past eighty years or so. In addition, every director and group of actors is working on a particular stage, and the uses and limitations of various types of stages will to some extent determine the kind of production mounted. Most important are the actors themselves and what they bring to a production, how they rehearse, whether they are a company or an *ad hoc* gathering. All these factors will deeply affect the end product, the show that you watch.

The director is a relatively new phenomenon really. He came to prominence after the First World War, with the decline of the actor–manager, that legendary nineteenth-century figure who, like Sir Henry Irving at the Lyceum in London, or Frank Benson in the provinces, was director and manager of a company of which he was also the star actor. (The real precursor of the modern director is less the actor–manager, and more the writer–director of the later nineteenth century, men like Tom Robertson, W. S. Gilbert and Arthur Pinero, none of whom acted in the plays they produced.) The dominant status of the actor–manager in the production of Shakespeare could easily, and often did, lead to a grandiose distortion for the enhancement of the actor. This was also the time of magnificently elaborate, 'realistic', scenery, the demands of which often led to wholesale rearrangements of Shakespeare's fast-moving inter-cut scenes, in order to reduce the number of necessary scene changes. Sir Herbert Beerbohm Tree's live rabbits released on the stage during the forest scenes of *A Midsummer Night's Dream* are simply the best-known example of the scenic extravagance that included, for *As You Like It*, 2000 potted ferns, large clumps of bamboo, and cartloads of fallen leaves, and, for *Julius Caesar*, 'real' on-stage clouds for the Forum scene, since it was held that the Roman Forum, being on high ground, could well (on that ominous day) have been in the fog![3]

Such extravagant verisimilitude was bound to be challenged; and it is really among the challengers, especially William Poel and Harley Granville-Barker, himself in the tradition of Robertson and Pinero, that the ancestors of the modern director must be sought. Poel was an enthusiast who wanted to return Shakespeare's plays to the Elizabethan conditions for which they were written – especially the open stage, which would eliminate scenic spectacle and thus allow for the fluid movement of actors across the stage, for the easy flow of one scene into another and for the development of intimacy between actor and audience. Granville-Barker, a follower of Poel's, but with a surer theatrical sense and a richer understanding of Shakespeare (his famous Prefaces are the mark of both), directed three West End productions between 1912 and 1914 (of *The Winter's Tale*, *Twelfth Night* and *A Midsummer Night's Dream*). These, in retrospect, can be seen as the crucial turning-point in the movement toward both the uncluttered, rapidly spoken style of production with which we are familiar, and the development of the director as *animateur*.

The key to the change was scenery. 'To invent a new hieroglyphic language of scenery, that, in a phrase, is the problem', wrote Granville-Barker at the time.[4] It was not just the awkwardness and extravagance of the traditional nineteenth-century set, or the long delays with curtain down while sets were shifted, that were under attack: underneath that distaste for romantic pictorialism which characterized people such as Granville-Barker and Shaw there was developing a new notion of the very meaning of stage illusion, one that was more in tune with the Elizabethan. 'We are less conscious of the artificiality of the stage where a few well-understood conventions, adroitly handled, are substituted for attempts at an impossible scenic verisimilitude', wrote Shaw in relation to one of

Poel's productions in the 1890s.[5] Peter Brook puts the matter succinctly: 'The Elizabethan stage was . . . just a place with some doors.'[6]

Through one of these doors comes a well-dressed gentleman who addresses the audience:

> Two households, both alike in dignity
> In fair Verona where we lay our scene . . .

and the audience is immediately transported to the burnished city of the Montagues and Capulets. That was the sort of thing Granville-Barker had in mind when he wrote in his Prefaces, 'Gain Shakespeare's effects by Shakespeare's means when you can. . . . But gain Shakespeare's effects; and it is your business to discern them.'[7] But he was no antiquarian. What he set out to do was to reproduce 'those conditions of the Elizabethan theatre which had a spiritual significance in the shaping of the plays'.[8] Brook, writing sixty years later, says something similar: Shakespeare's stage, he suggests, allowed the playwright 'free passage from the world of action to the world of inner impressions'.[9] The stage areas which Granville-Barker developed and utilized in his productions – the 'inner stage', the centre and the 'apron' – are still in use today and have led, in the design of some modern theatres, to the full development of the 'open stage', such as at Stratford Ontario, Minneapolis and Chichester. The apron especially required the elimination of the footlights and orchestra pit and the extension of the stage into the house. The result, wrote Shaw, was that, 'instead of the theatre being a huge auditorium with a picture frame at one end of it, the theatre is now a stage with some unnoticed spectators around it'.[10]

To eliminate the footlights was not just a convenience, but a gesture of defiance toward nineteenth-century stagecraft in general and a recognition of the growing importance of lighting on the modern stage. The advent of electricity had made possible a flexible, atmospheric style of lighting that could be integrated into avant-garde strategies of writing, acting and design such as characterized the 'new stagecraft' advocated by such theorist–practitioners as Adolphe Appia and Gordon Craig. Its principal aims were radical simplification and stylization, suggestiveness over direct statement; and lighting was of paramount importance. For Craig, it was 'the true and sole *material* of the Art of the Theatre'.[11] Light was potentially sculptural, expressionistic, decisive. The influence of the revolution in lighting and other aspects of staging proclaimed by Craig could hardly have escaped such innovators in Shakespearean production as Granville-Barker. And of course that influence, though tempered and transformed in a thousand ways, is still powerfully felt today.

Granville-Barker's attempt was to see the plays whole, rather than as a series of grand scenes with the actors 'in a new pictorial progress, sometimes compelling in its fashion, sometimes drowsily slow, and devised mostly at the expense of [the] text'.[12] The effects that could be gained by juxtaposing one scene with another, even by overlapping them slightly in Shakespeare's manner, by restoring the original text in its original order, by speaking the lines quickly and clearly, by sweeping 'the shadows from the stage as if they harboured germs',[13] by, especially, projecting the playing-space into the auditorium, these effects bespoke that 'spiritual significance' which Granville-Barker sought.

From there it was not long to the development of the Old Vic as a Shakespearean theatre and its presentation in the early 1920s of almost the entire Shakespeare canon, under the general directorship of Robert Atkins. Partly for economic, partly for aesthetic reasons, simplicity was the order of the day – as it was too at Stratford-upon-Avon, where W. Bridges-Adams throughout the twenties and early thirties was working according to the same principles. So dedicated was the latter to the integrity of Shakespeare's text that he earned the affectionate nickname of Unabridges-Adams. Thus the new movement launched by Poel and Granville-Barker began to dominate, assuring as it did so the central position of the director or 'producer'.

In the mid-twenties Shakespeare made his first appearance in modern dress, a garb which he has worn frequently but rather uncertainly ever since. *Hamlet* 'in plus-fours' from the Birmingham Repertory Theatre in 1925 was the shocker, alerting critics and public to a whole new set of possibilities and forcing them to think about the play in a new way. The flapper taste for outrageousness was lovingly met by Terence Gray at Cambridge over the following few years with productions that nearly match the wildest invention of the present day. There one could see the Duke of Venice playing with a yo-yo during Portia's famous speech on the quality of mercy, itself delivered from a swing, Sir Toby and Sir Andrew entering on roller skates, or Rosalind and Celia disguising themselves as a boy scout and girl guide.

By the thirties and forties, the old pictorial verisimilitude, the ponderous verse-speaking and the even more ponderous scene changes had disappeared. The public expected, and got, 'full texts at full speed, characters freshly considered, Shakespeare humanised'.[14] A new generation of actors, raised in the new school, had come to dominate – people as diverse as John Gielgud, Peggy Ashcroft, Laurence Olivier, Edith Evans and Alec Guinness. The director too, as the figure responsible for production and hence for the changes taking place, had established the critical importance of his position.

But the proscenium stage, modified to be sure and often fitted with a permanent, flexible set, still predominated. Some directors, notably Tyrone Guthrie, found it a hindrance. And in 1953 Guthrie had the chance to strike out in a new direction. Invited to Stratford Ontario to launch a Shakespeare Festival there, Guthrie, together with designer Tanya Moiseyevitch, created the first major 'open' stage, getting rid of the proscenium altogether, placing the audience firmly on three sides, providing a small projecting balcony and several entrances, two of which were downstage amid the first rows of seats.[15]

The open stage, it was felt, approximated the conditions of the Elizabethan stage for which Shakespeare's plays were written, without being slavishly antiquarian. Hence it would provide the flexibility, the freedom from the conventions of realistic illusion, the opportunity for continuous performance (one scene flowing smoothly, naturally, into the following one), and the intimacy between actor and audience characteristic of the Elizabethan theatre. The idea was not entirely new: Robert Atkins had staged three Shakespeare plays in a boxing-ring on the Blackfriars Road during the thirties;[16] and before that, in the early twenties, Nugent Monck had made out of a former chapel and baking-powder factory the Maddermarket Theatre at Norwich, with neither proscenium arch nor drop curtain, and with a balcony, an inner stage and a small intimate house.[17] Guthrie himself had some experience with 'in the round' theatre, beginning in 1937 with an improvised mounting of *Hamlet* in the ballroom of a Danish hotel after a planned outdoor production at Elsinore was rained out.[18] But the Stratford Ontario experiment was a major and much-heralded event; with its many successors, it launched a new trend which is now sufficiently well established for its drawbacks – mainly stemming from the fact that at any one time only a fraction of the audience can directly see and clearly hear any particular actor – as well as its advantages, to be apparent.

Nowadays, no matter what type of stage a Shakespearean play is presented on, some attempt will undoubtedly be made to reproduce the stage conditions for which the plays were originally written. In many respects, some form of the open stage is probably the easiest for this, but even within the proscenium, provided the theatre is not too large, most of Shakespeare's effects can in fact be gained.

Since the Second World War, and especially with the rise during the sixties and seventies of the Royal Shakespeare Company (RSC) as the major Shakespeare company in the world, the art of the theatre has become increasingly the art of the director. We now usually speak of Brook's *Midsummer Night's Dream*, Hall's *Hamlet*, Barton's *Richard II* or Nunn's *Macbeth*, and we refer in doing so to a unique stylistic approach that the director has brought to the play in question. The director deploys his or her actors and ideas about design, music, text, in the interests of a particular *concept* of the play, an interpretative idea about the play derived from and manifested in an extremely subtle attention to its details. Such ideas are often rather abstract, even academic, and it is no coincidence that the majority of RSC directors over the past twenty years have been university-trained, involved in the literary, as well as the theatrical, investigation of Shakespeare's texts. This has led to a close scrutiny of the poetic texture of the plays and an attempt to realize that texture in theatrical, often symbolic, ways. Production, in this view, becomes analogous to literary criticism, an attempt to illuminate the play from a particular vantage point. Few directors, however, would claim that their reading is definitive and all would agree that no production, any more than a work of criticism, can exhaust one of Shakespeare's plays.

As in the nineteenth century, and again in Granville-Barker's day, design is a key factor. Since about 1960, most notably at the influential RSC theatres in Stratford and, afterwards, London, there has been a strong movement away from naturalism toward a kind of symbolic or heightened realism in which designers have played a crucial part. Plays have been mounted in a glaring white box (*Midsummer Night's Dream*), in a large octagonal sand-pit (*Troilus and Cressida*), on a metallic structure fitted with staircases and a moving bridge (*Richard II*) and on a shaggy blood-red carpet (*Macbeth*), to cite just a few examples. The texture of the materials used, the stark geometry of the stage picture, and especially the possibilities provided by modern lighting techniques, have all been of major importance. One designer has written that the conviction throughout the period has been that stage objects ought to be given 'the dignity of objects in their own right' and that the stage itself should be given its 'reality' as an 'architectural extension of the auditorium rather than an illusionary life as a place elsewhere'.[19] This is certainly a very different notion of illusion from that of Beerbohm Tree. It is an illusion that makes no attempt to hide its fundamental theatricality.

Even those productions which set a play in a specific historical period, whether Elizabethan, modern, or some time in between, rely not on the illusion of, say, nineteenth-century Europe for *King Lear*, but rather on the solidity of those nineteenth-century objects themselves – chairs, tables, rugs, uniforms, cigars – to bring home the significance of the play to us in the late twentieth century. Whatever the choice that director and designer make about setting, lighting and costumes, it is likely nowadays to have some symbolic or conceptual, rather than illusionary value, the main aim of which is not to convince the audience of the actuality of what they are witnessing, but to embody some idea about the play.

As at the beginning of this century a reaction against the pictorial–illusionistic theatre set in, so, in recent years, there has been a good deal of persistent questioning, especially among academics, of the 'directors' theatre', with its tendency to impose intellectual and visual 'concepts' on the plays. Critics emphasize the distortion that can result from the act of interpreting, with its attendant temptation to cut the text to buttress the prevailing concept. A distinction has sprung up, but one in no way universally accepted, between 'open' directors, who let the play speak for itself, or at most simply make the choices it forces upon them, and 'interpretative' directors, who approach the play armed with a controlling idea.[20] The former are often seen as serving Shakespeare, the latter as serving themselves. Against this, Brook's pronouncement 'No play can speak for itself' perhaps speaks for itself![21]

Some writers have called for an end to the 'tyranny' of the director and a return to the actor; the cry is for a 'free Shakespeare', spontaneous, ambiguous, undirected, even unrehearsed.[22] But few would actually go that far, recognizing that the complex machinery and artistry of the modern theatre can hardly be forgotten, or abandoned to a kind of aesthetic Luddism, but recognizing too that it is upon the *actor*, even more than the director, that the life of the theatre ultimately depends. A balance, clearly, needs to be struck between the roles of these two central figures, and there is a good deal of evidence that this is what is happening. Simon Callow, himself a well-known and articulate actor, has recently made some radical proposals for changing the relationship between director and actors, arguing that the latter should hire directors rather than the other way round, and insisting on the primacy of 'the actor's delight in the opportunities afforded him by the writer'. If Callow's manifesto is unlikely to be put fully into practice, it may encourage a healthy new awareness on the part of directors and a fruitful partnership with the actor. In 1984, John Barton, a veteran RSC director, conducted a television series that was subsequently released as a book, on 'playing' Shakespeare, concentrating on the actor's handling of the text's rhythms and nuances. Although he remained the 'director', the whole project was a good example of co-operation with actors.[23] The directors' theatre has yielded a rich harvest of insights into the text as well as plenty of splendid theatrical experience, but it is true that its excesses have sometimes obscured both the actor and Shakespeare himself. If some redress of that imbalance seems in progress at the present time, then so much the better.

The same period as has seen the director take on such primacy in the RSC, at Stratford Ontario and elsewhere has also seen the development of a strong *company* of actors in such places, each with its own distinctive, evolving style. The advantages of a company, where actors get used to working intensely together, where major actors can, and often do, take on minor parts, where casting can be effectively planned, where a distinct style and even ideology can be developed (as with the RSC in the sixties) are many and obvious. The difficulties, both economic and artistic (the danger of self-satisfaction, of inbreeding and insularity), are equally apparent. Despite such problems, the established company has become the norm, and is overall far better for the production of Shakespeare. The kind of continuing training and self-examination that actors undergo within a company is simply not available outside such a structure, and serves to counterbalance the weight of the director.

We come back then, finally, to the actor. Our *experience* rests with him or her. That is what we treasure, and what we return to, what we mention at the intermission or as we push out through the doors, looking for a taxi or our car keys. The actor does two crucial things: he presents a character and he uses his own body, most especially his voice and his movements, to do so. How he views these functions – whether, say, he gives priority to character or to rhetoric – will affect the way in which he projects himself from the stage. Nowadays, acting is more introspective than it used to be, less overt and, speaking generally, less grand. There is less attention to formal rhetoric, and more to the minutiae of character. A contemporary actor will often break up the verse in order to go after a particular psychological effect – again we are at the opposite pole from the eighteenth- and nineteenth-century habit of coming downstage and delivering famous passages right to the audience. The modern actor, like the director, will usually try to express a complex of ideas about the character in a consistent theatrical way. This approach means some diminution in the glory of verse-speaking, often bemoaned by older critics who recall the vocal richness of Gielgud or Ernest Milton, and it can also involve too much simplification, a sacrifice of affectiveness for effectiveness.[24] But it can mean as well a gain in subtlety and flexibility, an adroit and perceptive handling of shorter speeches, and a realistic, if insufficiently musical, conception of the verse.

The temptation to impress the audience by simplifying, by concentrating on only one feature of the character and developing that brilliantly, thus reducing the complexity of the Shakespearean conception, can be encouraged by the way audiences receive such actions as well as by the way actors rehearse. Often both actors and audience want a clear picture, a 'through-line' that distinguishes the character and carries him through the play. Inconsistency, contradiction, 'chaotic fullness', these essentially Shakespearean characteristics, are often resisted, just because they aren't neat and clear.[25] But the actor has to be able to do more than one thing at a time. Even Shakespeare's small parts are multifaceted, irradiated by moments of sudden insight or hidden generosity; look, for example, at the booby Aguecheek in *Twelfth Night*, whose 'I was adored once' provides the actor with a whole precious history, or the sycophant Nathaniel in *Love's Labour's Lost*, of whom we are told that 'He is a marvelous good neighbor, faith, and a very good bowler', a description that illuminates a segment of his life in the village which we do not otherwise see. The best actors and directors do not shun this 'inconsistency' but embrace it, following the filaments of what Brook calls *les mots rayonnants*.

To follow these rays, it is not necessary to 'sing' the verse, or to speak in an upper-class British accent (that of Richard Burbage, Shakespeare's leading actor, was undoubtedly closer to modern Newfoundland than to modern Oxbridge). But it is necessary to train the voice and to develop techniques of metrical control which can handle sustained rhythms and broken phrases, produce both speed and clarity, and highlight meaning without awkwardness or gabble. As an audience, we may not be particularly aware of such techniques, important as they are, but see them as serving the primary ideal of significance. Probably we are greedier for meaning than previous audiences were, more suspicious of grandeur, rhetoric and spectacle, more comfortable with the psychological nuance than with the passionate gesture; and, if that is the case, we are doing nothing more than living in our own time, and it is no surprise that our theatre reflects and even embodies such widespread cultural attitudes.

1

A Midsummer Night's Dream

'There's nothing wrong with capering rustic sprites and traditional mischief in the wood – except that Brook's production [of 1970] has so clobbered the convention that it may never recover.'[1] So wrote Charles Marowitz, a one-time associate of Peter Brook, apropos of the 1977 RSC production of *A Midsummer Night's Dream*. Not all critics agreed with this point of view, but there is no doubt that Brook's bold, striking and utterly original version has changed for ever our notion of what can be done with the play. Probably no single Shakespearean production of the last fifty years has been so influential, or so controversial. Even a production such as the one Marowitz was reviewing, which attempted a return to 'enchantment', with 'bark skinned, frond-waving earth sprites that [froze] into stumps or exotic foliage when mortals approached',[2] could not help feeling the influence of Brook, even if only to reject it.

What did Brook do with the play? Briefly, he turned it into a circus – not in any crude sense, but in order to evoke the magic and the delight in performance for its own sake that mark the circus at its best. The play, he knew, had been too long clogged up by romantic conventions, and he looked for a way to free it:

> Today we have no symbols that can conjure up fairyland and magic for a modern audience. On the other hand there are a number of actions that a performer can execute that are quite breathtaking. So we went to the art of the circus and the acrobat because they both make purely theatrical statements. We've worked through a language of acrobatics to find a new approach to a magic that we know cannot be reached by 19th century conventions.[3]

Accordingly, the stage, designed by Sally Jacobs, was a brightly lit white box; Puck and Oberon, dressed in brilliantly coloured suits, flew on trapezes (see Plate 1); the lovers became fiercely acrobatic tumblers; Puck directed the confusion from giant stilts; and characters who were not on-stage appeared on a gallery above,

15

occasionally 'shooting blue and silver darts across the space', hanging and twisting coiled wire 'trees' which 'produced metallic music as they . . . settled', or 'making sounds with musical saws and plastic tubes'.[4] One critic gives a striking example of the way circus techniques signalled the magic:

At II, i, 246, Puck swings down on a trapeze, spinning a plate on a rod. Oberon, on a lower trapeze, looks up to ask, 'Hast thou the flower there? Welcome, wanderer . . .' and Puck leans over to tip the still spinning plate on to Oberon's rod – 'Ay, there it is.' The plate does not *become* the flower. Instead, the act of passing it becomes the *magic* of the flower.[5]

Nothing was hidden from the audience – there were no behind-the-scenes stage tricks. Everything underlined the fact, and the fun, of performance. It should also be noted that, with all its emphasis on physical action, the production still never forgot the crucial importance of language. Even the most hostile critics agreed that the verse was superbly spoken.

If one were pressed to single out a person in this century who has done even more than Brook to change the course of Shakespearean production, Harley Granville-Barker would undoubtedly come to mind. And perhaps it is no very great coincidence that Granville-Barker also produced an epoch-making *Midsummer Night's Dream*. In fact, it was he who in 1914 first 'clobbered' the extravagantly decorated conventions that had increasingly weighed down the play during the previous century. In the 1840s Samuel Phelps had brought in gauze and moonlight, and around the same time Charles Kean introduced 'innumerable fairy legions . . . light and brilliant as gossamer; and a 9-year-old child, Ellen Terry, as the "merry goblin" Puck, who was belted and garlanded with flowers'. Toward the end of the nineteenth century, Frank Benson provided among other things a 'protracted fight between a spider and a wasp', Augustin Daly 'fitted the fairies with portable batteries and incandescent lights' and Beerbohm Tree 'had a wood of cushioned moss, bluebell thickets, and scurrying rabbits'.[6] Granville-Barker changed all this, eliminating the green gauze, training his actors to speak the verse quickly and sensibly, substituting English folk tunes for the Mendelssohn music which had become *de rigueur* (Brook used it ironically to celebrate the coupling of Titania and Bottom), and turning his fairies into strange, golden, mechanical creatures who moved like marionettes. Foregoing realistic illusion, he devised a stylized and dreamlike forest, and occasionally made Puck into a kind of stage manager who motioned for lights to be dimmed or a curtain to be raised. As Brook was to do many years later, he thus built into his production an awareness of the performance going on, a modern 'Brechtian' feature that we may be surprised to encounter as early as 1914, since it is still so very modish. Indeed, in one recent production, Puck carried out Oberon's instructions to 'overcast the night . . . With drooping fog as black as Acheron' by manipulating a fog-machine in full view of the audience.

Granville-Barker recognized that 'one's understanding of *A Midsummer Night's Dream* is to be measured by one's perception of the fairies',[7] and his own were odd and otherworldly, all gold with crimson eyebrows and metallic curls, inspiring disgusted comments from critics such as William Winter, who called them 'steamheat radiators cast in human form'.[8] Brook's were more like puppet-masters than puppets, unobtrusively dressed in grey, entrapping the mortals in their steel coils, or acting the part of stagehands or roustabouts. Company slang christened them the 'audio-visuals' and in creating their effects they became an essential part of the deliberately non-illusionary atmosphere.[9] Other recent productions have stressed an erotic, sensual element in the fairies or have depicted them as sinister and bizarre. In general, the trend has been to treat them seriously, to downplay their decorative role and to make their activity a crucial part of both the magic and the threat of the forest, however that may be conceived.

The notion that the forest is threatening and not just pretty is a characteristic of the modern perception of the play. Taking their cue from critics such as Jan Kott, whose essay on *A Midsummer Night's Dream* in his influential book *Shakespeare Our Contemporary* stressed its erotic and aggressive elements, directors have taken a closer look at what the lovers actually do and say, and have reassessed the comedy of Titania's languishing love for an ass. The lovers, who before 1920 were treated as primarily romantic, gradually developed after that into comic figures. Now, in productions such as Brook's, the comedy has become darker, the fun crueller – madness and pain are not far away. The 'fierce vexation' of the dream has come to the fore. When Hermia awakes at the end of II.ii, after having been abandoned by Lysander, she is caught in the toils of a frightening nightmare. Brook emphasized this by ensnaring her in the metal

coils of the forest's wire trees; since the fairies manipulated these
trees from above, they were implicated in her pain.

So too with Bottom's dream. Once a harmless ballet or a comic
version of beauty and the beast, it has developed into an erotic
fantasy in which Titania's sexuality is rudely and roughly
awakened. This does not mean that the comedy disappears, only
that it is paired with something far more unsettling. In Brook's
version, Bottom (the traditional ass's head replaced by a clown's red
nose and earmuffs) was carried to Titania's bower of scarlet ostrich
feathers in a

> celebratory ritual of the most complete sexuality – supported by
> the wild percussion of the two 'musicians' seated on either side of
> the gallery and the active participation of the entire cast:
> '. . . Titania's body arches with desire, she cries out, the fairies
> carry Bottom in state to her bed, an arm raised through his legs
> like a giant phallus, with Mendelssohn's "Wedding March"
> bursting triumphantly on the audience and huge confetti paper
> plates showering down from the gallery.'[10]

Some critics reacted violently to this kind of bold-faced deviation
from Shakespeare's fairly clear intentions. There is nothing in the
text, complained John Russell Brown with some justice, to indicate
that Oberon's plans for Titania include an intention to have her
'fucked by the crudest sex machine he can find'.[11] But it did fit in
with the extravagant and pointed theatricality of the whole
conception.

A very different note was sounded in a later RSC version of the
play (1981), in which the fairies (Oberon, Puck and Titania excepted)
were represented by hand puppets, held, manipulated and spoken
by virtually expressionless actors dressed in black.[12] Since the
lighting was kept fairly low, this led to uncanny movements when
the fairies really did seem small enough to war with reremice for
their leathern wings. One could hardly imagine a more pointed
difference from Brook's fairies than this. Nevertheless, magic,
eeriness and even brutality were successfully evoked. There was a
chilling sequence when Oberon came in to streak Titania's sleeping
eyes with the love-juice. One fairy, standing aloof as 'sentinel', set
up an alarm, and a swarm of small bodies quickly converged on
Oberon. He kicked and beat them off, then grabbed the sentinel and
wrung his neck, dropping the lifeless body to the stage. At this the

handler suddenly assumed a character, wailed, picked up the body and carried it off. The extraordinary thing about this approach is that one can actually develop a relationship with a puppet, simultaneously recognizing and ignoring the handler. The puppets come easily to dominate one's perception, and a connection is mysteriously established. The 1981 *Midsummer Night's Dream* thus found a theatrical image for what a fairy is, which is the essential thing. And it did not sidestep the sharp cruelty of the fairy world.

If the fairies are in many respects the determining feature of a production's approach, they are still only a part of the multiple world of the play. We have also the court of Duke Theseus and his impending marriage to Hippolyta, which provides a frame for the rest of the action, and we have the separate plots of the lovers and the 'mechanicals', which intersect with the fairy world certainly, but are distinct from it. Four different plots, all dealing with the trials and tribulations of love. Theseus has wooed Hippolyta with his sword but hopes to wed her in another key, the lovers suffer the hell of choosing love by another's eyes, the fairy king and queen endure a cosmic falling-out which leads to her being erotically bound to an ass, and, finally, the Athenian workmen rehearse and present a comic play of tragic love (Shakespeare's parody of his own *Romeo and Juliet*). How unite all these various strands?

They are, indeed, connected thematically, but directors will seek ways of connecting them theatrically as well. Here Brook made a bold decision. He doubled the court characters and the fairies, so that the two very different worlds of daylight and moonlight, practical life and dream, were visibly intertwined. Theseus, Hippolyta and Philostrate became respectively Oberon, Titania and Puck, and Theseus's courtiers became the fairies. This device has now become standard practice, avoided mainly by those productions, such as John Barton's in 1977, that seek deliberately to remove themselves from Brook's influence. The effect of the doubling is to emphasize the dream, to make it a dream *of* someone, Theseus and/or Hippolyta, for example, or the lovers. And often the power of the dream will bind together the play's disparate elements. This can lead to excellent effects: at some moment in the play scene, for example, will not Bottom suddenly, eerily, recognize Hippolyta? Frozen by a powerful feeling of *déja vu*, he may pause in his acting, or momentarily forget his lines, thus adding an unexpected poignancy to the comic tragedy of Pyramus and Thisbe. The hilarious confusion of Bottom's speech when he wakes up from his dream will then be seen in retrospect as expressive of a truly unfathomable mystery which he has touched upon, is aware of, but cannot comprehend. His experience of the dream, though less articulate than that of the lovers, can thus be revealed as deeper than theirs.

Robin Phillips, directing the play at Stratford Ontario in 1976, made the whole thing a dream in the mind of Queen Elizabeth I. This was taking the doubling one step further, not only making Titania a dream image of Hippolyta, but making Hippolyta a dream image of Elizabeth. Posters and programme were emblazoned with Elizabeth's portrait, costumes for the production were magnificently and authentically Elizabethan, and Hippolyta was deliberately made up to look like the virgin queen. Even Hermia and Helena were conceived as young versions of Elizabeth and Mary Stuart.[13] The play opened with the lights coming up on Elizabeth–Hippolyta, stiff in her ornate black brocade, her head moving restlessly as she wove the whole play.[14] It ended with her alone on-stage with her fool – the sad dream of an old lonely woman now faded away. The sense of unfulfilment was sharply pointed just before the end, as Oberon pronounced his blessing over the house of Theseus – 'And the issue there create, / Evermore be fortunate' – and Titania–Elizabeth's hand 'moved to her childless womb'.[15] In the wood, Titania's hair was down, her clothes loose, her stiffness replaced by eroticism. This emphasis, according to Martin Knelman, gave the scene with Bottom a sudden electricity as well as an affecting sadness as part of Elizabeth's dream.[16] But many critics also sensed a strain in the overall interpretation, and some noted the difficulties of integrating the mechanicals into the dream.

Indeed, the problem with too rigid or singular an interpretation of the play, i.e. one that makes it a dream of one particular character or figure, is precisely that it tends to isolate the workmen and their plot. How to weave them into the whole tapestry is another problem for the producer. They can be extremely funny – the play within the play is one of Shakespeare's most uproarious comic scenes. But, as the fairies were for so long stifled with gauze and gossamer, so the humour of the mechanicals still tends to come weighed down with old gags, some of which actually go all the way back to Shakespeare's own time. A comedy of 1607 mentions someone who 'like Thisbe in the play . . . has almost kil'd himself with the scabbard', a joke that is still in common use. In Wright's promptbook of 1854, Thisbe 'Takes Pyramus' sword up . . . stabs herself three times (2nd time a guttural sound of, oh!), lies down alongside of Pyramus (having arranged her dress first), lays her head on his breast, he raises his head and removes her head from him and lies down again. Thisbe places her head again on his breast.'[17] A 1980 production in Vancouver followed this business almost exactly. When Granville-Barker did the play in 1914, he treated the mechanicals simply: he cut all the old gags and presented them as countrymen rather than clowns. Brook also treated them more seriously than usual, making them less butts of the humour and more participants in it. The play scene, far from being a burlesque, was done with an absurd, simple dignity and was met, not with the usual smug condescension on the part of Theseus and the court, but with a genuine, concerned courtesy.[18] If the workmen were circus clowns, they were so in the best tradition – dignified, unruffled, admired by the other performers, and an essential part of the show.

Nowadays, we may see either approach to the mechanicals: all the old gags, or an attempt to play them more seriously. The former course is easier certainly, and avoids the problem of having to fit them into an overall conception. But the latter, especially in regard to Bottom, seems to be the current trend. Bottom is now more often understated than not, played with puzzled sensitivity as well as loud bravado. In John Barton's production, Bottom's self-absorption was conveyed 'not by boisterous rant but by solicitous advice to Quince and the others', and the mechanicals in general were credible and quiet.[19] This reading fitted well with Barton's emphasis on the unforced humanness of the mortal world, and the exotic enchantment of the fairies. But, as Brook showed, a plain, true approach to the workmen can also be effectively integrated into a conception which seeks to stress mystery, magic and even an occasional patch of darkness through an imaginative identification of the courts of Theseus and Oberon.

For all the advantages to be derived from doubling the characters and connecting the play scene with Bottom's experiences in the woods, there is the supreme disadvantage that to do so clearly deviates from Shakespeare's text.[20] One moment in the play makes this clear. At iv.i.101, Titania, Puck and Oberon exit, and immediately Theseus 'and all his train' enter. Undoubtedly, on Shakespeare's own stage their entrance would have been through another door, simultaneous with the fairies' exit. This moment obviously poses a problem for productions that go in for the now popular doubling. Brook, emphasizing throughout his production the act and art of performance, took the simplest, boldest and most consistent course: Oberon and Titania walked up to the stage doors at the back, donned cloaks and turned to walk downstage as Theseus and Hippolyta.[21] Other productions have had more difficulty. The elaborate Elizabethan dress of Phillips' production required a long costume change, which was covered by a tape of Oberon's 'Come my queen' and a dance of the courtiers, before Theseus and Hippolyta could re-enter.[22] In Vancouver in 1980, Theseus had to shout his first few lines from backstage as he and Hippolyta were zipped and buttoned through a quick change while the last of the fairies flitted over the scaffolding. How well a production that does the doubling manages this moment will be a mark of how well it has really integrated the ideas set in motion by the original decision.

With or without doubling, the most difficult parts of the play to get off the ground are probably those with Theseus and Hippolyta. Take, for example, their dialogue about hounds and hunting following their Act IV entrance: it announces the arrival of daylight and the world of actuality, but, for all its thematic relevance, it is likely to fall a little flat. Perhaps, though, the actors can make use of the sly humour that the exchange aims at these mythological heroes – Hippolyta dropping names such as 'Cadmus' and 'Hercules'; Theseus, not to be outdone, boasting of the superior quality of his hounds. For those productions that want to show an unwilling Hippolyta, or a general bristliness in her relationship with Theseus, this short dialogue can be useful; it is indeed possible that Hippolyta, in challenging her conqueror, is expressing an edgy, not quite suppressed, hostility. At the beginning of the play, Hippolyta is Theseus' captive, and this has led to interpretations that stress the distance between them. Hippolyta has appeared in manacles and chains; she has been ritually stripped under a spotlight, her Amazon hunting-clothes replaced by a flowing gown; or she has simply stood aloof and spiritually unbeaten. All of these approaches point to an insensitive male domination at the basis of the action, a motif that is continued through the play in the behaviour of Egeus toward his daughter, Oberon toward Titania, and the young male lovers toward the women they at first love and then as easily scorn. Hippolyta's original unwillingness can lead as well to a clear, though unarticulated, sympathy for Hermia's plight in I.i, and to a disgust with Theseus for taking Egeus's part against the poor girl. But the problem is that, except for a slight suggestion in Act ιν, her disgruntlement would seem to end there – certainly by Act v she has accepted Theseus and her fate with grace and even love. The decision to double her part may arise from a perception of this difficulty: it can be used to point toward a resolution to her original hostility. What changes Hippolyta, according to this interpretation, is the dream experience she goes through as Titania. But this is hard to play and is likely to remain unconvincing. If, on the other hand, there is no doubling, initial conflict between Hippolyta and Theseus seems even harder to resolve.

Brook made the doubling more a theatrical than a psychological process, a wise decision given the rather thin justification for psychological pronouncements that the text allows. Accordingly, he began the play by having his whole company swoop onto the stage dressed in long white capes. Flinging off their capes, the actors suddenly became the characters, dressed in brilliant colours against the pure white background. Theseus and Hippolyta knelt on cushions facing the audience, speaking their opening lines in a kind of ritual.[23] There was gravity certainly, but no reluctance on Hippolyta's part. Psychological interest was raised not by conflict between the two of them, but by the unsettling relationship established between the dream fantasy that they later experience and their daylight world of rulership and imminent marriage.

So, though there is some justification in the text for what might be termed a feminist production, favouring Hippolyta and Titania and their rebellion, there is no very effective way of resolving the issues that such an approach raises. The ending is unremittingly celebratory: Titania is won to Oberon as her counterpart is to Theseus. Still, in one sense at least, the irony turns on the men at last: one of the male lovers, Demetrius, is left for ever under the magic spell. (It will be pleasant if a production finds a subtle way of reminding us of this.) Added to this, Hippolyta clearly gets the better of the important exchange with Theseus concerning the mystery of imagination (v.i.1–27). Hippolyta, we feel, sees farther – she is willing to let the strange stories of the magic night touch her in ways that the stolid Theseus refuses. If there has been doubling, the contrast between their daylight and moonlight selves might be effectively increased by this moment – though under Brook Theseus made up in gravity and courtesy (especially in his treatment of the mechanicals) what he lacked in imaginative insight.

Although Theseus and Hippolyta provide the frame, Oberon and

Puck drive the play forward to its dreamlike conclusion, where we are left partly under the magic spell, like Demetrius, and partly liberated from it, like Lysander. As a character, Puck continuously straddles the line between performance and audience. He controls the action, giving it at times a deliberately theatrical shape – by, for example, emphasizing its comic predictability: 'Yet but three? Come one more; / Two of both kinds makes up four.' He also comments on the course of the action even as he participates in it: 'Shall we their fond pageant see? / Lord, what fools these mortals be', or 'Jack shall have Jill; / Nought shall go ill; / The man shall have his mare again, and all shall be well.' Coming out of English folklore, he has a different lineage from the classical fairies like Oberon and Titania. He is the hobgoblin, the mischievous sprite who sometimes lurks in a gossip's bowl and 'on her withered dewlap pour(s) the ale'. For these reasons, he is often conceived of and played as distinctly different from the rest of the fairies. As I mentioned, Granville-Barker thought of him partly as a stage-manager figure, and many directors since have followed his lead, using Puck to underline the pure theatre of what is happening. In line with this, his first appearance in ii.i is often sensational: he rises from a mushroom, is discovered behind a fan, emerges from a flower or, in a spectacular effect, seems to drop in a bag from the flies to the stage. This last was accomplished by dropping a large stuffed bag from above, which fell with a thud as the previous scene ended; there was a lighting change and forest fairies emerged, dancing with a large cloth held between them. The cloth masked a quick exchange, by means of a stage trap, of the dummy bag for an identical one containing Puck. His opening line was spoken from within the bag, puzzling and frightening the one fairy left on stage. Mimic stretchings and contortions of the bag, as though it was itself alive, eventually led to the discovery of the mischievous spirit. This introduced a Puck who was athletically, indeed gymnastically, conceived throughout the production, and one who was full of sportive tricks.[24] Brook and Sally Jacobs dressed Puck in a bright yellow clown suit with a blue skull-cap, and for the scene when he harries Lysander and Demetrius (near the end of iii.ii) gave him six-foot stilts on which to dart around the stage 'in a new-established convention of invisibility that makes stage poetry out of a scene normally surrendered to a dead convention'.[25] At the end of the same version, Puck and all his colleagues deliberately broke the magic – the magic created by the *theatre* – by advancing into the audience on his final lines ('Give me your hands, if we be friends / And Robin shall restore amends') and shaking hands with everyone they could reach. But of course such a tactic subtly continues the magic as well, making it linger in a way analogous to Puck's last speech, which both breaks and extends the illusion.

We are a long way from the girlish Pucks of the last century, of whom the nine-year-old Ellen Terry is the most famous. Since Granville-Barker, Pucks have begun to have something startling, at times even threatening, about them. In Granville-Barker's revival, Puck was a man in scarlet against the fading gold of the last scene; he seemed 'sinister and alien among the golden elves . . . the play absorbed him as music absorbs discords'.[26]

This last metaphor might serve as a key to the play and its productions. It is one in fact that Shakespeare himself provides: 'Merry and tragical?' asks Theseus of the mechanicals' interlude; 'How shall we find the concord of this discord?' Modern productions have unearthed many discordant elements: not only Puck, who has his cruel side, but Oberon too, whose attitude toward Titania is harsh and aggressive; Titania, whose row with Oberon is cosmically and sexually disturbing; the lovers, who attack each other with a vengeance born of misunderstood rivalry; Theseus and Hippolyta, whose own relationship arises from conflict and perhaps has not sufficiently risen above it; even the mechanicals, whose play of love is tragical as well as merry. All of these provide an element of discord, notes to be struck and, if desired, emphatically struck; but in the end these darker tones are resolved in a harmony that is the more inclusive because of the very discords that it embraces. We come again to that magical ending – the clock tolling twelve; Puck with his broom ('Not a mouse / Shall disturb this hallowed house'); Oberon's blessing ('With this field-dew consecrate, / Every fairy take his gait, / And each several chamber bless, / Through this palace, with sweet peace'); and, finally Puck's two-sided epilogue, half in the play, half out of it:

> If we shadows have offended,
> Think but this, and all is mended,
> That you have but slumb'red here
> While these visions did appear . . .

Brook's actors, coming out to shake our hands as Puck finished speaking, caught, as precisely and as theatrically as anything could, that feeling of discord resolving itself into harmony that is the essence of this midsummer night's dream.

2

The Merchant of Venice

The Merchant of Venice is one of the relatively few Shakespeare plays that has never been absent from the stage for too long, and it is also one of the very few, if not the only one, to provoke at least some distaste among most audiences at the present time. This does not mean that it is rarely produced. On the contrary, it is still popular, still interesting – simply a little distasteful. Its ambiguous sourness may indeed account for some of its current popularity. But this was not always the case. During the eighteenth and nineteenth centuries, the play was admired for the opportunities it provided a star actor to shine in the role of Shylock. Charles Macklin, in the 1740s, for example, was malignant, sullen, malevolent; powerful and unshakeable, he 'stood like a tower'.[1] Edmund Kean, in the early nineteenth century, was fiery and sardonic, full of lightning shifts from one point to the next, driven more by family love and racial pride than by malevolent cruelty. Later in the nineteenth century, in one of his most famous roles, Sir Henry Irving turned Shylock into a dignified elder, calm, majestic, pitiless and implacable, a figure of tragic stature. Dazed and unconscious after his defeat, he at last tottered out, 'a broken man, only gathering himself together for one steady look of scorn at the mocking Gratiano'.[2] That look, by the way, came from Kean (an indication of the power of theatrical traditions throughout the period), who also sought a sympathetic and quietly dignified retreat. So successful was the emphasis on the defeat of Shylock that frequently the whole fifth act, containing the reunion of the lovers and the elaboration of the comic 'ring plot', was simply cut, so that the play ended with Shylock's shuffling exit. When Irving first produced *The Merchant of Venice* with the sparkling and graceful Ellen Terry as Portia, he retained the last act. But, as the run continued, the emphasis on Shylock's tragic loss increased and the last act was cut, despite Terry's sending the play dancing to a moonlit conclusion.[3]

At present, of course, we are not likely to see such wholesale cutting, nor is Shylock likely to be portrayed as a tragic figure. But he is still the central focus, the play's chief interest, and the touchstone of a director's conception. The problem that Shylock poses for us is not only theatrical, but social as well. We are in general acutely sensitive to anti-Semitism, more so than our predecessors generally were. It seems to me at best naïvely academic to claim about the play, as has so often been done, that the issue of anti-Semitism is irrelevant to it. When, in the late twentieth century, we hear and watch professed Christians mocking and attacking a man because he is a Jew, we can hardly not be aware of the blight of anti-Semitism as we have seen it in action during the last eighty years. The academic position that has often been taken, that Shylock is a 'blocking character'[4] who impedes the fulfilment of the comic action and must therefore be eliminated, contains a germ of truth but is far too simple. Equally, however, it is a romantic oversimplification to present Shylock as a sentimentalized tragic figure, as the nineteenth century tended to do.

What to do with Shylock, then, will be a major concern of the director. But the conception of Shylock must, of course, mesh with the conception of other features of the play. In terms of character, Portia is the only other figure who matches Shylock in strength and importance, and a decision to lay heavy stress on her role, making her attitudes and values central to the production, will necessarily lead to a diminution of Shylock's pre-eminence. Shylock might thus emerge as an energetic villain rather than a victimized moneylender. This in turn might condition how the Christian men of Venice are treated; they could be portrayed as relatively benevolent and Shylock's malignancy could be seen more as a deep-rooted personal hatred than as a result of vile treatment by the Christians. On the other hand, our sympathies might be more with Shylock than with his enemies, as Hazlitt's were for Kean's Shylock: 'he is honest in his vices; they are hypocrites in their virtues'.[5] In such a case, Portia might stand out distinctly from the Venetians, as a pool of virtue in her own right, or her virtues might be shadowed by the general sense of hypocrisy. It is, of course, possible, and these days even likely, that no character will emerge as particularly justified in his or her behaviour – that, for example, Shylock will be a shrewd, harsh moneyman, Antonio a nasty anti-Semite, Bassanio an egoistic treasure-seeker, Gratiano a vicious mocker, and even Portia a cynical, bitchy, manipulative, young (or not so young) woman of the upper classes, given to dishonesty to get what she wants. (Does she hint at the right casket for Bassanio through her

use of the key word 'hazard' or through the rhymes of the song that
is sung while he chooses?)

Clearly a play that admits of such radically different
interpretations cannot easily be pinned down to a single,
unambiguous meaning, and clearly, too, different periods will find
their own emphases. The conception just sketched comes, I think,
from a relatively recent perception of the importance of *money* in the
play, and how the quest for money undermines the motives of those
characters who don't have enough, while the use of their money
calls into question the actions of those who do. (This aspect was
strongly emphasized in Jonathan Miller's National Theatre
production of 1970, leading, according to some critics, to
distortion.[6]) Shylock lends out money at interest, at a time when all
such lending, despite widespread practice, was considered a form
of usury. He is tolerated as a necessary evil in society, but, like the
great Jewish bankers of the nineteenth century, he is deeply
resented as well. Bassanio is a wastrel who first uses his friendship
with Antonio to get money, and then quite consciously goes in
search of a rich woman and her 'golden fleece'. Lorenzo and Jessica
steal money and jewels from her rich father, seemingly justifying
their behaviour on the grounds that he is a Jew. At the end, after
Shylock's defeat, they show little compunction for his straitened
situation (they even adopt a pose of moral superiority), but they are
perfectly happy to live off his money. Other characters, such as
Antonio and Portia, treat their money, or the fact that they have it, in
questionable ways. Antonio spits on Jewish moneylenders in the
marketplace, and Portia lolls in luxurious self-pity at her country
house. Add to all this a general distaste for commerce, and you have
the ingredients for a nicely cynical treatment.

Consistent with this emphasis on commerce, Miller decided to set
his National Theatre production, with Olivier as Shylock, in the late
nineteenth century. Since then, many directors have followed suit.
The choice works well because, as critic Ralph Berry points out, the
nineteenth century is for us 'the great age of property . . . you can
illustrate great wealth, or bourgeois comfort, in an effective way', a
way that is immediately recognizable and meaningful to a modern
audience, but that still has a sense of remoteness or vanished
grandeur about it. The past century, says Berry, 'is more tenacious
of meanings than any other'.[7] What Berry says applies very well to
The Merchant of Venice – frock-coated businessmen sitting around in
rich leather chairs at the club, sipping port and smoking expensive

cigars; Shylock appearing as a liberal banker rather than an outcast, or perhaps a private moneylender working out of a small, crowded office; Portia relaxing at her country estate, surrounded with all the trappings of a life of leisure. But there are problems too; just because the play has such a firmly commercial, realistic base, anachronisms arise. During the great age of *laissez faire* capitalism, Shylock would hardly be condemned for charging interest on his money; furthermore, Antonio, embarrassed for cash to pay Shylock back, could simply see one of his banker friends; and, if he lost his argosies, he would surely have insurance to cover them. Such criticisms sound like cavilling, of course, and similar objections could be made to the story as Shakespeare originally conceived it, which, far from being completely realistic, is woven around two ancient folklore motifs. But the nineteenth-century setting invites criticism just because of the implicit claim to greater realism that it makes. So it's a trade-off really. Details such as the 'thread-thin' cigarettes that Patrick Stewart (playing Shylock at the RSC Other Place, 1978) took from a little box, extinguishing the butts and returning them for further use,[8] can suggest in a neat, economical way a precision of meaning unavailable in a more traditional setting (see Plate 2).

If the commercial, Venetian scenes of the play can be, despite anachronisms, enhanced by a nineteenth century setting, the more remote and romantic Belmont scenes might seem to work better in a less solid and recognizable environment. As in several other Shakespeare comedies, there are two distinct 'worlds' in *The Merchant of Venice*: one in which law, authority, commerce and other concerns of the 'real' social world play a dominant role; the other more the domain of romantic love, poetry and fantasy (Venice and Belmont have their analogues in, for example, the court and Arden in *As You Like It* or Athens and the wood in *A Midsummer Night's Dream*). The comic interplay generally rests on contrasts between the two worlds, leading to some sort of reconciliation between them, although many recent critics of this play have stressed the links and similarities between Belmont and Venice, and have questioned the final reconciliation. Portia is not only the key figure in Belmont, but the only character who fully and successfully bridges the gap between the two worlds of the play, and thus has some claim to central importance. In Belmont, she is something of an imprisoned princess, and, if the setting is nineteenth century, we might easily get an impression of a bored and worldly young woman, accomplished but useless, a bit like Rosamund Lydgate in *Middlemarch*. But for the play to work she must be more like Dorothea than Rosamund, with a little of Austen's Elizabeth Bennett thrown in. Her action in the real world is crucial – it is she who solves the play's major problem – and an actress's conception of the character has to spring from that success.

This means that at the beginning Portia must be chafing somewhat under the cruel terms of her father's will. Her first few lines in the play are important, and the way they are played will condition our reading of what follows: 'By my troth, Nerissa, my little body is aweary of this great world.' How are we to take this pert opening? How is it to be delivered? No director will fail to notice that Portia's speech here at the start of the second scene echoes that of Antonio at the start of the first: 'In sooth, I know not why I am so sad.' Melancholy is the keynote in both. On Antonio's part, it is a kind of motiveless depression that his friends go to some lengths to try to explain. (Critics and directors have also sought explanations; among the most popular these days is Antonio's latent or not so latent homosexuality, and his consequent sorrow at the imminent loss of his beloved Bassanio.) Portia is much clearer about the reasons for her sadness:

> O me, the word 'choose'! I may neither choose who I would nor refuse who I dislike; so is the will of a living daughter curb'd by the will of a dead father. Is it not hard, Nerissa, that I cannot choose one nor refuse none? (I.ii.22–6)

In both cases the plot begins on a down-note; both Belmont and Venice are plagued by uncertainty, and closed off to experience.

Portia, however, in her first speech, can easily suggest a playfulness about her melancholy. Phrases such as 'by my troth' and 'my little body' may indicate an amused self-awareness which contrasts with Antonio's more pained and self-involved consciousness of his condition. On the other hand, the line can be read with genuine feeling – a serious sigh and an anxious frustration – showing that the restrictions placed upon her really do bother her and their possible consequences frighten her. When, in response to Nerissa's good-natured attempt to cheer her up, she spells out the details of her uncomfortable situation, she seems to feel the hard edge of her father's 'curbs'.

There are at least three possible approaches to the part. First, and this works well in a nineteenth-century setting, is the bored, rather self-pitying little rich girl. This leads to a petulant reading of the expository lines about her father's will, and to a smug, perhaps even nasty, and self-consciously clever presentation of the caricatures of her various suitors that make up the rest of the scene. This would establish a basis for a negative reading of Portia, one that fits her in with an ironic attitude toward the Venetian gentlemen and probably toward Shylock too, though the latter may, in such a version, turn out much cleaner than the hypocritical parasites that victimize him. I once saw a production (in Vancouver in 1977) which adopted a wholly cynical attitude toward all the characters, with Portia appearing as an indolent, ageing Victorian woman of leisure, her harshness and bitchery presumably a cover for a growing desperation about sex and marriage.

A second, median position on Portia would be one that handles the first line with graceful self-irony, stressing playfulness rather than boredom or cynicism. This is perhaps the most common strategy. The caricatures might then follow naturally from a sense of her witty irrepressibility (that Elizabeth Bennett spark). Such an approach might have some difficulty with the passage about her father's will, but even there a certain *esprit* would be appropriate, or a naïve earnestness not at all inconsistent with her wit. This Portia is in general a younger, more innocent one than the first, not intensely bothered by the terms of the will and quite ready to fall in love with a handsome, dashing young man like Bassanio, who is remembered by Nerissa and Portia near the end of the scene as 'the best deserving a fair lady'.

A third approach, based on a serious reading of the opening line and the later speech about the harshness of her father's will, would emphasize the restrictions she feels, her inability to act freely in the world and control her own life. A possible problem with this is that the passage about her various suitors does not suggest a Portia that is too weighed down or distressed. However, the fact that, after getting free of the will, Portia does take significant action in society supports the conception of her as a mature woman, straining at the bit that keeps her in check. In the 1981 RSC production, Sinead Cusack delivered the lines about the will with impatient scorn; she was prepared to follow her father's injunctions out of filial piety, even though it was obvious she didn't consider them in the least just. And she 'laughed at her suitors to stop herself crying'.[9] Later in the play, this feeling led to a rich theatrical moment. Once Bassanio had chosen the correct casket, opened it and read the verse, Portia, who had been sitting in great happiness, suddenly sprang up, grabbed the little table with the other two caskets on it, and flung it upstage as far as she could. She followed it, looking down at the rubble, and then turned to Bassanio with her arms stretched out. There was no doubt about the sense of relief, of new-found vigour, that she felt.[10]

Most Portias will be alternately playful and serious, naïve and shrewd, engaged and ironical, thus combining various possibilities. If the trend these days is to play her as a bit of a minx, perhaps the real key to her character is not her tendency to tease, but her balanced straightforwardness, her common sense. She, more than any other character, can assess the actual value of varying claims of love and friendship, the real meaning of external signs (such as the rings at the end), and the true worth of individuals.

A basic choice in a production is whether to make it revolve around Portia or around Shylock. To give Portia the central place is to underline the values she represents – a balance of wit and good sense, reason and erotic fulfilment, action and retirement – to stress, that is, the *comic* aspects of the play. If Shylock is the main focus, the emphasis will likely be on victimization, on the racial tensions and commercial dealings among the Venetians, on the hypocrisy of the Christians, and on the partially tragic outcome.

When Henry Irving, who took the latter route, played Shylock, he inserted a non-Shakespearean scene right after the elopement of Jessica. Returning to his dark and empty house after the rush of revellers and torchbearers across the stage, Shylock stood alone and knocked, waiting, as the curtain fell, for the reply that never came. A dejected figure in strong contrast to the masked youth of the previous scene (it's worth remembering that Shylock is having dinner with Lorenzo's friends at the very moment Lorenzo is stealing his daughter and his money), Shylock met his sad fate with dignity. Irving's imitators took over the scene and extended it with curses, tears and anguished dashing from one window to another, thus destroying the bold simplicity of the idea. But Irving's original interpolation was a telling way of focusing interest on Shylock's plight, and on the callousness of his betrayers. The little scene successfully drew audience attention to Shylock – but in a way that Shakespeare carefully avoids in the actual text, where we are rarely, if ever, allowed an unmixed, unmediated response. Shylock is a difficult, and a fascinating, character, just because he shifts so much, inviting sympathy one minute and repugnance the next.

His opening scene, like Portia's, offers a variety of possibilities. We are presented with several different Shylocks: the careful businessman, the religious Jew who is proud of his tradition, the stage Jew who hates Antonio 'for he is a Christian', the wronged man who rightly condemns Antonio for the treatment he has received at the latter's hands, and the crafty, even malignant villain who conceives of the 'merry bond' by which Antonio promises him a pound of flesh if he is unable to pay back the loan. This last action admits of a wholly different interpretation as well: perhaps Shylock is honest in his claim that he is offering this bond in 'sport', expecting to get nothing from it. Is he then genuinely interested in being kind to his Christian enemy? The BBC Television Shakespeare production seemed to take this course, and hence put extra weight on the betrayal of Jessica, an event which embittered Shylock and drove him toward implacable revenge.

The disparity in the depiction of Shylock continues throughout the play, in the famous 'Hath not a Jew eyes?' for example, with its searing indictment of Christian hypocrisy; and, in the very same scene, the wild, almost comic, oscillation of his grief for the loss of his ducats and his daughter. Again in the trial scene, we have knife-sharpening wolfishness juxtaposed with sharp juridical perception and then with broken victimization. David Suchet, in Barton's 1981 production, was edgy but good-humoured in the first scene, prone to giggles as he acted the role of the genial Jew. (His tragedy, according to one critic, was that he was for once lured into dropping that mask.[11]) The possible weight and mystery of the slow opening lines were avoided, perhaps because Barton's aim seemed to be to keep Shylock from dominating the play, and to give Portia pre-eminence. To complement Cusack's Portia, Shylock was conceived rather narrowly, as unimaginative and tied obsessively to the notion of bonds in general. It appeared that, even if he had not loathed Antonio, he would have felt impelled to claim his pound of flesh because he was unable to think of what else to do.[12] He was as much a prisoner of the bond as Antonio, although in the trial scene he suddenly saw the emptiness of his position.

A very different approach was adopted by Sir Laurence Olivier in the 1970 National Theatre production. He was a prosperous Victorian banker, on uneasy but cordial terms with his Venetian merchant colleagues. Wary and sharp, those early moments played for shrewdness and a sense of uncertainty about what lay behind, Olivier remained 'uneasily sociable until, his racial and family pride really touched, he [became] a man of granite with a revengeful devil beneath it'.[13] Thus Olivier found in Shylock's Jewish pride a key to his motivation, linking his vengefulness to his betrayal by Jessica, and seeing her abandonment of his house and her theft of his goods as an act of the alien Christian society against him and his race. The symbol of Jessica's betrayal is the turquoise ring which Shylock's dead wife had given him and which his daughter callously trades for a pet monkey. In an interpretation such as Olivier's, the ring looms large, and contrasts tellingly with the ring Portia uses to trick Bassanio at the end.

The conception of Shylock links interestingly with that of Portia. Director Jonathan Miller has described how, long before rehearsals started, he first heard in his mind's ear a key phrase from the play which then acted 'as a sort of nucleus or crystal . . . [to] consolidate the rest of the text'. This process, he suggests, is a common one, where a director hears a certain inflexion, 'then other inflexions must follow from it in other parts of the text' until a full interpretation has developed. 'One evening', he continues,

I wasn't doing anything in particular, but I overheard in my mind's ear Portia speaking the line 'the quality of mercy is not strained' and in place of the ringing feminine rhetoric of the familiar version, I heard and saw a brief flash in which I saw a rather boyish figure leaning forward over a table on one elbow saying those first lines in a rather irritable, explanatory tone of voice, as if trying to push something which someone rather stupidly misunderstood previously, saying . . . 'the quality of mercy is not *strained*' and . . . certain consequences came from that. First of all, the visual image of the table meant that I could no longer place the thing in a courtroom. People . . . can only sit and lean across tables in small chambers, like Justices' chambers. . . . That meant that there were only certain settings which could accommodate that hallucination and this became a nineteenth century setting in which someone could quite realistically plead a cause in a judge's room and out of that suddenly the production began to take its form.[14]

Aside from the general import this passage has as a record of how a particular understanding of a key moment can lead to a full blown conception, it makes as well some valuable observations about Portia and Shylock. For her to say the famous lines in the way Miller describes is to make Shylock look not only venomous, but rather stupid as well. The effect clearly is to increase our appreciation of Portia's common sense, and to deflect sympathy away from Shylock. Olivier's granite-hard revenge was thus deftly incised by Portia's easily worn, practical virtue. It is noteworthy that, with a very different Shylock, Sinead Cusack approached this moment in a similar way. Upon saying her line 'Then must the Jew be merciful', she began walking away from the audience toward a table upstage, as if she thought her statement self-evident. Shylock's scornful dismissal of it ('On what compulsion must I? Tell me that') took her aback; she wheeled around and stared at him for a few beats before beginning 'The quality of mercy' in an almost incredulous tone, as if in exasperation at having to explain so clear a thing.[15] In both cases we get a strong, practical Portia, not a boring sermonizer, but a woman whose good sense defines the central values of the play.

This famous speech has met rather different fates as well. When Terence Gray, at Cambridge in the late twenties, had his Portia speak it from a swing, while the Venetian Duke played idly with a yo-yo, he was projecting his own boredom with the familiar pieties onto both the on- and off-stage audiences instead of looking for a working solution to the problems the speech poses. Unfortunately, the simple-minded sermonizing which Gray's iconoclasm was attacking has survived such onslaughts and is an equally weak response to the scene. Neither cynicism nor plaster holiness strikes the right note, nor will simply throwing the speech away (as I saw done at Stratford Ontario in 1984) quite do either.

At the end of the trial scene, the Christians impose conversion on Shylock, in return for allowing him his life and some of his goods. Instigated as it is by the bigot Antonio, the Jew-baiter who has seemingly made a habit of spitting on Shylock in the Rialto, this move has frequently disturbed both audiences and readers. And despite arguments that audiences of Shakespeare's day would have found it acceptable, because it might make possible Shylock's salvation, it seems to me that the dramatic import of the scene is once again to shift the emotional ground, to undermine the Christians and to put Shylock in a sympathetic position, even for an Elizabethan audience. How Shylock reacts to this final indignity will of course depend on how he has been played up to this point. The more emphasis on the significance of his cultural and religious heritage for his life as a whole, the more devastating this blow is likely to be, and hence the more sympathy it will generate. Patrick Stewart, in Barton's Other Place production, stressed the idea of Shylock's greed throughout (one critic called him an 'opportunistic and avaricious maverick'[16]), so that gratitude for being allowed his money and his life prevailed over the distaste he felt at becoming a Christian. Another critic wrote that he was 'cool, unportentous and human . . . ready to ingratiate himself after the verdict, clearly believing that there are worse fates than Christianity and already planning new business enterprises. ("I am not well" is mere malingering.)'[17] The latter line thus becomes a kind of key; played as malingering, it gives us a harder, cooler Shylock than if it is played as a serious, shocked reaction to a bitter fate. In general, it has been said of Barton's production that it stressed the ambiguity of the central characters and evinced no desire to undermine or build up Shylock;[18] accordingly it is not surprising that some other critics saw Stewart's Shylock as more definitely broken. As he left the stage, he slowly, lingeringly, pushed his skull-cap off his head and let it drop to the ground; the effect is provocatively ambiguous – is he in pain, or is he quietly showing his willingness to accept the Christian verdict, to play their game? When Barton directed the play again three years later, with David Suchet as Shylock, he retained certain features of this sequence, such as the slow removal of the skull-cap, but added another dimension. Suchet's performance had stressed the legalistic strain, but the intent of the production was, according to Anne Barton's programme note, to show the inadequacy of Shylock's attitudes and to protect even him from them. The word 'charity' in the trial scene thus 'suddenly stabbed him' and he later accepted his punishment 'with wry, rueful resignation'.[19] When Portia, in a line that is often seen as the last cruel straw, asked him, 'Are you content?' she knelt before him and he answered quietly, still smiling, 'I am content.' Thus Barton managed to lighten the whole Venetian sequence, making a scene that is rarely palatable to modern tastes acceptable and even meaningful.

Portia's behaviour from the moment she turns the tables on Shylock is not always treated so positively. In the text itself it seems distinctly ambiguous. Her strong approval of Antonio's suggestion about forced conversion and her orchestration of the humiliation of Shylock can make her look harsh and manipulative. The darker mood can be carried over into the game with the rings that follows, so that the whole last act may be laced with distaste. Barton, in keeping with the direction taken in the trial scene, and playing against what has become almost conventional, treated the last act not as 'sour whimsy' but as festal, with Belmont bursting forth into spring.[20]

The major problem with Act v, however, is not a matter of tone at all; rather, it is the threat of anti-climax. After the powerfully engaging action with Shylock, what follows may easily seem trivial. There are important thematic links: the ring game replays the theme of loyalty and the motif of external bonds (Shylock's bond, Shylock's ring) in a comic key. But a production must find some way of making the themes count dramatically. This can be done by emphasizing the comic uplift, as in Barton's production, or by weighting the anti-climactic feelings themselves and thus trivializing the actions of the characters that remain. Act v begins with Jessica and Lorenzo's love poetry, which in itself is hard to darken, despite its references to tragic lovers. But we must remember by whom it is spoken – those wasteful and insensitive lovers whose self-interest stands as a paradigm for most of the behaviour in the play. In the Vancouver production mentioned earlier, this sceptical note was exaggerated to such a degree that the scene was twisted into barely recognizable shape, the two lovers standing at a distance from each other, facing different directions, and adopting distorted postures.

As the scene continues with the ring game, it is again possible to give it a hard edge, to make Portia cruel rather than graceful. The men too can be simply dupes, or defensive oafs. The sequence will necessarily take its cue from what has gone before. If Bassanio has been merely a treasure-seeker (in the Vancouver production, he made sure of getting the right casket by appearing in disguise first as Morocco and then as Aragon and choosing the gold and silver ones – a funny but clearly distorted gambit), then some suitably cynical put-down will be in order. Portia will perhaps turn out to be more of a problem than he bargained for! And Gratiano, if he has been less the clown ('Let me play the fool') and more the hissing sycophant, will get his come-uppance as well. Thus a generally cynical viewpoint will treat the ring plot accordingly, while a softer approach will yield here a graceful justification of Portia's unorthodox methods.

In my own view, the play works best with an admirable, common-sensical Portia, a woman who holds the comic key and knows what's what. But the play unquestionably admits of different interpretations. And a brilliant Portia does not preclude a note of sadness at the end. Perhaps the truest approach is to play each scene hard for itself, not concealing the unevenness of the whole, but allowing the different, even opposing, currents to run and eddy into each other. The final note will thus not be one of undiluted joy, or of cynical derision, but, more moderately, one of happiness tempered and muted by melancholy, recalling the beginning. In Miller's production, after the other characters had departed, Antonio and Jessica were left alone, separate and sad, each perusing their letters; Antonio wandered off to his solitude and Jessica remained behind to think of her humiliated father, as the mournful sound of the Hebrew *shofar* brought down the lights.

3

As You Like It

A moment that catches the full flavour of *As You Like It* occurs toward the end of the second scene. A wrestling-match, itself a highly theatrical display, has just ended. If the production is at all exciting, the audience has been caught up in the athletic dazzle of this event, as well as in the success of the hero, Orlando, in foiling the plot against him by beating both the odds and Charles, the Duke's wrestler. The wrestling-match is one example among many of Shakespeare's larding of the play with spectacular, witty or musical 'numbers'. *As You Like It* has some of the characteristics of a first-rate variety show.[1] But, as in the present instance, the different numbers are subtly integrated into the whole texture. For the acrobatic bravado of the wrestling-match leads immediately to a series of sharp intimate exchanges, which together create a complex effect. The shape and feeling of the scene shift rapidly. Upon Orlando's victory, the usurping Duke Frederick asks the victor his name. The simple reply, 'Orlando, my liege, the youngest son of Sir Rowland de Boys', falls coldly on the ears of the Duke and his careful court. For Sir Rowland has been a close friend of the former duke, now banished, who is the brother of the present one and father of Rosalind, Frederick's distrusted niece. Orlando then is the son of a man who has been Frederick's mortal enemy. In John Dexter's 1979 production at the National Theatre in London, at Orlando's words 'the puppet court froze into attitudes of obsequious horror'.[2]

The choice to emphasize the court reaction, and hence to draw attention to the dangerously sycophantic nature of Frederick's milieu, meant that the social and political background behind the love story was being taken seriously. The court's potential for harm, which bursts out into the open in the following scene with the banishment of Rosalind, was thus strongly signalled. More commonly, however, these scenes are skimmed over rather quickly – indeed, the whole of the first act is played more for plot and spectacular effect than for meaning.

If the danger of the court is played as real, then Rosalind's position in it will be the more precarious. And our attention will be

directed not only to her budding love, but also to her response to the
political pressures of her situation. At the beginning of I.ii, she has
appeared sad and uncomfortable in the court of her usurping uncle,
mindful of her banished father, yet witty and cheerful in her
conversation with Celia, especially when their talk has turned to
love – in the abstract, of course. Suddenly Orlando the wrestler
makes his appearance and Rosalind's knees begin to wobble. She
watches the wrestling with unwonted keenness and is naturally
relieved by its outcome. When Orlando subsequently reveals his
identity, her feelings are reinforced – he is the son of Sir Rowland,
her father's friend. Her budding love is therefore justified,
legitimized. But, given the response of the rest of the court, the
danger of her present circumstances becomes apparent; she must,
therefore, conceal from the court, though not from Celia, her delight
at Orlando's distinguished parentage.

Other directors have treated Duke Frederick's court more
humorously or more softly than Dexter did. In a jazzed-up
modern-dress version directed by Buzz Goodbody for the RSC in
1973, the Duke appeared as 'an elderly playboy in a black eyepatch',
while his dinner-jacketed guests smoked and circulated under a
showy chandelier.[3] The wrestling-match was a stagy TV affair
introduced by Charles's finger-stretching exercises and a histrionic
fist punched wickedly into the palm of his other hand. Charles was
actually played by a professional wrestler. A different atmosphere
was created at the New York Shakespeare Festival, where Joseph
Papp set his open-air version amid a grove of ghostly silver-white
branches. They were there for both court and forest, contributing to
the gentle, elegantly melancholy tone that prevailed throughout.
One reviewer commented that in this production the emotions as
well as the costumes were in pastel.[4] Neither of these versions could
quite uncover the sense of menace conveyed by the strict, unnatural
formality of Frederick's court in Dexter's interpretation. His
costumes and style were high Elizabethan, with ruffs, jewelled
brocade and curled wigs. But the decorative function of this style
was subordinated to its power to trap and fix the 'puppets' within it,
and force them into collusion with Frederick.[5]

What with evil dukes, heroic younger sons, love blossoming in
the midst of complicated familial hatreds and alliances, we are likely
to be reminded here of the typical procedures of fairy tales or
romances, and there is much in *As You Like It*, especially in the early
scenes, which will give us that impression. In I.i, for example, the

arbitrarily cruel behaviour of older brother to younger brother, and in 1.iii the equally unjustified and equally cruel behaviour of the Duke toward Rosalind, seem deliberately contrived to challenge our realistic expectations.

It is precisely this quality of contrivance which has led to the general tendency to de-emphasize Act 1 in both productions and criticism of the play. The common view has been that the initial scenes, given their rather arbitrary and unrealistic mode, exist primarily to get the main characters into Arden so that the real fun can begin. On the stage this has often meant hurried and superficial treatment aimed at laying down the lines of the plot while the audience settle into their seats. But it is important to discover and to register the truth under the contrivance. The play as a whole enjoys its own artificiality, but it has too a keenness of insight and a sharpness of observation that is never far below the surface. Indeed, one mark of a superior production may well be the sense that, from the very outset, the play is being seriously and fully scrutinized.

In the opening scene, Orlando complains that his brother, Oliver, keeps him 'rustically at home' without proper education. The reality of this was underlined in Dexter's production by having Orlando working the fields with the peasants, tying sheaves of grain in a 'Millet-like tableau'. His strength was suggested a moment later when he took his brother by the throat and hurled him to the ground in fury.[6] Oliver is an arbitrarily villainous older brother, a fairy-tale figure, but the deliberate artificiality of that kind of characterization was tied in this production to a firm naturalistic rendering. This approach drew out an important implication of the text itself: that the actual practice of Shakespeare's time – the tradition of primogeniture and the real injustice that often derived from it – could easily have harsh and ominous consequences for those affected by it; but modern productions and audiences can easily miss the relevance of this.

The full flavour of *As You Like It* is thus one that includes a blend of different tastes: elements of variety show, love story, and fairy tale are mixed together with close psychological observation and acute social awareness. During the central part of the play, an artificial convention, this time the 'pastoral', is offset by a sharply realistic set of attitudes toward *love* – the central subject of *As You Like It*, as it is of much pastoral literature. The play continually brings together the differing effects wrought by conventional forms and realistic presentation. In doing so, it uses widely various theatrical means,

such as athletic displays, elaborate set-pieces, disguises, mock
debates, songs, recitations, parodies and a masque. The essential
problem, and it is one that any director must contend with, is that,
once we are through with the fairy-tale twists and turns of Act I,
there is practically no *plot* whatever. Different energies must keep
the play afloat.

The play is a pot-pourri, and the performers must catch a style
that will make sense of it all and yet retain the play's humour,
lightness of touch and *charm*. There is no mistaking that charm, and
a production that lacks it is sure to founder. Rosalind is its exemplar,
the play's animating spirit; the audience, like Orlando, should fall in
love with her at first sight.[7] But the other characters must be worthy
of her. Orlando, who complains that his brother's mistreatment has
deprived him of education and refinement, is nevertheless no boor.
Still less is he a pretty boy. He needn't even be handsome, but he
does need to be attractive, vigorous, manly. Rosalind, after all, falls
in love with *him* at first sight too. He is extravagant, earnest,
impulsive, he takes himself too seriously, but he retains the winning
smile of the youngest child. Celia, so often played in the shadow of
Rosalind, actually has as much vivacity, and a gentler heart. It is she,
not Rosalind, who develops the plan to flee the court, and she who
is rewarded with a trouble-free love, after enduring for a time the
disconsolate but ironic role of fifth wheel. Even the more 'literary'
characters, such as Silvius and Phebe, parodies of types from
pastoral literature, are not without their charm: Silvius's naïveté, for
instance, or Phebe's amusing inconsistency.

Charm, however, does not preclude either scepticism or irony.
The best Rosalinds combine delight with comic detachment, and
Orlandos that are too sentimental are bound to drag. Although the
mooning, love-struck youth is still frequently to be seen, Orlandos
in recent years have begun to change, often bringing, as in Simon
Callow's performance in Dexter's National Theatre production, an
unexpected power to the role, a power that in his case was combined
with impish humour (for example, the trick of doing the obviously
expository speeches in I.i directly to the audience) and with naïve
earnestness (as in his habit of constant reading as though to catch up
on his education). In New York in 1973, Raul Julia played the part as
a high-energy youth 'straight out of West Side Story'.[8] Walter Kerr
praised his 'feline command' and a knowing, insinuating quality
that cast sceptical doubt on what was said and done – especially the
play-acting with Rosalind.[9] At one point during the false wooing, he

backed off shocked after Rosalind–Ganymede kissed him on the mouth, and he responded warily when Ganymede said with a knowing smile that he could do 'strange things'.[10]

It has been said that the essential thing in a production is to highlight the intense and ironic, warm and amusing, ultimately *real* relationship between the two principals, Orlando and Rosalind, by underlining the artifice of everything else.[11] This may have been the impulse behind a lavishly baroque, operatic version of the play that Trevor Nunn mounted in 1977. He provided, among other things, an allegorical prologue starring Hymen, Fortune and Nature, a large ensemble piece that turned 'It was a lover and his lass' into a choral celebration of spring, and a final masque with Hymen entering on a 'baroque cloud which opened and shut, attended by cherubs with absurd wings'.[12] Critics differed as to whether the essential combination of powerful erotic charge and ironic detachment was present in the central relationship, though one remarked that the intent of the production seemed to be to celebrate the baroque while at the same time suggesting its limitations in terms of human values.[13]

The usual approach to the play has indeed been to stress the 'reality' of Orlando and Rosalind in opposition to the unreality of the play's other elements, which accounts for its susceptibility to productions in which artifice is allowed to flower as in a greenhouse. One revival that I saw (at the Vancouver Playhouse, 1980) portrayed Duke Senior and his men as a bunch of left-over hippies, complete with benign young women with shawls, ineffable smiles and a baby (they looked always on the verge of saying, 'Have a good day!'); there was even a Hare Krishna adept in this forest, and Jaques, huge and bearded, looked like a graduate-student drop-out in search of hallucinogenic enlightenment. Touchstone was a new-wave Las Vegas-style master of ceremonies, Phebe appeared in a skin-tight scarlet jumpsuit on roller skates, and Rosalind and Celia were a pair of gum-chewing adolescents on the loose, their ears glued to transistor radios. The production substituted the humour generated by surprise for the necessary charm, and thus ended up being funny but trivial.

There is no doubt that the relationship between Orlando and Rosalind is the primary thing, and that their interplay in Acts III and IV is the very centre of the play's interest and idea, as well as its chief delight. It is also true that the extensive background – sub-plots, set-pieces and all – is more consciously artificial than the central relationship. A successful production can therefore be mounted which makes a clear distinction between foreground and background. Central to any version, however, will be the two scenes, iii.ii and iv.i, in which Orlando wooes the disguised Rosalind, thinking she is only a young man pretending to be Rosalind. (The artifice of the situation here does not take away from the reality of the interplay; in fact the scenes provide the best example in the play of Shakespeare's deriving human significance out of conventional materials.) Rosalind's disguise affords her a wonderful opportunity for ironic deflation but it doesn't completely cover her deep and growing feelings. The dramatic result is a constantly shifting movement from mockery to rapture, which both captivates and confuses Orlando.

In the National Theatre production to which I have already referred several times, Sara Kestelman gave Rosalind a dynamic, fast-talking power, as well as a persuasive 'androgynous eroticism' that fit in exactly with the overall approach. The conception was first of all serious. It was also passionate, sincere and, at the same time, formal (as revealed not only by the acting-style but also by the costumes, which reminded more than one reviewer of Nicholas Hilliard miniatures). Kestelman perhaps missed the softness and tenderness of the part, its sweeter and gentler tonalities, but this was in keeping with Dexter's emphasis on courtly Elizabethan style and rich country rites. The empty, even menacing, ritual played out at Duke Frederick's court was replaced in Arden by a hard-won spring, symbolized especially in the ritual slaying of a deer. Arden first appeared as a wind-swept and wintry tundra that was gradually tickled into life. 'After the interval a slender tree with white blossoms rose up centre stage . . . and later expanded into an umbrella of cascading leaves, the focus for country rituals, garlanded with flowers, and in the finale becoming a Maypole.'[14] Some critics felt that *The Golden Bough*, quoted in the programme, was putting in a too-obtrusive appearance,[15] though others saw the seasonal associations as integral to the serious purpose.

The high point of anthropological reference came in iv.ii, a tiny, usually unnoticed scene, where, instead of a modest hunters' song and a stuffed dear head, the Dexter production invented an elaborate ritual. William, almost always presented as a comic yokel in other revivals, was conceived of as a local country boy who had succeeded in killing the deer and who was therefore initiated and rewarded (in the text he is not even in iv.ii). The plump deer was cut open on stage; William was smeared with its blood and given an antler-crown, as other members of the exiled court group gathered around wearing deer masks. Some of the entrails, as well as a red garland, were hung on the central, sacred tree. For the final masque, William again appeared, this time as Hymen (recruited by Rosalind), an antlered, rustic god surrounded again by figures in deer masks.[16] Against this background, the Rosalind–Orlando scenes were played out with both wit and intensity; they probably ended up being slightly less gay, less delightfully mocking, less tender, than in more conventional productions, but at the same time they came across as more deeply erotic.

The love scenes culminate in v.ii, where the complications introduced by the Silvius–Phebe plot and the ambiguity of Phebe's love for Rosalind–Ganymede come to a head. In the famous 'quartet', as it has come to be called, the four as-yet unmatched lovers intone in a highly formal, rhetorical way what it means to love:

> SILVIUS. It is to be all made of sighs and tears;
>   And so am I for Phebe.
> PHEBE. And I for Ganymede.
> ORLANDO. And I for Rosalind.
> ROSALIND. And I for no woman.
> SILVIUS. It is to be all made of faith and service;
>   And so am I for Phebe.
> PHEBE. And I for Ganymede.
> ORLANDO. And I for Rosalind.
> ROSALIND. And I for no woman . . .
>
> (V.ii.84–93)

Despite Rosalind's high-spirited irony – she ends the recital with 'Pray you no more of this; 'tis like the howling of Irish wolves against the moon' – there is an important sense here that her and Orlando's love is parallel to, and continuous with, that of Silvius and Phebe. There is a sense of community, of shared values. The quartet is indeed just that – a quartet in which each member has an important voice, though Rosalind's is the first violin. It is also deliberately formal and therefore a challenge to modern, naturalistic production techniques.

The scene can certainly be played ironically – mocking or 'guying' both character and situation and refusing to take the romanticism

seriously. An alternative strategy would be to seek a style that suits
this scene not only to the Rosalind–Orlando dialogues, but to
various aspects of the 'background' as well. In Dexter's production,
the quartet was ritualized, each lover, as he or she spoke,
touching hands against the sacred tree. At the same time, the
powerful eroticism of the production was evoked in Rosalind's
promise to Orlando, just after the quartet and right on the heels of
her ironic remark about Irish wolves: 'leaning against that tree
among those white flowers and fixing her dark, piercing eyes upon
Orlando . . . she filled "I will satisfy you if ever I satisfied man" with
fierce, urgent desire'.[17] One can readily see how other elements of
the play – the songs, for instance, concerned as they are with
country life, with weather, love and fertility might fit into this sort
of conception.

All this may sound a little heavy for so gentle a play as this one,
but handled with delicacy, and not forgetting the subversive
ironies, such an approach could give both depth and seriousness to
a production without eliminating the charm. No doubt a certain
gravity is likely to characterize the kind of production that Dexter
mounted. But the advantage of taking the *whole* play seriously,
including the early scenes (which Dexter emphasized rather than
hurried over), can compensate for any loss of gaiety.

Shakespeare derived the basic plot and situation of *As You Like It*
from a prose romance called *Rosalynde*, published in 1590 and
written by Thomas Lodge. Two of the play's most memorable
characters, Touchstone and Jaques, do not, however, appear in
Lodge's work but are Shakespeare's own creations. Touchstone,
inventive, parodic, cheerful, and realistic, may owe part of his
character to the personality and capabilities of Will Kemp, the clown
of Shakespeare's company till about 1599, who probably created the
role, though the sharper voice of Robert Armin, who replaced
Kemp, can also be heard in the part. Touchstone's function is often
to deflate the romantic pretensions of his betters, but his 'love' for
Audrey leads him to join in with the other 'country copulatives', as
he calls them, in the final festive rites. Mockery and celebration, the
two poles of the play's attitudes, are neatly combined in him.
Audrey, who since at least 1825 has been seen wandering barefoot
around the stage peeling and eating a turnip or, more recently,
munching an apple, seems inevitably and incorrigibly a wench.

Touchstone, by contrast, has been played in many colours, including the traditional motley, but his outward guise hardly affects his essentially ironic, corrective and, at the same time, complementary role.

Jaques is a more difficult case. He has been played in a hundred different ways, often with a minimum of attention to the style of the rest of the production. There is a tendency for the lead actor of a troupe to take the role, with the result that it can get a trifle overweighted. It is, after all, a minor, though mysterious, part, whose main function is tonal. Still, tone can be important, especially in such a play as *As You Like It*, and one can understand the appeal of the role. A further difficulty, or challenge, is that Jaques has become famous for a single speech (the 'seven ages'), which has frequently been taken out of context and now presents something of a hurdle to the actor. It is, of course, a set-piece, akin to Touchstone's comic disquisition on the various 'degrees of the lie' in the final scene. Both provide entertainment, and both fill in time between an important character's exit and subsequent re-entry (Orlando with Adam in the first instance, Rosalind with Hymen in the second – she needs the time for a quick costume change). But of course Jaques' speech is much better known, and the actor has to get through it somehow, without having half the audience mouthing a *sotto voce* accompaniment. In the New York production mentioned earlier, Frederick Coffin, dressed in black against the predominantly white surroundings, bounced back quickly in answer to the Duke's clichéd comment about 'this wide and universal theatre', treating 'All the world's a stage' as an 'almost idiotically obvious explanation of the Duke's proposition'. He thus bypassed 'that awful split-second pause in which the actor steadies himself for a bout with what he feels to be a bromide'.[18] This type of approach allows the actor to play the elaborations in the speech as variations or improvisations on his performance, discovered as he goes along.

The basis of the character is a posture, parallel to the poses of Silvius, Phebe, and even Duke Senior with his praise of the value of country life and his rapid return to the court once conditions allow it. Jaques' posture is melancholy, a fashionable Elizabethan malady, indicative supposedly of profundity and complexity of character. His view of the world is therefore satiric, even cynical – i.e. he imagines he sees farther than others do; he distrusts pleasure, perhaps because, as we are told, he has once been a 'libertine' himself; and he enjoys the special place that his role as a malcontent and the eloquence with which he performs it create for him in the Duke's circle. Some actors prefer to see Jaques as ironically aware of the role he is playing. In the Dexter production, Michael Bryant's performance seemed to extend its cynical observation of the world to the fashion of melancholy that he himself had adopted.[19] Other actors have treated the melancholy as less of a pose, and more the result of Jaques' thirst for experience (as he claims it is in IV.i).

Whatever the approach, Jaques is clearly the centre of the Duke's exiled retinue. When he is not there, the others talk about him, and, when he is, they defer to him. One critic commented about Richard Pasco's Jaques in Goodbody's modern-dress version of the play that 'the party was never complete when he wasn't there, and never at ease when he was'.[20] There were reticent indications of a 'tensely loving relationship' between himself and the Duke, the latter enjoying Jaques' talk but always a bit nervous about what he might say. Pasco's conception of the part was built around the textual hints that he has been a libertine and a scholar. He 'had the air of a man faced with the alternative of alcoholism or indigestion' and knew, like a character out of Graham Greene, that 'every smile can accompany an unpleasant memory'. After the 'seven ages' speech, 'left alone at the dining table, [he] wheezed his way into a long belly-laugh – at the Duke, at life, at us – which became, in effect, the beginning of the interval.' The same derisive attitude toward sentiment appeared at the end, when Jaques' departure to join the converted Duke Frederick was edged with bitterness. The wedding had been staged with rock music and modern dancing which Jaques had watched from the side. He spat out, 'So to your pleasures / I am for other than for dancing measures', in a way that clearly disconcerted the Duke. A shadow thus fell over the little sequence that follows:

> DUKE. Stay, Jaques, stay.
> JAQUES. To see no pastime I. What you would have
> I'll stay to know at your abandon'd cave (*Exit*).
> DUKE. Proceed, proceed. We'll begin these rites
> As we do trust they'll end, in true delights.
>
> (v.iv.93–7)

Here, as so often, Shakespeare gives no hint of his intentions. Critics who argue that the text should be played 'straight' forget that much of Shakespeare is made up of just such moments as this. Pasco didn't hesitate before leaving. He was aloof and misanthropic, and, as an uncomfortable hush settled over the crowded stage, the Duke had trouble recovering enough poise to restart the dancing.

The importance of Jaques' role in the play can thus be measured by the effect that he can have on the ending. The most common approach to his decision to leave is to have it easily accepted, his exit only a brief comma in the action, the return to 'delights' genuine and normal. But, given a performance such as Pasco's, the predominantly festive tone of the marriage celebrations is a little soured by Jaques' harshness and Duke Senior's disappointment. If, on the other hand, Jaques is primarily an absurd *poseur*, his refusal to take part in the final festivities will be no great loss, and the tone of the ending will be uninterrupted by melancholy. A production that adds a concluding tinge of sadness – and to do so with the comedies is rather in fashion these days – will usually prepare for it by giving real weight to Jaques' weariness, or scepticism, or restlessness, earlier in the action. The tonality established near the beginning by the winter and rough weather, metaphorical or literal or both, will thus be carried through to the end, despite the indications of a general clearing. On the other hand, a more satirical or comic conception of Jaques will reduce his importance throughout the play, making him the butt of Touchstone's, Rosalind's and even Orlando's wit, and revealing his final exit as yet another self-deluding pose.

The complexity of the ending is elaborated by two other noteworthy elements. One is the masque of Hymen; the other, Rosalind's epilogue. The high formality and solemnity of the one, and the witty informality of the other, bespeak the play's delight in contrasts. The masque – at least in our time, when deliberate artifice is so much suspected – has generally fared worse in the hands of directors than the epilogue. It has been cut, sidestepped, curtailed or performed with a certain amount of embarrassment. But it has also been met head-on: highlighted, as at Ashland in 1979, by the descent on a trapeze of an eight-foot golden god, backed by a golden monstrance, who provided a sonorous benediction; or integrated into the country rituals, as at the National Theatre. Like the other 'variety' elements, the masque is partly a 'number' in itself, partly a figure to be woven into the overall tapestry. However it may be done, it requires subtlety and tact to fit it in. The epilogue depends entirely on Rosalind and, unlike the masque, is hard to spoil, though it loses something in the post-Elizabethan theatre, since

women's parts are no longer played by boys. (Nor will all-male
productions really serve to resurrect lost stage conditions.) Playing
ironically with the differences between men and women, and the
ambiguity she herself embodies, Rosalind ends the play with that
combination of wit and charm, mockery and celebration, which has
characterized it, and her, throughout.

4
Twelfth Night

How old is Feste? The director's answer to that question will be one indication of his or her attitude toward *Twelfth Night* as a whole. In recent years it has become fashionable to give us an aging Feste, a precarious, vulnerable, melancholy fool whose wit is the brighter for the dark background. And, if Feste is old, the general emphasis is likely to be autumnal, with a sense of winter coming on and people buttoning up against the cold. At Stratford Ontario in 1980, William Hutt's quiet, dignified and haunting Feste even wore a wool scarf knotted around his neck. His age was matched by that of Maria, played by Kate Reid, who was a gentlewoman well past her prime, rather desperately seeking a match with a much younger Sir Toby Belch.

'Autumnal' has, in fact, become something of a byword when applied to *Twelfth Night*. A play that in simpler days was primarily a high-spirited romp has, on more careful examination, revealed the latent melancholy and complexity of feeling that lie beneath the spirited surface. And this, I think, has meant a real gain in our understanding. The essence of *Twelfth Night* is the rich and delicate web of relationships that it spins. If the previous age took its cue from the revelry suggested by the festive associations of the title (the twelve days of Christmas), the present age looks to the wintry landscape outside the brightly lit windows and to the quandaries suggested by the ambiguous sub-title: 'What You Will'.

The play blends lyricism and mockery, sadness and wit, melancholy and revelry. And, as with so much else in Shakespeare, no production can afford to neglect one side completely, though most directors will tend to weight their reading in one way or another. The ideal, I suppose, is the approach John Barton described in talking about his 1969 production: 'The text contains an enormous range of emotions and moods and most productions seem to select one – farce or bitterness or romance – and emphasize it throughout. I wanted to sound all the notes that are there.'[1] What this might mean in practice is that even the purely comic moments will be shot through with unsettling emotion, and the more serious scenes

51

interfused with humour. Subtlety of tone becomes crucial in the
attempt to catch the shifting moods; what Feste says to Orsino might
stand as a motto for the play as a whole: 'the melancholy god protect
thee, and the tailor make thy doublet of changeable taffeta, for thy
mind is a very opal.' At Stratford Ontario in 1985, Feste pointed this
line with a series of sleight-of-hand tricks involving a taffeta
handkerchief: taffeta, opal – a play of light, colour and shadow.

Take, for example, the character of Sir Andrew Aguecheek.
Played usually as a goofy, foolish knight, often tall, gangly and
awkward, a butt of the comic games of his intellectual superiors, an
absurd yes-man to Sir Toby, he nevertheless has his dignified and
slightly pathetic side. When Sir Toby says of the intrepid Maria that
'she's a beagle, true-bred, and one that adores me', Andrew replies
wistfully, 'I was ador'd once too.' This line could be delivered as
simply another of Andrew's many attempts to keep up with Sir
Toby, but how much richer it is if we suddenly see a new side of the
bumbling fool – a man of some feeling who really was adored, once.
Stanley Wells comments that 'the role is one in which comedy and
pathos are often inseparable, because the pathos comes from a
realization of inadequacy which also has comic aspects'. He quotes
from a review of Barton's production: 'When [Andrew] hears that
Olivia cannot abide anything yellow he quietly and sadly conceals
the little bunch of primroses with which he has been hoping to woo
her, and thereafter carries only pink flowers.'[2] Poor Andrew is
perpetually behind, and this makes him funny.

But it also makes him vulnerable, and it is precisely this sense of
vulnerability that characterizes the emotional life of the play as a
whole – people's loves, fantasies and hopes are so easily bruised,
and even their triumphs, as at the end, are fragile and bring with
them a cluster of contrary feelings. The play ends with Feste's
evocative song of the wind and the rain, a reminder, as at the
beginning of *As You Like It*, of winter and rough weather. Precarious
happiness may make us think of Chekhov, and modern directors
sometimes turn to him in their search for the right tone. Trevor
Nunn has said of Peter Hall's trend-setting 1958 production at
Stratford that Hall 'touched a Chekhov-like centre in the play',[3] and
in the programme of Robin Phillips' Stratford Ontario production
Chekhov is quoted: 'It usually takes as much time to be happy as to
wind up one's watch.'

The image from Chekhov suggests another feature of the play,
also emphasized by Phillips – its sense of domestic life. Two

households dominate the scene, and nearly every character is connected to one or the other. One of these houses we get to know intimately – that of Olivia, with its great lady, her waiting gentlewoman, her steward, her licensed fool, her poor relation, and assorted servants and hangers-on. Orsino's world is more remote, but it is still a functioning house. The life of a household means a network of relationships and this we get *par excellence* in Olivia's palazzo, with its friendships, alliances, rivalries, hates and loves. Olivia, the queen of the hive, is served by Maria and Malvolio (between whom there is no love lost), amused by Feste, exasperated by Sir Toby and wooed by Sir Andrew Aguecheek, all of whom can claim some place in the network, and all of whom interact in multiple ways.

To take but one example, what is the relationship between Feste and Maria like? Each has a special place in the household and both have been there for some time. Maria is not a soubrette nor a buxom serving-girl; she is a gentlewoman of good family, a lady in waiting. Most modern productions get this right, avoiding the old tradition of making her merely a wench. Giving her her rightful dignity will make a difference in her relationships with the others in the house, including Feste. Theirs will not necessarily be a jocular, bouncy association based on clowning and witty exchanges, but may easily be one in which their mutual concern, based on a shared past, plays a central role. Feste, in turn, may be more than a fool – perhaps, like William Hutt, an 'impecunious gentleman' who has carved himself a place in Olivia's household and wants to stay there.[4] Their first dialogue together, at the beginning of I.v, will set the tone. Maria scolds Feste in a familiar, teasing way: 'Nay, either tell me where thou hast been, or I will not open my lips so wide as a bristle may enter in way of thy excuse. My lady will hang thee for thy absence.' Feste tries his clown's method of witty avoidance, which she enjoys, but she comes back in a minute to the point: 'Yet you will be hanged for being so long absent; or be turned away, is not that as good as a hanging to you?' The threat of losing his job, though he deftly brushes it astride, may indeed be a genuine one; economic reality edges in. In the 1985 Stratford Ontario production directed by David Giles, this whole dialogue was conducted as Maria helped Feste, who was distinctly old and frail, into his tattered motley. She held a pail up to him, he dunked his head in and came up white-faced. She was clearly his friend and knew his routines. Later, heeding her warning, he had to work hard to please Olivia and keep his job.

Both Maria and Feste are economically dependent, and each is aware of the other's position. Maria wants to marry Sir Toby – she 'adores' him, but perhaps also she is looking for some kind of economic security (though Sir Toby too depends on the generosity of his niece or the gullibility of chumps like Andrew). At the end of their little dialogue, Feste, in his characteristically oblique way, alludes to her none-too-secret desire, which some recent Marias have shown to be rather desperate: 'If Sir Toby would leave drinking, thou wert as pretty a piece of Eve's flesh as any in Illyria.' Her response, 'Peace, you rogue, no more o' that', shows again their familiar, teasing closeness and perhaps too a poorly concealed desperation (as Kate Reid played it), a quickly replaced dignity or an amused carefreeness.

As for Sir Toby, he is more than a comic drunkard, or a bumbling clown. As far back as Granville-Barker's important production in 1914, he was treated properly as a gentleman, though one who is slightly down at heel.'[5] Nevertheless, subsequent directors and actors have often followed comic tradition and played the caricature. His age is uncertain, though it seems fitting that, as Feste and Maria are getting older, he seems to be getting younger. He carries the play's revelry on his shoulders, but he can also display a harsh and bitter side which cuts against the general festivity. The strongest example of this is his outburst in the final scene: 'I hate a drunken rogue', he says in reference to the besotted Dick Surgeon, who never appears. But many actors have seen in the line some justification for a vein of self-hatred in Sir Toby's character. The notion is strengthened a moment later by his sudden unmotivated attack on the innocent Andrew, who has merely offered to help: 'Will you help? An ass-head and a coxcomb and a knave, a thin-fac'd knave, a gull' (v.i.203–4). If Maria is on-stage here (again this is a matter for a director to decide, since the text is silent), she may well take over, helping Sir Toby out or, perhaps, be rejected in her turn. She has won herself a husband, but she may already be regretting it.

Thus the interplay of feeling established early on, say in the little scene between Feste and Maria discussed above, can have interesting consequences in the finale. Such subtlety can be extended as well into what used to be called the 'kitchen scene', the night of drunken revelry that Malvolio so rudely interrupts (II.iii). The traditional way of doing that scene was to load it down with exaggerated comic business, though at present we can hope for some signs of other feelings along with the madcap humour – a touch of sadness in Feste's song, an edge of belligerence in Sir Toby, or, again, a sense of solidarity between Feste and Maria. In Barton's production (see Plate 3), there was a good deal of boisterous singing, including an extension of the old ballad, 'There dwelt a man in Babylon', of which Shakespeare gives us only the first line, and there was much else besides. I quote from Wells' description:

The old ballad to which [Shakespeare] alludes continues:

> Of reputation great in fame;
> He took to wife a fair woman;
> Susanna was her name.

But here the name was varied to Maria; the episode became a mock-courtship of Maria, who stood on a chair as the revellers danced around her. Complexities of emotion emerged. The mock-courtship by Sir Toby was something in which Maria would have liked to believe; a clasp of hands between Feste and her suggested a sympathetic understanding between them.

Later in the scene, when Malvolio scolded Sir Toby, a hard edge appeared in the latter's genial hedonism. His famous response to Malvolio's rebuke, 'Art any more than a steward? Dost thou think because thou art virtuous, there shall be no more cakes and ale?' was spoken 'with a passion that was the more impressive because it was clear from Maria's reactions that in thus challenging Malvolio he was endangering his own place in Olivia's household'.[6]

By the end of this scene, after Malvolio's repressive interruption, the comic energies seem to have flagged and yet another set of feelings emerges. Andrew's 'I was ador'd once' introduces a note of pathos, and Sir Toby's 'Let's to bed, knight. Thou hadst need send for more money', reminds us again of the economic realities behind the high-jinks. There is a sense of depletion, of lethargy; Toby's last line is 'Come, come, I'll go burn some sack. 'Tis too late to go to bed now. Come knight; come knight.' It is not hard to imagine Andrew, like run-down clockwork, trailing slowly out, while Sir Toby, his heart no longer in it, tries to make the best of the situation. Alternatively, of course, the two can exit cutting a caper, still looking for fun. Such energy will be appropriate for a high-spirited production showing no more than a touch of melancholy. There is perhaps more subtlety in the first way, more innocent delight in the second.

We have been neglecting Malvolio. What of him? More than any other character, he is subject to a variety of interpretations. Is he simply a pompous ass, and hence a fitting butt for the practical joke that undermines his hard-earned dignity? Is he a fool, a puritan, a man of some sensitivity, even if too earnest and self-concerned? Whatever he is, his is the star male part, and he has therefore been played by an array of brilliant actors. He has often evoked sympathy as well as laughter and contempt, especially at the end, where the treatment he undergoes at the hands of the comics seems to outweigh his crimes, and has thus reminded some critics of the treatment of Shylock. Overall, he has been played more for comedy than pathos, though usually comedy with an edge. Gielgud, in 1931, was 'sere and yellow', a 'Puritan to the core'; Olivier, in 1955, was the lower-class fellow who had worked his way up, his affected speech sometimes slipping to reveal the broader vowels of his upbringing; Donald Sinden, in 1969, was 'a Victorian cartoon Humpty Dumpty', pompous and absurd; Nicol Williamson in 1974 was, in the Gielgud vein, a 'pinched Scottish elder', very tall and gangling with a ruff around his neck giving him a small detached-looking head on a grotesque body; Brian Bedford at Stratford Ontario in 1980 was broadly comic, complete with a teddy bear half-concealed under his nightshirt in II.iii, which inevitably led to a good deal of funny business. Back in the early part of this century, Beerbohm Tree played Malvolio with an earnest dignity that was both impressive and absurd; he was attended by 'four smaller Malvolios, who aped the great chamberlain in dress, in manners and in deportment'; nevertheless, his ultimate loss of Olivia was emotionally telling. Shaw describes one wonderful moment: while descending a magnificent staircase, Tree slipped and fell; 'without betraying the smallest discomfiture, [he] raised his eyeglass and surveyed the landscape as if he had sat down on purpose'.[7]

When Malvolio exits at the end, the subject of the Fool's ridicule and the others' laughter, his hopes to gain the fair Olivia (like those of the hapless Sir Andrew Aguecheek) for ever dashed, he shouts 'I'll be reveng'd on the whole pack of you.' The festivity of the ending is at least temporarily disrupted, and a note of grievance and distaste enters in. Just how much a director will allow this mood to intrude upon the dominant feeling of joy will affect profoundly the final taste of the production. Some modulation of the mood is inevitable and desirable. Even the most comic Malvolios are likely to bring to this moment some feeling of pathos, as with Bedford's wince at Olivia's friendly touch, which underlined his loneliness and the shame he felt at his exposure. Nicholas Pennell's performance at Stratford Ontario in 1985, though it stressed Malvolio's absurdity, elicited a sympathetic 'oh' from the audience as he appeared dirty, downcast and bedraggled. His final line, with a significant pause after 'reveng'd', was restrained and bitter. Pinched and puritanical Malvolios, such as Gielgud's and Williamson's, are the least likely to excite sympathy. Gielgud, for example, went out snarling and spiteful. With his patrician presence, Henry Irving in the last century made his exit frightening and vindictive – he clearly meant mischief. No sympathy there, but a sense of danger undermining the final peace. Olivier's final words were 'the pained cry of a man who . . . refuses to see himself as others see him'.[8] An element of tragic feeling thus mingled with the comic. And Donald Sinden left 'the right bitterness in the mouth when the play's flight from realism might have seemed too precipitate'.[9] It is hard, then, to say how Malvolio should, or predict how he will, be played. But any performance will have to take account of both the comic absurdity – especially in the famous letter scene and its aftermath, when he appears smiling foolishly, in yellow stockings and cross-gartered – and his earnest vulnerability, veiled as it may be by pomposity or self-congratulation.

Malvolio and Feste are natural enemies, living in the same household, each competing for place, and, presumably, taking any available opportunity to goad one another. At the outset, Malvolio turns up his nose at Feste – 'I marvel your ladyship takes delight in such a barren rascal. I saw him put down the other day with an ordinary fool that has no more brain than a stone' (i.v.80–2). At the end Feste reminds Malvolio, rather cruelly, of his earlier words and the price he has paid for them: 'and thus the whirligig of time brings in his revenges' (v.i.373–4). Perhaps we could say that these two characters represent two poles of the play, and a director's choices will lead him or her to weight one or the other. The tendency over the last twenty years or so has been to make Feste the spiritual centre (one production even had him stationed on-stage throughout).[10] And Malvolio's role, though obviously important, has been correspondingly diminished.

One other character in Olivia's household – the very minor but puzzling figure, Fabian – deserves a brief mention. He turns up at the end of Act ii to take part in the plot against Malvolio, presumably because the latter has brought him 'out o' favor with my lady about a

bear-baiting here'. Directors have not always known what to do
with him, but he cannot be cut, since he is crucial to the trick played
on Andrew and Viola (their 'duel'). One of the most inventive
answers to the question of who Fabian really is was Hugh Hunt's at
the Old Vic in 1950. He made Fabian into a second fool, a younger
rival to Feste, seeking the latter's spot in the household. This
emphasized again the economics of Feste's position, and led to a
nice moment in the last scene when Fabian is preferred over Feste in
the reading of Malvolio's letter. The final song, poignant but
unsentimental, thus seemed to suggest that Feste had been
succeeded, and faced alone the 'wind and the rain'.[11]

Twelfth Night presents us with a tangled web of unfulfilled desire,
of blind alleys and frustrated hopes. Among the principal characters
these discontents are for the most part overcome, as the conventions
and structure of comedy demand. But the feelings that they have
induced remain, and the uneasiness of many of the characters
(Malvolio, Andrew and Feste we have already mentioned) gives us
pause. To choose another telling, if minor, example, we might ask
what happens to Sebastian's friend Antonio. He seems quite clearly
in love with Sebastian, following him to Illyria despite the personal
danger this puts him in: 'But come what may, I do adore thee so /
That danger shall seem sport, and I will go' (ii.i.45–6). After
suffering, as the others do, the confusions occasioned by the
similarity between Viola and Sebastian, Antonio, unlike Orsino or
Olivia (but very much like that other Antonio in *The Merchant of
Venice*), remains unrewarded, a silent observer of the final
heterosexual pairing-off. Again, a production can emphasize the
pain and loss of this moment – and there are lots of hints in the play
to justify an approach which underlines the sexual ambiguity of
many of the relationships – or it can, in a more purely comic fashion,
transform Antonio's disappointment into delight. I prefer the more
sombre approach because, in general in the play, it is the
impossibilities of love that stand out, its self-created obstacles and
perverseness. These are neatly and happily cleared away by the
magic of the story, with its identical twins fulfilling and rounding
out the fantasy. But the reality of the wind and the rain has its say
and is still around at the end to shadow the conclusion.

Orsino loves Olivia, who loves Viola, who loves Orsino. There
you have the problematic circle of the main plot. The entrance of
Sebastian clears away the difficulties by, as it were, doubling Viola,
giving both Olivia and Orsino a legitimate and possible (i.e.

heterosexual) love object. At the beginning, Orsino and Olivia are drowning in a sea of comic self-indulgence, Orsino nursing his love-melancholy not to cure it but to keep it alive, Olivia exaggerating her mourning for her dead father and brother and forswearing all male company. Each of them avoids real emotion by constructing a set of artificial 'poetic' feelings with a defined code. Orsino's cultivation of melancholy keeps him from seeing Viola's devotion for what it is (though more than one production has seen him as bisexually attracted to him–her), and Olivia's grief is easily shown to be a comic sham by the alacrity with which she falls for Viola–Cesario. Viola is the catalyst for both, engaging ambiguous feelings that disturb the equanimity of the measured but illusory worlds that each has created.

The interpretative question for both Orsino and Olivia concerns the degree of satire or comic mockery that may be directed at them. Orsino can easily be played as a luxuriating, slightly absurd, pampered aristocrat, with nothing more to do than lie around on this or that couch and have music feed his melancholy. The fact that he is the ruling duke of the principality seems to play almost no part in his life. One production that I saw had him constantly and elaborately mirrored, even directly above, so that when he lay down, as he often did, he could watch himself suffer. But he can also be given a degree of strength and presence, making Viola's love for him more credible, and turning his love-madness into, perhaps, a charming obsession, a brooding aberration, or even the inevitable result of a loving nature. Colm Feore, in David Giles's production, was strong, and used to command; his obsession with Olivia was clearly aberrant, stemming perhaps from the fact that he was unable to command *her*. His growing interest in Viola–Cesario thus suggested a truer relationship, blocked though it temporarily was by the confusion of sex. In general, though some 'gentle satire' is certainly mingled with the 'lyric strain',[12] a winning, masculine Orsino is preferable to a swooning one.

As for Olivia, she has occasioned a wider range of interpretations. For many years, she was played as a dignified countess, somewhat older than the others, commanding her house with a sensible firmness and gaining from characters and audience a fair amount of respect. Peter Hall, in his 'Chekhovian' production at Stratford in 1958, revised all that, making her into 'a pouting doll, a gawky, giggling coquette',[13] much younger than she had traditionally been. In Barton's 1969 production, which developed some of Hall's ideas, she was also young and silly. Such an Olivia will necessarily affect our view of Orsino and his love, making him seem blinder and more foolishly obsessed than ever. She is now usually young, though at Stratford Ontario in 1980 she was considerably older and coolly dignified once again. This allowed for a distinctly agreeable Orsino, who lost little of our estimation despite his obsession. Nor was the silliness of either of them completely neglected. In Olivia especially, the sight of an older woman making a fool of herself in the face of such youngsters as Viola and Sebastian (though the former, unfortunately, was no spring chicken either) had both ironic and slightly distasteful consequences.

Both of these characters, and indeed the very life of the main plot of the play, revolve around Viola–Cesario. Her quickness, her lyricism, her good sense, her loyalty define the tone and dominate the action. She is one of Shakespeare's great comic heroines, but unlike the others she is remarkably helpless. For all her initiative and daring, her wit and resourcefulness, she seems less dominant, more at the mercy of events than Portia, Rosalind, Helena (in *All's Well*) or even Beatrice. And she is the only one of these to become the butt of a major joke – the mock duel in Act IV. Beatrice is fooled by her friends, tricked into loving the man she is already half in love with. But Viola is actually made fun of by the comic rowdies, her helplessness made manifest. It is an unusual state of affairs to have the most attractive, most positive character in the play turn for a while into one of its dupes, but it is a measure of the kind of play we are dealing with. That mixture of lyricism and revelry, invocation and mockery, that I spoke of at the beginning is nowhere so richly embodied as in the person of Viola.

In II.iv, the many moods of the play gather softly around the heroine, and the trick will be for actress and production to hold and carry as many as possible: the gentle comedy of mistaken identity, the lyrical evocation of the shortness of youth and beauty, the deep sadness of Feste's song ('Come away, come away, death'), and especially Viola–Cesario's artfully ironic and melancholy story of his–her 'sister' who 'sat like Patience on a monument, / Smiling at grief'. This is one of those moments, infrequent but crucial, when the action stops and its opalescent tonalities are allowed to eddy freely:

> ORSINO. For women are as roses, whose fair flow'r
> Being once display'd, doth fall that very hour.

VIOLA. And so they are. Alas, that they are so,
To die, even when they to perfection grow!
(II.iv.38–41)

Later, the lyrical voice is countered by the comic: 'Say that some lady', says Viola, 'Hath for your love as great a pang of heart / As you have for Olivia' (ll. 89–91). But Orsino refuses to believe in such a possibility: 'There is no woman's sides / Can bide the beating of so strong a passion / As love doth give my heart . . . they lack retention.' The joke, of course, is on him. And Viola proceeds to tell her own story in a disguised way. Orsino is engaged by it; as Colm Feore and Seana McKenna played the scene at Stratford Ontario, he moved in towards her: 'But died thy sister of her love, my boy?', to which she replied mysteriously, 'I am all the daughters of my father's house, / And all the brothers too – and yet I know not.' A pause; Orsino was standing *too* close to her. Deliciously confused feelings filled the moment. Then she broke away, returning to more comfortable ground: 'Sir, shall I to this lady?' – 'Ay, that's the theme.' His constructed plot and artificially created emotions were easier for Orsino than these unfamiliar stirrings. Judi Dench, speaking the above lines in Barton's 1969 production, gave 'a tiny pause followed by a catch in the voice as she said "brothers" ' – a reminder, in the midst of her fiction, of the reality, to her though not to us, of her lost brother.[14] Such subtle interplay between illusion and reality is both appropriate and necessary for a scene, indeed a play, in which the lyric and ironic voices are so finely modulated.

We get the same mixture in the final scene, where the recognition and unravelling are sandwiched between the climactic outbursts first of Sir Toby and then of Malvolio. Even within the recognition itself, there are ironic underlinings of the conventional features of such scenes. Can Viola really say to Sebastian with a straight face, 'My father had a mole upon his brow?' She can and does, and the ironic reminiscence only adds to the sense of an exquisite stateliness, a measured formality which prolongs and encircles the act of recognition itself. J. C. Trewin describes how in the hands of an actress such as Peggy Ashcroft the moment can be magical indeed; after Sebastian's wondering question, 'What countryman? What name? What parentage?' there was a long pause before Viola, 'in almost a whisper (but one of infinite rapture and astonishment) answer[ed]: "Of Messaline!" ' Trewin comments, 'Practically for the first time in my experience a Viola [had] forced me to believe in her past.'[15] Viola, in keeping with the measured quality of the scene, forbears an embrace with her brother until 'each circumstance / Of place, time, fortune, do cohere and jump / That I am Viola' (v.i.248–50). Orsino adopts the same manner as he moves to the faithless boy turned faithful woman: 'Give me thy hand, / And let me see thee in thy woman's weeds' (ll. 269–70). Again the embrace is postponed, the formality allowed. The scene, like many others in the play, manages to be both moving and funny, and calls for the kind of subtle playing that can evoke both reactions.

Feste and Fabian re-enter with the letter from Malvolio, and the mood again shifts. The latter's entrance and revengeful departure introduce a bitter note which echoes behind the processional exit of the happy couples, and we are left alone with the clown, who moves downstage, or stands in a spotlight as the other lights dim. Edward Atienza's poignant and versatile Feste, the spring of the 1985 Stratford Ontario revival, simply sat on a step, raindrops falling on his lute (his fingers tapped the wood as he looked quizzically to the sky). He sang, in a variety of appropriate voices, that last song, with its wonderfully ambiguous and evocative refrain: 'With hey, ho, the wind and the rain . . . For the rain it raineth every day'. Youth, marriage, revelry, the passing of time, all take their place under the sky and its unpredictable weather. But the play ends on an upbeat, with a reminder of the joy of playing, and of playgoing:

> But that's all one, our play is done,
> And we'll strive to please you every day.

5

Measure for Measure

Measure for Measure is a deeply ambiguous play, a fact that has assured its popularity in recent years. In the nineteenth century, and even in the early twentieth, its frank handling of sexual encounters and its complex questioning of sexual morality kept it for the most part off the stage. Now, however, it is frequently produced. And, because of its perceived modernity, it is also one of the plays that continues to receive thoughtful treatment. Directors do not have to seek outlandish styles in a quest for relevance or audience involvement, although they sometimes have; the issues that the play engages and the psychological dimensions that it explores are enough to guarantee attentiveness.

The 'modernity' of *Measure for Measure* derives from its approach to both moral and aesthetic questions. It is profoundly distrustful of moral absolutes, like chastity and justice, and recognizes the self-delusion and hypocrisy that dependence on such absolutes can lead to. The play continually confronts its absolutist characters, Isabella and Angelo especially, with an intransigent reality that defeats their absolutism. It is, at the same time, sceptical about the pragmatism of the Duke, and casts a cold eye on the manipulations by which he attempts to mould the lives of the other characters. The Duke's role, in fact, is the chief means by which the comic form of the play is called into question. Aesthetically, the play feels modern because it undermines the conventions of the very form it adopts, conventions which determine the plot and its comic outcome, but which do not sit very comfortably on the play's events. When, for example, the Duke at the very end decrees the marriages of Angelo to Mariana and of Lucio to Kate Keepdown, and when he then twice offers his own hand to the silent Isabella, who seems an unlikely partner for him, we may feel that the traditional Shakespearean comic ending, the festive marriage rite, is being imposed on the material. This tactic is likely to lead us to question rather than to celebrate – to question both the morality of the Duke's manipulation and the validity of the comic convention under which he pursues it.

The ending of the play has in fact become notorious in recent years, and the way it is treated is probably the best yardstick by which to gauge a particular interpretation. Ever since 1970, when John Barton had Isabella turn away in confusion from the Duke's marriage proposal, instead of silently accepting it as she always had before, actress and director have had to choose, and critics have taken note of their choices. A decision now to have Isabella accept the Duke, as in the BBC Television Shakespeare version or Barry Kyle's RSC production in 1978, must be taken in the light of Barton's production and the mini-tradition it has spawned. Thus the final marriage becomes more of a 'statement' than it would have been before there was any questioning of the ending.

Why has an ambiguous view of the ending developed? One answer, of course, is that our time has, though with some discomfort, embraced moral uncertainty, and distrusts simple and ready-made resolutions. But that would hardly excuse undermining the ending of a comedy unless there were some justification in the text. It has been argued, for example by Anne Barton in the programme note for her husband's production in 1970, that because Isabella says nothing in response to the Duke's proposals, though he asks her twice, it is 'at least possible' that her reaction is one of 'dismay'.[1] Here we have one of those many places where Shakespeare's intentions are unclear, where what he offers us is tantalizingly incomplete. In a classroom or a study we can take note of Isabella's silence and show how Shakespeare leaves things open, but on the stage a choice must be made. And in the 1970s and 1980s the predispositions of the time have led predominantly, though not exclusively, to the 'darker' alternative.

The Duke's first proposal comes immediately upon his revelation to Isabella and the others that her brother Claudio, whom she had thought dead, is alive and present. Claudio is unmuffled and the Duke says,

> If he be like your brother, for his sake
> Is he pardon'd; and, for your lovely sake,
> Give me your hand and say you will be mine,
> He is my brother too. But fitter time for that.
>
> (v.i.495–8)

The Duke's timing is clumsy at best. Isabella, in a turmoil of emotion at finding her brother alive, when she earlier had had to struggle to forgive his cruel and unjust execution, can hardly be expected to be

open to an unlooked-for marriage proposal. We cannot resist the
impression that there ought to be an awkward pause just before 'But
fitter time for that'; the line seems to indicate that the Duke realizes
that he has made a social gaffe – or perhaps he perceives that his
chances are slim. His words feel like a hurried cover-up, a transition
to other matters. Forty lines later, just as the play is ending, he tries
again:

> Dear Isabel,
> I have a motion much imports your good,
> Whereto if you'll a willing ear incline,
> What's mine is yours and what is yours is mine.
> So, bring us to our palace. . . .
>
> (ll. 539–43)

But again Isabella says nothing. As Barton handled it, the first
proposal was ignored, Isabella simply leaping to Claudio's arms.
Duke Vincentio's long pause and heavy sigh before 'But fitter
time . . .' signalled his forlorn love and underlined Isabella's
unconcern. Later, 'he made his last bid: "What's mine is yours and
what is yours is mine." After a long . . . silence, he uttered a
resigned, "So", put on his glasses, and departed with all the others,
leaving a bewildered Isabella alone on stage looking out at the
audience.'[2] The break between 'So' and 'bring us to our palace'
capped the interpretation; not necessarily called for by the syntax or
punctuation of the line, it was nevertheless compatible with it.

At Stratford Ontario in 1975, Robin Phillips took the ending even
further. There the Duke's apparent predilection for young boys,
noted by some critics, combined with his enjoyment of power and
his 'meddling and unfathomable' nature to compromise the
proposal and darken the ending.[3] Isabella's reaction was
accordingly more extreme than it was in Barton's production. At the
end, everyone else went off, leaving only a trembling Isabella who
removed her glasses and put them on the table, took off her nun's
cowl (a symbol of her repression throughout), and slowly began to
revolve, 'her mouth tortured by . . . helpless agony', as the lights
dimmed.[4] The same year saw Jonathan Miller's production, set like
Phillips' in early twentieth-century Vienna, in which the Duke's
designs on Isabella mirrored Angelo's; at the end, he dismissed his
underlings and propositioned her in a 'gloomy Thurberesque variant
on the boss and secretary routine' from which she retreated in
horrified silence.[5]

To treat the ending in such ways depends on a certain conception of the Duke. Broadly, there are three or four ways of seeing the character, and much in a production will depend on the way he is interpreted. Is he to be a godlike figure, allegorically related to that 'power divine' to which Angelo compares him; is he to be a man of integrity and wisdom, basically human, amiable, a worthy ruler; is he to be an ineffectual meddler whose plans continually go awry, or worse, an authoritarian manipulator who toys insensitively with people's lives? The basic question really is, does the production criticize him in any way, does it mark what he does with shadow and ambiguity, or does it see him as generously and honestly motivated?

Those, such as I, who argue that the Duke's behaviour and morality are questionable will usually cite the fact that he leaves the responsibility for cleaning up the city to Angelo, even though his own laxity has allowed public morality to decline. They will question his motives in appointing and testing Angelo, in eavesdropping on Claudio and Isabella, in devising the 'bed trick' whereby one virgin is surreptitiously substituted for another, and most of all in tormenting Isabella by telling her that Claudio has been executed when he has in fact just been saved. They may point, for examples of his ineffectuality, to Juliet's apparent rebuff of his spiritual advice in II.iii, to his inability to manipulate Barnardine in IV.iii, or to his sententious assurance that Claudio will be reprieved, which is almost immediately undercut by Angelo's letter calling for instant execution.

On the other hand, those who see the Duke as an enlightened, or even a divine, figure will stress the moral purposiveness of his actions; they may, however, have to strain a bit to do so – 'If the play is to mean anything,' wrote Richard David in a review of Peter Brook's 1950 Stratford production, 'we must accept the Duke's machinations as all to good purpose, and himself as entirely wise and just.'[6] The way that Brook encouraged the audience to do this was to place the emphasis strongly on Isabella and what she was able to achieve through the Duke. Setting the action in a base and harshly realistic world, underlining what he calls the 'rough' elements, Brook was able to create a 'Dostoyevskian' background, in which the sacredness of Isabella's plea that the Duke forgive Angelo, even though the latter has, as she believes, unjustly executed her brother, took on additional meaning. The moment is climactic. After an intense internal struggle, Isabella acquiesces to

Mariana's entreaties and kneels before the Duke. In order to stress the value as well as the intensity of the stuggle, Brook directed the actress, Barbara Jefford, to pause as long as she felt the audience could stand it before beginning her speech. Brook later wrote that the pause, which on some evenings could last as long as two minutes, 'became a voodoo pole – a silence in which all the elements of the evening came together . . . in which the abstract notion of mercy became concrete'.[7] Thus did the Duke's 'machinations' bear fruit.

But in order to make his conception work consistently, Brook was led to cut many short moments, or lines from various scenes, bits that reveal the Duke to be clumsy, self-important, temperamental, faintly absurd or morally questionable.[8] An interesting example was his omission of the direct proposal to Isabella, 'Give me your hand, and say you will be mine', a cut which greatly reduces Vincentio's awkwardness and makes his second offer altogether more handsome. Would Brook have been able to achieve the effects he did if he had retained all the cut lines? I would say probably not, since, once the Duke's project begins to look discreditable, the ironic mode of the play is likely to make itself strongly felt. However, a more recent production by the RSC, directed by Barry Kyle in 1978, did succeed in creating a consistent positive interpretation of the Duke, by emphasizing a combination of practical good sense and moral concern for his subjects as his most salient characteristics. Michael Pennington made him a 'man who in putting others to the test discovered himself'. While avoiding the temptation to play God, he sought to make his subjects '*experience* the gravity of breaking the law'. His vigorous working-out of his plans, his humanity, and most important the 'natural relationship' with Isabella that developed out of their shared activity, combined to overcome any nagging sense of discomfort at the means the Duke employed.[9]

Thus the line that a given director and company take on the Duke will determine the course of the whole production. Seeing him as flawed or even perverse will lead to an ironic, ambiguous reading of the play and a darkening of the ending, while presenting him as essentially well-balanced and genuinely concerned will result in a more traditionally comic reading, though the sharp, low realism of the play need not be scanted. Our third alternative, mentioned earlier, that the Duke is an allegorical, semi-divine figure, has pretty well gone out of fashion. We are likely these days to get a human Duke, no matter what the attitude taken toward him. The symbolic interpretation was popular during the 1960s, and reached its apogee in Tyrone Guthrie's 1966 revival, where the Duke was 'the Heavenly Bridegroom' to whom Isabella was betrothed.[10] But, whether purposely or not, Guthrie's godlike Duke, as played by John Franklyn Robbins, turned out to be more of a jovial eccentric than an immanent presence – or so the critics thought. Thus an interpretation that looks good in theory (in a critical essay or in the mind of a director), can, when it runs up against the physical and psychological reality of the actor and his reading, have its current turned awry. The play in fact is too intransigent to support a purely allegorical presentation (as Guthrie seemed implicitly to recognize). It is precisely the obstacles that it puts in the path of any one version, any comfortable or 'definitive' mastery, that make for the play's ambiguous fascination.

Measure for Measure is remarkable for the fact that a large portion of it takes place in a prison – hardly a setting conducive to a full comic tone. Furthermore, the overweening presence of the law is felt throughout, not only in the perversion of justice that is the centre of the main plot, but also in the handling of the low-life characters of the sub-plot. Mistress Overdone is hauled off to prison in the third act and we hear nothing more of her fate; Pompey is brought twice to trial for procuring, and ends up exchanging his vocation of bawd for that of executioner, though he maintains his irrepressible vitality throughout. And Lucio, whose illegitimate child Mistress Overdone has generously been caring for, is forced to marry a 'punk' as a punishment for his crimes. The exuberance of such characters is a typical feature of Shakespearean comedy, but rarely is it so tinged with vice or so harshly repressed. Seldom do we feel, as we do here, the iron hand of the law so rigorously restricting the vitality and good humour of the low-life characters.

This feature of the play contributes to its overall ambiguity and must somehow be marked by any particular production. Brook emphasized the rough, teeming life of the city, and the cruel power of the law, by introducing into i.ii a Breughelesque crowd of peasants, beggars, whores and cripples who shouted and jeered as the Provost and his men showed them the 'criminals', Juliet and Claudio.[11] From tiny hints in the text (Juliet's silent presence and Claudio's brief complaint that he is being shown 'to th' world'), Brook thus made a telling point. In the prison itself, Brook replaced the 'usual Dickensian . . . stage prison' with 'the wheels, the fires, the whips and the racks of a still cruder epoch'.[12] Further, he animated Pompey's catalogue of prisoners in iv.iii by actually having them on the stage from the beginning of Act iii, when they entered in procession. They thus formed a mostly silent, occasionally clanking chorus to what goes on in Act iii and most of Act iv (see Plate 4). Barton, in 1970, also brought on a parade of felons, but lightened the sombre tonality with something of a *Beggar's Opera* air.[13] Stressing the ambiguity of the Duke's behaviour, as Barton did, thus led to a softer approach to the city's vices. If, that is, the city seems in reasonably good shape, the Duke's project becomes accordingly more questionable. When Robin Phillips directed at Stratford Ontario in 1975, the ambiguity surrounding the Duke was further heightened, and the life of the city considerably cleaned up, making Vienna seem, in the view of one critic, 'well-run and bent on reform, a veritable Toronto'.[14] If the Duke is seriously implicated in, and compromised by, the corruption of his city, as he was in Michael Bogdanov's production at Stratford Ontario in 1985, both may seem equally bad; and then his project will be motivated less by a desire to clean things up and more by a voyeuristic desire to watch, and play with, people's lives.

Lucio, in Phillips' production, fitted neatly into the whole conception. Neither perverse nor superficial, as he often is, Lucio impressed the critics as 'paradoxically moral' – a 'fantastic champion against the masquerading Duke'.[15] Richard Monette, who played the part, saw Lucio as the moral voice, the only person who penetrates the Duke's disguise, and whose mockery therefore is a way of puncturing the Duke's pretensions. (It is noteworthy that the first time Lucio is alone with the disguised Vincentio he immediately asks 'What news, friar, of the Duke?') This approach makes Lucio more intelligent than he is usually played and makes interesting sense of the scenes where he attacks the Duke. (The same strategy marked Richard Macmillan's performance at Stratford Ontario in 1985.) The final crushing of Lucio thus emerges as an official 'You're right, but now you're going to be silenced.'[16] Such a reading does not make Lucio into a hero. He still tries to weasel out of his responsibility to Kate Keepdown and their child; he still betrays Mistress Overdone and refuses to help Pompey. Furthermore, there are places in the text where it is difficult to reconcile Lucio's words with the kind of penetration Monette gave him. But to create a morally perceptive Lucio is to redistribute the weight of the play as a whole, to introduce a questioning, paradoxical element into the character, and hence to underline more forcefully the play's multiple ironies.

Because of its ambiguous outcome, its sceptical tone, and its uncertain structure, *Measure for Measure* has long been considered a 'problem play'. Angelo and Isabella, more even than the characters and characteristics we have been discussing, are the focus of the problem. The dilemma of their situation and the intensity that it fosters catch the audience more immediately than anything else in the play. But, just when their choices seem to be leading to inexorable consequences, their responsibility is suddenly swept out from under them, and they become players, witting or unwitting, in the Duke's comedy. When the Duke steps forward in III.i with a plan to save the situation, he creates a hurdle for readers, producers and audiences alike. A break appears in the play's continuity which directors must decide either to patch or to widen. And from that decision will flow interpretations that are predominantly either comic or ironic.

Though each is introduced to us earlier, we see Isabella and Angelo together for the first time in II.ii, when she comes to plead for her brother's life. Crucial questions arise. When does Angelo's feverish desire for Isabella first strike him? Is Isabella in any way implicated in the sudden onset of Angelo's desire, or is she entirely innocent? Is her hesitation shyness, strategy or indifference? What is Lucio's role in the scene?

In Brook's production, Barbara Jefford's Isabella was young, ardent, warm and sympathetic, innocent of the effect that she was having on Gielgud's Angelo, grasping his hand and not noticing his barely perceptible response.[17] Isabellas of the sixties tended more to worldliness, often appearing in secular dress; while those of the seventies, as the tonality darkened, became more repressed and rigid. Sexual repression in particular could account for the electrifying effect that Isabella has on Angelo (he responds to her tension), and could also explain her tentativeness, her initial unwillingness to deal with the issue at all (a few lines into the interview she seems ready to give up). In Barton's production, Isabella's 'hysterical fear of sex' emerged as a dominant characteristic, motivating her entry into the nunnery, colouring her behaviour in the scenes with Angelo, and underlying her final rejection of the Duke's proposal.[18] But such a view might miss her canny side, her sense of strategy and her skill at persuasion (mentioned by Claudio in a previous scene). It is these latter, as much as fear of sex, that lead her to join with the Duke's bed-trick plot later on. On hearing that her brother's betrothed is pregnant, her first reaction is in keeping with her concern for practical solutions: 'O, let him marry her.' She hardly seems horrified. When she begins her plea to Angelo with the words, 'There is a vice that most I do abhor', she may, then, be saying what she thinks Angelo wants to hear, rather than describing her own psyche.

As for Angelo, he is struck by some kind of repressed desire in himself which is unlocked by Isabella. His first words to her – 'Y'are welcome. What's your will?' – are bland enough. He is probably seated at a desk, shuffling papers, somewhat preoccupied. He looks up at her. Is it at that moment, with a brief pause before 'What's your will?' that the process begins? So it was in Barton's production; the idea is attractive. More likely, though, it is Isabella's ardour, her *heat* as she warms to her cause (and here Lucio's ambiguous interruptions lend a cunning sexual note), that possesses Angelo.

How sympathetic his obsession is likely to make Angelo is very much up to the actor. The character is rigid and humourless – of that there is little doubt. But for me this scene, and even more the next scene with Isabella, ii.iv, can bring Angelo very close to an audience by focusing on a horrifying self-awareness, a revelation of himself to himself. Brian Bedford, in the 1975 production at Stratford Ontario, experienced his passion 'like an attack of fever'; he sipped water; he tried 'to examine his malady'.[19] A strange combination of cerebration and violent emotion makes the character fascinating, if not exactly sympathetic, and the actor who can catch both should succeed in bringing Angelo uncomfortably close.

Ian Richardson, playing opposite Estelle Kohler in Barton's production, was a cold-blooded, precise Angelo, 'whose disdain for baser men was signalled in the carriage of the head . . . and the sparse, carefully expressive gestures'. He began ii.iv with the quick fever of his desire closely covered; 'seated on his desk, he pulled a chair towards him with his foot, and indicated with a flick of his right hand that [Isabella] should sit'. But later the control completely disappeared, as he seized her hair, pulled her down unto the desk and 'stroked her body from breast to groin'.[20] Barton and his actors were going too far here. Better, I think, for Angelo to maintain decorum, as Julian Curry did in Miller's 1975 revival: at one point he touched 'her skirt with one hand, and then deliberately replaced the ruffled cloth'. This approach holds the electric tension that marks the whole scene. Penelope Wilton, in response to Curry's carefully

circuitous arguments, listened 'as if at a seminar', but, when she
finally understood, was 'all knife-blades and arrows'.[21]

Such interactions touch on the emotional centre of the play. The
pretence, the repressed feeling, the elaborate argumentation, the
careful sidestepping and verbal chess-playing – the slightly
hysterical *pitch* of the scene – are typical and crucial. At its end,
Isabella is exhausted. Angelo's desire has exploded into cruelty, and
she is left alone. She will not sell her body to reprieve her brother:

> Then, Isabel, live chaste, and, brother, die;
> More than our brother is our chastity.
>
> (II.iv.184–5)

It is hard not to see sexual repression behind these lines. But there
are different ways of handling them. Barbara Jefford's ardent
Isabella turned and hid her face against the wall, 'as if . . . ashamed
that her intellect could find no more adequate expression of her
heart's certainty';[22] whereas Estelle Kohler twenty years later
emphasized the lines and hence, in Robert Speaight's words, 'let us
see that her chastity . . . is corrupted by pride'.[23] The lines are not
easy for a modern audience, nor were they, I am convinced, for an
Elizabethan. But it will not do to cut them – some accommodation
will have to be made, and in the process a great deal of Isabella's
character will be revealed.

When Martha Henry played Isabella under Phillips' direction, she
found a telling piece of business for the end of II.iv, which, for
Phillips, was a 'crystallization of what the scene is about'. Of
Henry's Isabella it was said that you were always aware of the body
under the nun's habit, though she was at all times correct and
leashed in. As she came to the end of the speech, including the
resolution to live chaste, she removed her glasses and splashed cold
water from a jug on the desk onto her forehead. She was, as Phillips
stressed, *hot*. The water, the same that the self-examining Angelo
had at first sipped matter-of-factly (before meeting Isabella) and
then feverishly (after his upheaval), thus became a concrete marker
of the emotional interplay between the two characters.

Since drama is a physical as well as a verbal art, the theatre has
continually to find such physical correlatives to give added weight
to the language. That, of course, is an important function of settings,
costumes, props, and so on. Phillips placed his production in
Freud's Vienna in 1912 (it is an interesting twist of history that

Shakespeare should set his play of sexual repression in the city of its most illustrious anatomist), a city of high-buttoned propriety, starched collars and pristine cuffs, of military uniforms and frockcoated bureaucrats. But a city too with a celebrated and, to a modern audience, easily imagined low-life – 'a smell of romance, gaiety'. Even the architecture of the city embodied for Phillips 'the strictness but delicacy of texture' that he saw as typical of the play's language. To re-create the period on the open Stratford stage, there were gas lamps and metal grilles, stylish boulevard scenes complete with a street coffee vendor, and, for the official scenes, 'massive writing desks which vibrated with power'.[24]

Within this precisely imagined setting, the Duke exercised his questionable authority, Lucio probed the disguises of the stiffly formal aristocrats, and Angelo and Isabella fought their grim, repressed duel. Mariana, as she ought to in a production, provided a contrast, a moment of 'fertile luxury'; but her world of wicker furniture and elegant indolence could hardly compensate for a dominantly impersonal Vienna. Furthermore, the sense that she was also the Duke's mistress (picked up by at least one critic) added an ambiguous tonality to the little oasis that the 'moated grange' usually represents.

Miller's production at Greenwich in the same year, though coincidentally set in the same era, was interestingly different in conception. Instead of the gaiety of the boulevards and the strains of the 'Merry Widow', the design stressed the seedy, bureaucratic interior of government buildings. The main set was a corridor office with low grey walls, a battered green bucket in the corner, a nondescript desk, a hat stand and departmental doors – 'prison there, executive suite here'. The play was handled as a 'comedy of government', with Angelo the model bureaucrat and Lucio an ex-public-schoolboy with knitted sweater, chatting away while awaiting promotion. All this gave credibility to the repressive sexual laws – they seemed to belong to the 'dusty oppression of the place, [its] sinister good behaviour'.[25]

Phillips and Miller wanted as much to pose as to answer questions about this provocative play, and the approach that each took to character, language and setting was designed to do just that. Phillips' production in particular was praised because it managed a wholeness without dissolving the play's ambiguities. That approach has marked several fine recent revivals, one of which I want to look at by way of conclusion. The Bogdanov production at

Stratford Ontario (mentioned above) built on the insights of previous actors and directors, but added its own original, even outrageous, twists. With its leather-clad transvestites and whores adorning brothel and street, its suggestive dancing and punk music, the production drove some Shakespearean purists to near-apoplexy.

The whole theatre was turned into a kind of brothel–nightclub. An extended, suggestive and quite unwarranted prologue, involving a frenzied sexual dance, culminated in a circle closing in on the club's number-one patron – Duke Vincentio himself, clad in blazer and grey flannels, who gradually subsided to the floor amidst a rhythymically attentive knot of whores and transvestites. The Duke (as played by Alan Scarfe) was a sly fellow, more than slightly voyeuristic, who took an unhealthy interest in his snooping and manipulating. His power was absolute, and he clearly enjoyed the theatrics of experimenting with people's lives – something he had ample opportunity to do as the play went on. There was a marked ambiguity about his motives and style (the smirk at 'I have confessed her [Mariana] and do know her virtue', for example – did it mean he 'knew' her all too well?). He had a characteristic savouring and suggestively sensual movement of the mouth and a habit of tasting little candies which he took from a small silver box. The streak of perversity that seemed to mark him did not, however, make him disagreeable; he was actually quite engaging in his knowing way. The production put the Duke back at the centre of the play, but not as a providential guide, a bumbling stage manager or a man of practical moral concern; rather he was the embodiment of the play's elastic ambiguity.

He was interested in Isabella from quite early on. In their first scene together, seemingly innocuous lines were given a sexual edge: 'The hand that hath made you fair hath made you good . . . grace, being the soul of your complexion, shall keep the body of it ever fair.' Scarfe gave a slight savour to words such as 'beauty', 'fair' and 'body' here, as he stood extremely close behind a rigid and uneasy Isabella. The moment seemed subtly to repeat Angelo's more blatant proposition in the previous scene. Isabella herself was an innocent, at sea in a rampant, sexist world. She was embraced by everyone, by Angelo first of all bending her back over his desk, then by the Duke in a later prison scene ('Command these fretting waters from your eyes / with a light heart . . .' – iv.iii.146ff.). They were interrupted by Lucio, who raised his eyebrows, and then in his turn embraced her – in sympathy with her for the presumed death of Claudio. When the latter appeared alive in Act v, this would-be nun was once again held in a man's embrace, now for the first time willingly – in fact she fled the Duke's wandering hands and ingratiating proposal to run to her brother, and at the very end she again recoiled from the Duke's touching her hands. He and the others exited upstage and she was left alone and pained in a faint light; a sudden, bright tableau of the brothel denizens behind bars clinched the irony.

The final act was a grand theatrical show managed by the Duke on the same polished nightclub floor as the opening gambit, thus linking the theatrical deviousness of the finale with the sexual perversity of the prologue. This was where the seemingly irrelevant sensationalism of the beginning paid off and in retrospect made good sense. The scene was done as if at a fascist rally; the houselights were brought up in an effort to disallow the ordinary comfortable distance the audience normally enjoys. There were microphones, amplified voices and media lights; characters spoke from the aisles and the balcony. The point was to emphasize the embarrassing inappropriateness of the scene, all this private revelation and gossip being publicly reviewed. The vulgar theatricality of the presentation signalled an ironic attitude toward the Duke's highly theatrical and public imposition of power – over events, other characters, and even the comic form itself. Angelo's dour glumness as he stood with Mariana's proprietary arm through his, Isabella's confusion, and the punishment of Lucio (the Duke's canny challenger throughout) all contributed to the ironic tone. Lucio, a sassy boulevardier in a white suit, had seen through the Duke's disguise early on, and insulted him seemingly on purpose to goad him into taking action on Claudio's behalf. Implicitly questioning the morality of the Duke's project, Lucio probed and pushed, but went too far and was slapped down, too harshly it seemed, at the end.

Some will certainly say that this production went too far, substituting perversity for ambiguity. Halfway through I found myself feeling that the sensational elements seemed extraneous (the intermission began as a result of the interruption of a striptease act by the arrival of the morality squad!). But by the end I could appreciate their connection to the main action and its ambiguous

theatricality. The production may have been outrageous, but it was
sharply successful in extending and improvising on the doubts and
ironies that have characterized most of the best performances of this
intriguing play.

6

Richard II

In the 1590s *Richard II* was something of a political hot potato. When it was first printed in 1597, and again in subsequent quartos, the 'deposition' scene, in which Richard is forced to resign his crown in favour of his rival Henry Bolingbroke (later Henry IV), had been carefully excised. The scene was not reinstated until the First Folio of 1623. When the play was mounted on the public stage some time in 1595–6, the deposition scene was undoubtedly presented, but its political reverberations proved too dangerous for print. Queen Elizabeth, the aging but still skilful monarch, saw herself in the person of Richard II, though her political shrewdness might be thought to belong more properly to Bolingbroke. In 1601, her former favourite, the Earl of Essex, led an abortive rebellion against her, and the analogy between the Queen and Richard, and Essex and Bolingbroke, was sealed by a timely production of *Richard II*, commissioned by Essex's followers and performed by Shakespeare's company. There seems little doubt that the deposition scene was included in that performance! Interestingly, members of the company escaped reprisals, because the authorities accepted the view that they had simply been hired to do a job and were not implicated in the political crimes of their employers.

The sort of relevance that *Richard II* then enjoyed is not likely to be recaptured today. We are no longer much interested in the *fate* of kings – though public interest in their private lives still runs high. This lack of feeling for the essence of kingship is, in fact, an impediment to the appreciation of *Richard II* on the part of a modern audience. For the real dilemma of the play is built on the conflict between the demands of the 'king's two bodies' – i.e. his sacred, sacramental body, the symbolic manifestation of the abstract idea of kingship, and his personal, physical body, subject to time and decay.[1] A simple, though less accurate way of putting this is to say that the play investigates a conflict between the public and private roles of the king. What we miss today is a sense of the overwhelming importance of the monarch, his or her absolute centrality. Without that sense we are all too likely to see Richard as merely a whining, self-pitying child, and if that happens the play is spoiled.

There is another impediment to our appreciation of this play and of the other history plays. That is simply our ignorance of the history behind them. Especially for North American audiences, the grand file of Richards, Henries and Edwards, of Gloucesters, Yorks and Warwicks, can easily lead to bewilderment. For *Richard II*, it is important to know that Richard and Bolingbroke are both grandsons of Edward III, father of seven sons, who survived his own eldest son, also named Edward (and called the Black Prince). By the laws of succession, the Black Prince's son Richard became the next king. Thus it is that the young King Richard has to contend with some powerful old uncles, men such as John of Gaunt (Bolingbroke's father), Thomas, Duke of Gloucester, and Edmund, Duke of York. Before the play begins, Richard has contrived the murder of his uncle Gloucester, who had been held in Mowbray's custody. The exact circumstances of the murder are left unclear, but what *is* clear is that behind the elaborate formality of the opening scene lies the lurking suspicion of Richard's own guilt. Bolingbroke, in accusing Mowbray, is thus pointing a finger at Richard as well, and the whole court knows it.

In 1973 John Barton directed a production of *Richard II* for the RSC that met the problem of kingship head-on and tried to find a language that was both suitable to the play and understandable to modern audiences. Barton started with an idea about the play, and gradually developed, along with designer Tim O'Brien, a visually striking, symbolic representation of the central concept. In a programme note, the director's wife, Anne Barton, herself a distinguished critic, spelled out the general idea: Shakespeare, she argues, in confronting the notion of the king's two bodies, 'seized upon . . . the latent parallel between the King and that other twin-natured human being, the Actor'. Both king and actor have an ambiguous attitude toward their roles – each is defined by his role but at the same time stands outside it. Thus Richard's consciousness of his role as monarch is, as Queen Elizabeth's was, essentially that of an actor. Barton sees Bolingbroke as suppressing his 'voluble individuality' in the role of king, and thus becoming remote. 'Like the two buckets filling one another that Richard imagines in the deposition scene . . . Richard's journey from king to man is balanced by Bolingbroke's progress from a single to a twin-natured being. Both movements involve a gain and a loss. Each, in its own way, is tragic.'[2] Thus the parts of Richard and Bolingbroke were seen as symbolically interchangeable – as mirror-images of each other. The formally patterned and symmetrical features of the play itself, plus the many verbal images which express this fundamental balance between Richard and Bolingbroke – these were ingeniously emphasized to epitomize the theme.[3]

The initial production idea that Barton had in order to represent these rather abstract notions was a simple but effective one. The two actors chosen to play Richard and Bolingbroke would alternate the parts, making the *role* of king dominant.[4] The idea would be that the two levels of play-acting, that of kingship and that of the players themselves, would both be emphasized. The play would not be simply Richard's tragedy, but the tragedy of kingship itself (and, by extension, of all authority): the necessary veneer of falseness that it imposes on him who adopts the role. The text as it stands, however, doesn't provide the crucial insight into Bolingbroke, the usurper, and the suffering that taking on the kingly role exacts from him. In order to give the shadowy Bolingbroke more presence, Barton added several speeches to the part, taken mostly from *2 Henry IV*, where Bolingbroke, by then an old and guilt-ridden king, looks back over his reign. Thus Bolingbroke, at the very beginning of his time as king, manifested a sense of the 'cyclical nature of history'. Barton was clearly tampering with the text here, but by doing so he succeeded in making Bolingbroke more sympathetic and complex, with a strong sense of the dangers and cares of kingship.[5]

The opening of the production strongly emphasized the twin features of kingship – play-acting and ceremony. A 'portable pyramid of golden steps' was set downstage with the royal robe and crown mounted on it. The play began with 'Shakespeare', in an appropriate mask, coming on with a book, and the actors filing on after him. The two leads went up to 'Shakespeare' and one was 'selected' to be King Richard for that performance (the original idea was to leave the actual selection each evening till that very moment, but it proved impracticable). The 'King' was then robed, crowned, and seated on top of the pyramid as on a throne. The other characters assumed their elaborate costumes, all knelt and proclaimed, 'Long Live the King'; then the book was held up to Richard, who, finding his place, spoke the first line.[6]

The stiff formality of the opening scene was thus precisely caught, and a rich metaphor for the grip that kingship has on a human being emerged. The metaphor worked, as it were, both ways. As the actor is defined by the costume he wears and the words he must speak, forced to be both himself and not himself, so too the king. And, conversely, the formal ceremony associated with kingship, emphasized in the first scene with the knightly challenges and in the third with the tournament, found a suitable analogue in the formality of the stage presentation. Originally, masks were to be used extensively in the production; and, though they ended up being mostly discarded, their formality, developed in rehearsal, contributed to the overall effect. Though the masks were dropped, other modern variations on the techniques of Greek tragedy were kept. The most remarkable of these was the 'hobby-horses', used for example by Bolingbroke and Mowbray in the tournament scene (I.iii), and by the 'plumed King' on his return from Ireland, when he appeared astride a 'life-sized effigy with white trappings' (see Plate 5). Northumberland, in another spectacular effect, turned into 'a great black raven in a feather cloak with claws on his buskined feet'.[7] Other rebellious barons appeared on stilts. Such ritualistic ways of externalizing the action, of finding a performed, symbolic equivalent for it, sought to confront the audience with a theatrical equivalent to the issues that Shakespeare's contemporaries would have felt immediately in their blood.

The play ended as it began, with a ritual. Richard is now dead, and Henry IV was crowned by 'Shakespeare' with the same ceremony accorded the former king in the prologue. As he turned to the audience, however, he showed not the golden mask from the beginning, but a skull mask; then two hooded figures on either side revealed themselves as Richard Pasco and Ian Richardson, the actors who had played the two main parts (and whose very names continue the motif of mirroring), with between them the crowned skull-king. The 'hollow crown / That rounds the mortal temples of a king' could hardly have been more graphically illustrated.[8]

The above account of what Barton did with *Richard II*, in particular what he *added* to it (additions are often an effective measure of what a director is getting at), provides a striking example of the way a single concept about a play can determine the choices that directors and designers make. Elements such as the provision of benches at the back for the actors to retire to, a bowl of earth downstage (the earth that Richard kisses on his return to England), or the central design feature itself, a high, sliding bridge connected at both ends to sharply sloped walls at right angles to the proscenium,[9] all grew out of the initial concept. The formalized, symbolic mode extended to characterization, acting-technique and verse-speaking as well. For example, famous speeches, such as Gaunt's on 'this sceptred isle' or Richard's on 'the hollow crown', were either spoken straight out at the audience, or the speakers themselves were in some way isolated, as for an aria.

It is of course possible to take a very different approach to *Richard II*. Barton's conception, for all its originality and bold images, was a highly intellectual one, beginning with an idea and designed to put that idea across. It left mostly to one side what might best be described as a strongly lyrical strain in the play, epitomized in John Gielgud's many performances as Richard. There the emphasis was on the patterned, lyrical and self-conscious poetry, and on Richard himself as a kind of poet. Actors like Gielgud have tended to present Richard as a man keenly aware of his own ability to weave words together. One critic has suggested that there have been two basic treatments of Richard in the English theatre: the man who watches his own grief, standing 'aside from himself, entranced by the complexity of his own arias', the other a man who suffers more directly and 'refuses to luxuriate in his imagination'.[10] The first of these tends to be the more common – in North America as well (a fine example was William Hutt's performance at Stratford Ontario in 1964). Treating the play lyrically tends to reduce the importance of the political element, emphasizing rather the personal, tragic plight of the protagonist and his clumsy groping toward self-knowledge. Bolingbroke will be more a shadowy, though powerful, instrument in the King's downfall than a full-scale antagonist. An advantage, however, of exploiting the 'poetic aura' which Shakespeare has wrapped around Richard is that some of the strong feeling for kingship, usually lacking in modern audiences, can be partially revived.[11]

One strength of Barton's production, as I indicated, was the weight it gave to Bolingbroke. He is an enigmatic, ambiguous and relatively silent character. For one thing, just how ambitious is he? Is he already a contender for the throne *before* Richard banishes him, so that Richard is consciously getting rid of a major threat? The question is tantalizing because we never get a clear answer to it. When he returns after his banishment, he declares that he has come only to claim his rightful inheritance, which Richard has illegally seized. But it seems understood, at least by many of his followers, that he is marching directly toward the throne. Already when they are planning Henry's return, shortly after Gaunt's death, the rebels seem to look forward to his gaining the crown. Northumberland says to his fellows,

> If then we shall shake off our slavish yoke,
> . . .
> Redeem from broking pawn the blemish'd
> crown,
> Wipe off the dust that hides our sceptre's gilt,
> And make high majesty look like itself,
> Away with me in post to Ravenspurgh.
>
> (II.i.291–6)

Northumberland's words are careful – he *could* be talking about restoring Richard's majesty to himself, by eliminating the base flatterers with whom Richard has surrounded himself, and placing the barons once more in their rightful position of power. The nobles have just been discussing how the King is being grossly misled. But here too there is ambiguity. For, although everyone is always complaining about how the flatterers are dragging Richard down, we never actually see them do this. On the contrary, what we see is Richard acting very much on his own initiative. His rude and insensitive treatment of his uncle Gaunt before the latter's death, and his totally illegal seizure of Gaunt's lands and revenues afterwards – the very crimes the barons have been condemning – seem to have sprung entirely from Richard's own wilfulness. So, when Northumberland talks of making majesty look like itself, it sounds as though he is talking about the very dangerous business of replacing one king with another.

Barton emphasized the shadows here by playing the King's 'flatterers' as honest attendants – so that when Bolingbroke, in III.i, read the charges against them ('You have misled a prince . . . You have in manner with your sinful hours / Made a divorce betwixt his queen and him . . .'), he recognized the falseness of his accusations, but was fully aware of their political necessity. Consistent with this approach to the King's followers, those of Bolingbroke were considerably darkened. Northumberland at one point turned into an ominous black raven, and Exton, Ross and Willoughby appeared as a 'sinister underworld . . . a grim band of supporters for the cold dogged Northumberland'.[12] From this it might appear that Barton conceived of Bolingbroke as crown-hungry from the start, but when he deliberately gave him a full and anxious awareness of the cares of kingship as well, and so left the matter undecided.

What then is Bolingbroke? Is he a man who knows what he is doing and is willing to look the other way when unsavoury methods are used in his support? Unwilling to sully himself, and determined to maintain a high moral tone, he is ready to love Richard murdered, though he hates the murderer – as he says to Exton at the end of the play. That cynical comment can colour a whole interpretation. On the other hand, he can be played as more or less innocent at the start, only gradually falling into the inevitable track that his initial decision to return from banishment and defy the King has laid down – a victim as it were of impersonal political forces. Since, nowadays, idealistic conceptions of politicians and political behaviour are rare indeed, the common tack on Bolingbroke has been to see him as shrewd and manipulative, a 'new' politician. He thus becomes a political, as well as a personal and theatrical, contrast to the ceremonial Richard, who depends on hierarchical and divinely sanctioned notions of political behaviour. Barton chose to take an intermediate ground, equalizing the two characters as much as possible.

The more positive the portrayal of Bolingbroke, the more negative that of Richard is likely to be, and *vice versa*. The trick is to balance them properly. Richard's illegitimate action justifies Bolingbroke's revolt, at least in emotional and theatrical terms, if not in terms of the traditional political theory on which Richard relies. The first and third scenes of the play will establish the tone. Richard can easily be weak, showy and effeminate, and Bolingbroke cool, strong and manly. In the opening scene, despite his protest 'We were not born to sue, but to command', Richard is unable to command the peace he seems to seek (though that too may be simply an act). Thus all he can do is set the day for trial by combat. Similarly, in I.iii he sets up the elaborate pageantry of the tournament only to abrogate it at the last minute, seemingly unable to sit comfortably in judgement. He then passes out sentences, more, it seems, from motives of fear and self-protection than desire for a just settlement. In order to counter the negative tone associated with these failures of royal responsibility, Richard can be presented, as Gielgud did it, as richly eloquent and grand; otherwise, Bolingbroke will get the upper hand at once. Some directors, however, will be seeking this latter effect, so that Richard's eventual reversal of fortune will bring with it a concomitant reversal of spirit. His tragic stature will thus grow as he sloughs off the trappings of kingship, and his previous behaviour will be seen as the necessary flaw leading to both suffering and insight. This was the approach taken by the BBC Television Shakespeare production, in which Derek Jacobi's Richard was at first distinctly irritating; he came across as all show, completely without substance, and smug about his own strutting. But, as the action progressed, some other self emerged, and in the final scenes he was powerful and direct.

The two scenes (III.iii and IV.i) in which the falling Richard and the rising Bolingbroke confront each other are the real backbone of the play. Both depict the rising and falling action in symbolic ways. In the first, the abandoned King, having taken refuge in Flint Castle, appears on the walls to parley with Northumberland and then descends to the 'base court' to meet Bolingbroke. The scene is a tricky one to stage: Richard, on the walls above, is clearly visible to Bolingbroke, who describes him appearing 'As doth the blushing discontented sun'; Richard, however, speaks only to Northumberland and is barely able to discern Bolingbroke in the distance. Northumberland moves between the two principals with messages, culminating with the announcement that Bolingbroke attends the King in the base court. Richard's histrionic 'Down, down I come, like glist'ring Phaethon . . .' seems to precede an exit from on top and a subsequent re-entry on the main level. On Shakespeare's stage, Richard probably appeared above at a window or on a small balcony. A quick dash down some hidden stairs and a dignified entrance below would complete the movement. Some similar treatment has been the norm on the modern stage as well. But Barton wanted to keep Richard on-stage the whole time, and his designer worked out a symbolic platform–lift that bespoke the ceremonial significance of the theatrical moment. As the doomed King was saying, 'Come down? Down, court! Down, king! / For night-owls shriek where mounting larks should sing' (ll. 182–3), the wide (eight metres) platform on which he was standing descended diagonally towards the waiting Bolingbroke on the stage floor. A sense of balance between new and old king, even of direct connection between the rise of one and the fall of the other (remember the image of the two buckets in the well, which the Barton production seized on as a paradigm) was thus graphically illustrated.

Before he comes down, Richard has a long speech which we may take as typical of the problem he poses for a modern actor or a modern audience:

> What must the king do now? Must he submit?
> The king shall do it. Must he be depos'd?
> The king shall be contented. Must he lose
> The name of king? A' God's name, let it go.
> I'll give my jewels for a set of beads . . .
>
> (III.iii.143–7)

and so on for twenty-five more lines. At the end he pulls himself up sharply with 'Well, well, I see / I talk but idly and you laugh at me', though Aumerle has apparently been weeping at the wretched spectacle. It's hard for Bolingbroke not to seem preferable here. And it's easy, all too easy I think, to discredit Richard. One can, of course, rescue him by cutting the speech almost entirely, but it is precisely this part of Richard, his tendency to self-dramatization and to poetic elaboration of his predicament, which must be faced throughout the play. It is this which defines him and gives him his particular life. He must to some extent captivate us, as he does his on-stage audience – though Northumberland as always remains unmoved.

The same is true in the next great confrontation scene, the deposition itself (IV.i). Again Richard's heart and mind range and rage, again his predicament is a source of poetic inspiration. Again Bolingbroke waits quietly, ominously, patiently, while the dogged Northumberland does the hatchet work and Richard flutters under the knife. The scene is weighted by sinister silences – such as that which follows Carlisle's loyal and brave defence of Richard's rights (l. 151), or that which attends Richard's cry of 'God save the king' (l. 173). The first is broken by Northumberland's sardonic comment 'Well have you argued, sir; and for your pains, / Of capital treason we arrest you here'; the second by Richard's own, 'Will no man say amen?' Everyone is *watching*: watching each other; watching Richard; watching, especially, the new king, ready to take their cue from him.

Bolingbroke tends to command respect and salutary fear among his followers, in contrast to the love that Richard can frequently attract. The so-called gage scene (IV.i.1–91), which serves as a prelude to the deposition itself, is an indication of this. It needs to be handled with care or it can easily degenerate into a piling-up of meaningless gauntlets and result in embarrassed giggles in the audience. The point is that Aumerle, who is devoted to Richard, is under pressure from the lords connected to Bolingbroke, who himself listens quietly and then deftly asserts his power as the judge (in contrast to Richard's bungling a similar chance in Act I). Barton rearranged the scene to make it deadly serious, a mounting of court loyalty and militarism against Aumerle, some of the gages being dropped silently and ominously. He thus made us interested in the power struggle surrounding the throne, and made us care what happened to Aumerle.

With this moment as prologue to the deposition, it comes as no surprise that, after it is over and the day of Henry's coronation fixed, the scene ends with the hatching of a new plot, in which Aumerle takes a key role. It is this plot that the wavering York discovers in true 'comic father' fashion and determines to expose to Bolingbroke. His action leads to an imbroglio before the king, which even the humourless Bolingbroke sees as a comic interlude: 'Our scene is alt'red from a serious thing, / And now chang'd to "The Beggar and the King" ' (v.iii.79–80). York himself is an uncertain character. He has been played for comedy because of his absurd solemnity in these scenes, as well as his tendency to fall into line with the prevailing powers despite ideological protests against the behaviour of both Richard and Bolingbroke. But, as Gielgud has said, what is needed is 'a tactful compromise between comedy and dramatic effect'.[13] A farcical York will weaken the play. In the early acts he vacillates, caught between powers over which he can exert no control. And he bows to the winner. But this makes him an apt representative of the confusion of loyalties engendered by civil war and usurpation.

The most common recourse in the face of the problems posed by York has been to cut his scenes from Act v altogether. (They were cut from all British productions between 1934 and 1955, but appeared occasionally in the sixties and seventies.[14]) Barton retained them and had them played naturalistically, in contrast to the predominantly ritualistic mode of his production. This made them stand out, emphasizing the eruptiveness of political feeling and the dangers of kingship, while at the same time giving Aumerle a stronger presence. Rather than turning the serious political ramifications of the incipient rebellion into comic absurdity, as some directors have done, Barton thus chose to reveal the pitfalls of Aumerle's course and the shrewdness of Bolingbroke in forgiving him and thus making him perforce into a kind of reluctant ally.

The end of the play, like the rest of it, offers us our choice between the tragedy of one character and the triumph of another. It is, of course, possible to complicate this, as Anne Barton argued in her programme note, by suggesting that Richard's tragedy involves its own triumph, just as Bolingbroke's gain involves a loss. But the play clearly divides, in the last two scenes, between a new, inner, personal concern for Richard, and an external, political interest in King Henry. The weight, in terms of length of scene and intensity, falls on Richard, but Shakespeare ends the play with an ambiguous scene in which Bolingbroke accepts with relief the murder of the former king but condemns the useful murderer: 'With Cain go wander thorough shades of night, / And never show thy head by day nor light.' Once again ambiguity surrounds the enigmatic Bolingbroke. Is he sincere when he says, 'Lords, I protest, my soul is full of woe, / That blood should sprinkle me to make me grow'? Or is his promise to make a penitential voyage to the Holy Land nothing more than a propaganda ploy, a shrewd way of averting criticism? Most productions will go for the latter alternative, leaving us nostalgic for the poetic ineffectuality of Richard, whose end is strangely moving. He dies fighting, which is an agreeable surprise given his penchant for words. And the short, quiet scene with the former groom of his stable just before the murderers arrive (v.v.68–94) once again adds that dimension of devoted loyalty which Richard, unlike his rival, has frequently been able to inspire. Barton made the groom into Bolingbroke in disguise, thus undermining the all-important loyalty and implicating Henry directly in Richard's murder; but this was to overstep his bounds in the interest of bringing home his concept.[15] The plight of the two men was intimately linked together, but Shakespeare has quite deliberately separated them here, giving each a scene, and leaving the contrarieties for the audience to resolve if they can.

7
Henry IV, Part 1

At festivals and repertory theatres, *Henry IV, Part 1* is often presented together with *Richard II* and the other two plays, *Henry IV, Part 2* and *Henry V*, that make up Shakespeare's great historical tetralogy. If this is done, it naturally provides a perspective that a production of just the one play does not. There will be a sense of large historical sweep, of characters, usually played by the same actors, continuing and changing from play to play, of the growth and decay of ideals, and above all a sense of the conflict and complexity of *rights* in the protracted struggles for succession. Issues which pertain particularly to *Henry IV, Part 1*, as for example the development of Prince Hal in relation to the King, his father, and to Falstaff, his surrogate father, or the question of the value of chivalric ideals, will be connected to broader considerations about the place of Henry's reign in history, or, more immediately, the problem dealt with decisively at the end of *Henry IV, Part 2* – the rejection of Falstaff. Similarly, *Part 1* may be presented along with *Part 2* only, as it was by Trevor Nunn and the RSC at the Barbican Theatre in 1982, or it may be produced as the first play of a trilogy culminating in the triumphant *Henry V*, as it was by Terry Hands and the RSC in the mid-seventies. (In fact, Hands did the three Henry plays along with *The Merry Wives of Windsor*, thus creating a Falstaffian tetralogy, but most critics thought such a series contrived and misleading.) As a part of a larger whole, *Henry IV, Part 1* will be seen as leading *to* its companion pieces, and the reading it is given will be coloured by the producer's feelings about the final play in the series. Thus Nunn's *Part 1* seemed infused with the dominant anti-heroic tonalities of his *Part 2*, while Hands' treatment of the whole sequence took its cue from how he saw *Henry V*; a clear indication of the priority of the latter play was that it opened the season, despite the chronological disruption of the story.

Henry IV, Part 1 on its own achieves a wonderful comic balance. It loses something important when it is not seen as whole and autonomous. The equilibrium it establishes is, however, disturbed in *Part 2* and thus in retrospect the achievement of *Part 1* may come to be seen as a good deal more precarious when the two plays are paired. Nunn gave us a Hal who throughout *Part 1* wavered desperately and unsuccessfully in relation to his hard, decisive and unreachable father; Hal was for the most part grudging and irritable, never gallant or heroic. The production repudiated any moments of possible reconciliation between father and son, even during the climactic battle, presumably so that the complete failure to resolve the Hal–Henry relationship could lead to an important moment in the second play when a reconciliation finally did take place just before Henry's death. So too Falstaff's humour was deliberately underplayed or played against – a reading that seemed to originate from the darker tones of *Part 2*. When Hands did his trilogy, in the years immediately following Barton's success with *Richard II* (discussed in the previous chapter), he adopted some of Barton's ideas about the king's relationship to the actor, and the importance of roles and the presentation of self in both spheres. His overall emphasis was, as the programme put it, on 'the education of a king' through role-playing and experimentation, with Hal coming across as a 'complex man educating himself for monarchy'. Thus the moment when Hal finally does become king, at the end of *Part 2*, was strongly emphasized, and the reading of both plays was pitched to that of *Henry V*, when Hal learns gradually how to *be* a king.[1]

If *Part 1* is played by itself, we are much more likely to see an equilibrium established between the various forces in the play, represented by the major characters, Henry, Hal, Falstaff and Hotspur. Out of the clash of these characters, Hal eventually emerges as the winner, defeating the chivalrous Hotspur, forgiving his enemy Douglas, embracing his father, and excusing Falstaff with a smile. The fragility of this temporary victory is unnoticeable, and the sense of a comic ending strong. When *Part 1* is combined with *Part 2*, the vulnerability of this stasis becomes clear, since the second play begins with another rebellious eruption, and the new emergent Hal of the final acts of *Part 1* is cloaked in mutability and returns to his previous ways.

The story of *Henry IV, Part 1* continues from *Richard II*, but the tone is different. Bolingbroke, now Henry IV, the most important character to carry over from *Richard II*, is subtly changed. Still hidden and secretive, he keeps himself out of the public eye as a matter of policy. And he retains his reserved, calculating mind and his authoritative presence. But he is considerably weaker here. The first line of the play announces the new attitude – 'So shaken as we are, so wan with care'. Gone is Henry's easy confidence. Although he restates his avowed intention to visit the Holy Land 'To wash this blood off from my guilty hand' (*Richard II*, v.vi.50), he is soon forced to abandon this project in order to attend to new civil broils. Nunn's production seized on the element of religious guilt for its ceremonial opening. As the lights went down, different actors (who had been wandering around the uncurtained stage while the audience entered) were spotted with lighted candles on different parts of the large, open set – bits of light in a general darkness. A Latin hymn filled the auditorium, the candles moved together in a slow procession and the stage lights gradually came up to reveal the dressing of the King and Archbishop in priestly robes. The procession continued behind a large crucifix while the King (played by Patrick Stewart) spoke the first part of his opening speech almost as a soliloquy. Then, bitterly, he diverted himself from this passionate religious interest to the unwelcome demands of state business. Thus the first scene was broken into two parts, with Henry being disrobed as he questioned his councillors on the progress of the latest rebellion. What this approach tended to hide was the fact that Henry already knows about Hotspur's refusal to deliver over his prisoners. He tells us this toward the end of the scene and thus in retrospect we realize that his project to go on a crusade is either wishful thinking or, more likely, deliberate obfuscation. Jon Finch, in the BBC Television Shakespeare production, made it clear that Henry did know what was what, and was staging this scene quite purposefully. Furthermore, everyone else present was aware of the calculation. Here the television medium helped considerably, since subtle eye contact and hesitation could be used to get the point across. Thus the scene reveals, I think, that Henry is still politically very canny, but Nunn's production, in over-emphasizing his religiosity, obscured that point.

Nunn's treatment of the scene was, however, an apt introduction to his and Stewart's conception of the title role. Here was a man of deep but impenetrable and unexpressed feeling, cool, hard and decisive, whose only display of warmth was a moment in i.iii when he was *almost* won over by Hotspur's contagious charm. He showed not a touch of tenderness in his relation with his own son. In the scene (iii.ii) where he upbraids Hal for his misdeeds, which ends with a guarded reconciliation, Stewart washed his hands very carefully at a silver basin and dried himself with a white towel as he derided Hal, tossing the towel contemptuously into the basin for emphasis. (Jon Finch too was a compulsive hand-washer, hinting at his guilt over the usurpation.) Stewart's antiseptic religiosity seemed a substitute for his inability or unwillingness to reveal any human softness. Quite different was the conception of the part in Hands' production; most critics saw Emrys James's Henry as a psychologically crippled neurotic, ranting and rasping, a 'snarling . . . hyena-like . . . autocrat' whose most consistent characteristic was his temperamental instability. He was by turns gleeful and suspicious, wily and emotional, authoritative and mean. At one point in his argument with Hotspur in i.iii, he threw a coin down to enforce a point; later he broke a formal, ceremonious exit to return and pick it up.[2]

What both these productions realized about Henry is that he is more than just a clever politician. The choice to explore his complexities was in both cases consistent with Shakespeare's interest in the play as a whole – at every level he develops *character* with a flourish, much more so than in the earlier *Richard II*, making this very much an actors' play. Dynastic struggle, chivalric rivalry, low-life boisterousness are all there, but seen always in terms of human character in all its varied and contradictory manifestations. From bit parts such as Francis the drawer, or Gadshill, to middle-level roles such as Poins, Glendower, Vernon, Worcester, Bardolph and Lady Percy, to the major parts – Henry, Hal, Hotspur and Falstaff – Shakespeare is prodigal and wide-ranging in his portrayals.

As a tiny example, let us glance at the anonymous Carrier who enters with the Sheriff at the end of the great tavern scene (ii.iv). He has only one line, and only this one brief appearance. The part is a superfluous one and could easily be cut (as it was by Terry Hands). But it is a telling one all the same. Prince Hal inquires what men the Sheriff is seeking. 'One of them is well known, my gracious lord', the Sheriff replies; 'A gross fat man.' And the Carrier, with a grave emphasis, adds, 'As fat as butter.' In Nunn's production, the actor took a longish pause before 'butter' as if searching for an effective comparison, and when it came the common-place simile was a humorous deflation, especially when set beside Hal's monstrous description of Falstaff earlier in the scene ('that swoll'n parcel of dropsies, that huge bombard of sack, that stuff'd cloak-bag of

guts . . .'). Supercilious, wanting to be noticed by the Prince, a bit
self-righteous – the Carrier is all these, and amusingly inadequate to
boot. Stanislavski once remarked that there are no small parts, only
small actors, and here is a case in point. Shakespeare has, in fact,
with only four little words, given the actor more to go on than other
playwrights often manage with extensive speechifying.

In the creation of the man whom the Carrier calls as fat as butter,
Shakespeare has outdone himself. Among all his characters, Falstaff
is second only to Hamlet as a source of endless fascination. He is, as
he says of himself in *Part 2*, not only witty in himself, but the cause
that wit is in other men. Falstaff is full of contradictions – he is a
thief, a cheat and a coward, a liar, a glutton and a drunkard. But, far
from making him distasteful, his disreputable activities contribute
to his liveliness and charm. He has winning ways, a disarming smile
and an endless wit. And he loves Prince Hal. Most of all, he is
transcendently *alive*. (One eminent Stratford director, William
Bridges-Adams, wrote of Balliol Holloway's performance that 'there
was in every stroke that jubilant *brain* that is the essential thing in the
part'.[3]) Now, it is possible to stress various sides of Falstaff at the
expense of others, nearly impossible to embody all of him
(figuratively or literally!). He is, for example, a knight, a gentleman,
and hence higher in station than the companions he surrounds
himself with. Most productions ignore this, but to give him back his
knighthood and to bestow some dignity on him means that he is
likely to be distanced from his cronies and hence nearer to Prince
Hal as well as more deferent with him (knowing his place, playing
his proper role). Such an approach might reduce the comic side, or
at least the low-life side, of the character, introducing a detached,
ironic element into his activity in the taverns and stews. Hands'
production played Falstaff that way, and accordingly improved his
military image, eliminating some of the fat knight's impertinent
interruptions of martial parleys and even having him (improbably)
challenge the fierce Douglas to single combat during the battle.[4]

More commonly, Falstaff is the large zestful comic figure,
wonderfully sympathetic just because he is so full of vitality. He
lives by, and represents, a subversive set of values – subversive at
least to the dominant ones of order, hierarchy, good government,
honour and chivalry. His unconventional allegiances make him a
threat, and it is this which worries the King. But it is just this
subversiveness that appeals to *us*. Too much solemnity in the upper
reaches of society finds a pleasing antidote in the Eastcheap tavern.

For a prince bent on kingship, however, such charm can be dangerous. In the programmes for both Hands' production, and an earlier RSC one (1966), the threat posed by Falstaff is stressed: 'Falstaff *is* paganism, the natural force of unguided appetite.' He 'embodies every aspect . . . of Vanity'. If Hal is set in a strongly favourable light, as he was in the 1966 revival, or if he is struggling seriously to find his way, as in Hands' version, Falstaff's considerable seductive power may be turned against the Prince; if he recognizes that he is fighting for Hal's favour against the King and court, his comic vitality can become a weapon in his battle and hence lose some of its pure appeal. Just because of his comic exuberance, he becomes a darker character altogether.

An alternative reading has been to exploit to the full Falstaff's inimitable capacity for puncturing illusions, giving a deliberately anti-war, anti-establishment flavour to whole productions. Such an interpretation is bolstered by emphasizing cold manipulation and betrayal at the centres of power (undermining both Henry and Hal, for instance, as well as Northumberland, Worcester and the rebels) and by transforming Hotspur's gallantry and honour into foolhardiness and rant. Falstaff's values thus become the only tenable ones. To some extent this is what Nunn in 1982 did with the text, though he significantly depleted Falstaff and treated the rebels quite generously. Falstaff had life, but too often threw it away. The robbery scene was flat and the tavern scene harsh. With the bravura humour gone, Falstaff failed to engage audience sympathy, and Hal was frequently sneering and contemptuous. The result was that the rebels emerged as the most winning characters in the play. Hotspur was strongly charming, likeable and brilliant without, however, being particularly honourable; Worcester was cool, rational and admirable in his politic way; and the Welsh scene was attractively intimate and magical.

As with so many of Shakespeare's plays, balance between the major forces seems the best policy. Hotspur, Hal, Falstaff, even King Henry – each has his appeal, each is right in some important way. If any one of them is simply discredited from the outset, the play's dramatic interest will be diminished. At the same time, each major character has an ambiguous, shadowy side which complicates his appeal and encourages alternative assessment. It is precisely the conflict of *rights*, the feeling in the audience of a divided sympathy, that gives emotional resonance to the story.

An excellent example of the complex tonality of the play, and a

telling moment from the point of view of interpretation, occurs at
the end of Hal and Falstaff's improvisatory scene in the tavern (just
before our Carrier's moment of glory). Hal, pressed to the limit by
Falstaff's insistent self-justification – the adopted roles of prince and
king have half slipped away – turns abruptly on his friend, just as
the harsh knocking on the door ends their play-acting:

> No, my good lord [Falstaff in the persona of Hal speaks to Hal in
> the persona of King Henry], banish Peto, banish Bardolph,
> banish Poins; but for sweet Jack Falstaff, kind Jack Falstaff, true
> Jack Falstaff, valiant Jack Falstaff, and therefore more valiant
> being, as he is, old Jack Falstaff, banish not him thy Harry's
> company – banish plump Jack and banish all the world.
> PRINCE. I do, I will.
>
> (II.iv.68–76)

This is a crucial interchange and there are as many ways of dealing
with it as there are productions and actors. It will of course grow out
of the relationship between Falstaff and Hal that has already been
established. But how? Does Hal realize the full import of what he is
saying? Is he warning Falstaff? Or is he more casual, throwing off
the line in his father's voice as a neat climax to the playlet? Does he
realize the implications of what he is saying while he is saying it, or
afterwards? Or is he calculating the effect before he speaks?
Technically, this comes down to a pause and what happens during
it. Does Hal pause before speaking, thus giving the line all the
deliberate force he can muster? Or between the two phrases, as in
Nunn's production, implying a dawning realization that he *will*
banish Falstaff? Or is there a general pause after the line, an
awkward, perhaps puzzled silence which affects not only Falstaff
but the on-stage audience as well and which is only broken by the
Sheriff's knock? (This is an approach I have seen several times – for
example, at Stratford Ontario, in 1979.) As a final alternative,
perhaps there is no pause at all – at Edinburgh in 1964, Hal simply
spoke the line quickly as he got down because of the knocking.[5] This
deliberately reduces the weight of the moment, and is set up by
introducing the knock a little earlier than usual, perhaps at the end
of Falstaff's speech. (The knock is nowhere specified in Quarto or
Folio and can occur wherever the director wants, though most
editors and productions place it after Hal's rejoinder.)

Another set of questions: how desperate is Falstaff? Does he seem to be fighting for his life? Is he aware of Hal's cool detachment and pushing for unconditional acceptance, or is he still playing for the grandstand? It will depend, of course, on Hal's attitude – whether there has been a clear imbalance in the relationship all along. In one production that I saw (in Vancouver in 1979), Hal was basically sympathetic and clearly liked Falstaff, but even so this moment had a chilling effect as Hal's true loyalties surfaced. Falstaff seemed to realize his vulnerable position for the first time. This was registered especially well in the business that followed the knocking: while other characters scurried to and fro, Falstaff kept still and insistent, wanting keenly to say more 'in the behalf of that Falstaff'. Sensing perhaps that this was his last chance, he didn't want to give it up. The obscure speech 'Dost thou hear, Hal? Never call a true piece of gold a counterfeit. Thou art essentially mad without seeming so' (ll. 486–8) took on a desperate poignancy, unnoticed by the other tavern denizens, and a significance beyond its ordinary suggestion that Hal should cover up for Falstaff in front of the Sheriff. It was a real plea for acceptance which was cheerfully, jokingly, thrust aside by Hal.

In Nunn's production, where Hal was basically unsympathetic, and ambivalent in his attitude toward Falstaff, 'I do, I will' was spoken with a rising emphasis, a short pause between the phrases, and the adolescent sneer that characterized the whole portrayal. Out of his own insecurities, Hal was perhaps protesting too much. Falstaff stood firm till the Sheriff was announced and then the issue became simply whether Hal would shelter him. A questioning tone on Falstaff's 'I hope I shall as soon be strangled with a halter as another' led to a truce and a hug as the Prince agreed to hide Falstaff. In Hands' version of the moment, to take a final example, Alan Howard, playing Hal as decent, rational, genuinely in search of a way to be a king and also a man, was distinctly friendly with Falstaff and in general was having a great time in Eastcheap (see Plate 6). Nevertheless 'I do, I will' carried with it a 'chilling authority'.[6] He took a pause before speaking, shook the cushion that had been serving as a comic crown from his head, and spoke regally. At the same time, everyone on-stage, except Falstaff, knelt. This was a clear forecast of the end of *Part 2*, when Hal appeared in golden armour, a stiff but dazzling image of his newly acquired kingship and the apartness that goes with it. The important thing was that Hal's detachment seemed justified – unfortunate perhaps, but a necessary part of his struggle to come to terms with himself and his role.

The exact tenor of this moment – the vibrations it sets going – will largely depend, as I have said, on what has already been established about the relationship between Hal and Falstaff, though it might, as in the last example, redefine that relationship somehow. Falstaff, for all his endless variety, is not that *complex*, and his attitude toward Hal is fairly straightforward – he loves him, not unselfishly of course, but loyally. So their relationship depends more on Hal, and *he* is much trickier to place. Though he doesn't lie as Falstaff does, he is less open, more deceitful, more difficult to read.

In recent decades, Hal has often appeared as a bit of a prig, or, worse, a hypocrite who uses everyone he comes into contact with for his own ends. (It was precisely this sense of the character, which has become a bit of a cliché, that Howard's performance sought to complicate.) Hal's dallying with Falstaff becomes in this one-sided reading primarily a mode of making himself look brighter when the time for reformation comes around. His new self will thus emerge as a theatrical coup, and Falstaff's main function will be as a foil. This Hal never lets himself go, never seems really to enjoy himself, always has his eye on his own advantage. The little scene with Francis the drawer (in II.iv) offers a small but salient example of the teasing, perhaps cruel, manipulation of which Hal is often capable. But the crucial scene in establishing this side of Hal is his first one (I.ii), and especially the final speech, a soliloquy in which he declares his essential detachment from his tavern cronies and his intention of throwing them off when the time is ripe:

> I know you all, and will awhile uphold
> The unyok'd humour of your idleness;
> . . . .
> So, when this loose behavior I throw off
> And pay the debt I never promised,
> By how much better than my word I am,
> By so much shall I falsify men's hopes
> . . . .
> I'll so offend to make offense a skill,
> Redeeming time when men think least I will.

His whole project can seem quite deliberately manipulative. But Howard made the speech 'more a good resolution than a real plan of action'. What he did seemed 'always capable . . . of a decent interpretation'.[7] In the Vancouver production mentioned earlier, the actor took the audience into his confidence in a boyish, intimate way, making up in charm what he might have seemed to lack in integrity. A more negative reading of the character will treat Hal as showing his true hand in the soliloquy (the real politician under the veneer of fellowship). In Nunn's production, Hal was brisk in the first part of the speech as he reset chairs and stools, and then became markedly shrill, with a contemptuous edge. In the scene leading up to the soliloquy, the primary emphasis might be on youthful teasing and companionship, or on the distance that separates Hal from Falstaff. The question is how much bite there is to the banter. For example, when Falstaff is teasing Hal because of his refusal to take part in the robbery, and says, 'I'll be a traitor then, when thou art king', Hal replies, 'I care not.' Part of the fun? Or a true statement with a hard edge?

Hal and Falstaff's relationship continues, of course, after the moment of truth in II.iv, but it is tempered by the new, serious context of impending and actual battle, and by the new role that Hal adopts in relation to his father and his princely responsibilities. Some of the old banter remains, but we hear in Hal a new, even more distant voice:

> Jack, meet me tomorrow in the Temple Hall
> At two o'clock in the afternoon.
> There shalt thou know thy charge, and there receive
> Money and order for their furniture.
> The land is burning. Percy stands on high,
> And either they or we must lower lie.
>
> (III.iii.199–204)

It is hard not to respond positively to this new, gallant Hal who from here to the end of the play sails along with effortless and impressive power (although in Nunn's production any sense of gallantry and honour was shot down). Falstaff's response to Hal's call to arms – 'Rare words! Brave world! Hostess, my breakfast, come! / O, I could wish this tavern were my drum' – is a delightful mockery, setting Hal's words in perspective, but it undermines Falstaff himself as much as it does Hal. From here to the end of the play, Falstaff is less Hal's equal, and more an ironic commentator – a brilliant, witty reminder of the folly and delusion of war and the 'grinning honour' of heroic death. As such he remains a very powerful voice, but it is questionable whether he measures up to Hal's new image. He has, in a sense, already been banished.

Now it is possible, as I said earlier, to put the full pressure of a production behind Falstaff's critique and show the madness of war and the hollowness of the kind of chivalric bravery manifested by Hotspur and Hal. In such a reading, the nasty manipulative Hal of the first part of the play merely changes costume, but retains his sharp eye for personal advantage; Hotspur is a fool, and King Henry a coward who has many marching in his coats in order to save his own skin. But, again, this loses the ambiguous balance of the text, however it might satisfy our own preconceptions about war and honour. When, at the end of the play, Hal stands over the dead Hotspur and the presumably dead Falstaff, we have an emblematic moment of great significance, Hal gathering life as it were from the failed energies of the two vital companions over whom he speaks such eloquent epitaphs. But Falstaff pops back up in comic refutation, seizing his own life for himself and calling into question Hal's highmindedness. Later, though, he undoes his own status as ironic critic by stabbing the dead Hotspur and trying to take credit for the latter's defeat. In his famous interrogation of honour a few scenes earlier, Falstaff had very tellingly put the value of life above that of honour; but, when he tries to collect on glory without paying his dues, he discredits himself. The ironies run thick, and a production had better be alert to them. Hands' production, in its stress on Falstaff's knighthood and dignity, went too far in these scenes, by having him challenge the fierce Douglas in the course of the battle. Since Falstaff has to fall down 'dead' during his skirmish with Douglas, this seems a bit misguided. And how mesh a really chivalrous Falstaff with the venal overreacher who stabs Hotspur?

Hotspur is an easy character to make fun of. Simpler than Hal and devoted to a single ideal, he might tempt the actor into the charmlessness of the obsessive personality. This will be especially true in an interpretation that seeks to give Falstaff's values and views the most weight. If the production takes a strong stand against the folly of war, then it is to be expected that the chief exemplar in the play of the glory and honour of chivalric battle will emerge as a fool, though perhaps an impressive one, who simply cannot see reality clearly.

It used to be the fashion to play Hotspur with a stammer, an old tradition that goes back to Beerbohm Tree's production in 1914, and which is based on Lady Percy's description in *Part 2* of her husband's 'speaking thick, which nature made his blemish'. Undermining his heroic gestures and grandiloquence with a diffident stutter might easily make him look ridiculous. But Laurence Olivier, when he played the part in 1945, gave it a more poignant suggestiveness. Aware that stutterers generally have trouble with just one or two sounds, Olivier chose to falter only on the letter 'w', which led to a superb effect at the end; Hotspur is one of only two characters in all Shakespeare who die in mid-sentence: 'No, Percy [he says of himself], thou art dust, / And food for –'. And Hal finishes for him: 'For worms, brave Percy' (v.iv.85–7). Olivier, stammering on the 'w', struggled to pronounce 'worms' and died with the word unspoken. Hal's finishing the sentence was a tender gesture as well as a subtle mark of his own superiority.

Hotspur, almost by definition, is hot-headed; he is impulsive, excitable, easily angered, but just as easily forgiving and generous. He is much given to honour and loyalty, and is above petty scheming. He loves his wife but teases her mercilessly, and fails to recognize her value. Two scenes (ii.iii and iii.i) give us a glimpse of the rebels at home, in their more relaxed moments. Hotspur especially benefits from the fuller view that these scenes provide. The setting humanizes the rebels, making them not just members of a faction, but men and women with a richer, more complex life than any we see at the royal court. Even their council takes place in a domestic environment and is concluded by the lovely singing of Glendower's daughter and the joking of Hotspur. Hotspur is clearly enjoying playing the tease, as he lies with his head in his wife's lap and listens to Lady Mortimer singing in Welsh, although, he says, he would 'rather hear Lady, my brach, howl in Irish'. Kate responds to him in kind, he tries to get her to sing, he mocks her for her tame 'sarcenet' oaths, and she becomes obstinate and silent. She is probably only play-acting, but the moment can be given a serious edge. Perhaps he has gone too far and hurt her feelings. In one production I saw, Hotspur leapt up and moved briskly away from her, leaving for the war without even noticing her genuinely pained reaction. His familiar, even endearing, kidding with her seemed therefore to cover a gap in his understanding, a failure to recognize who she was – and this weakened and complicated him from our point of view. In Nunn's production, this whole scene was quite lovely, especially the lyrical Welsh singing and the magical music which seemed to be drifting through the air from Prospero's island. The result was to secure our sense of the rebels' *value* in relation to the play's other forces. But the moment was transitory and the effect was quickly dissipated by a businesslike exit. The end of the scene works better, I think, if the two women who are losing their husbands to the war, Lady Mortimer and Kate, are left alone and silent on a gradually darkening stage.[8] Hotspur has stepped eagerly off; Mortimer, despite the bravado in his last line ('With all my heart'), has moved more hesitantly, with a sad look over his shoulder as he follows his father-in-law out. The lone women focus what Hotspur, in going gaily to his death, has never fully recognized – the inevitable blindness at the basis of his most treasured project.

In a rather odd move, Nunn brought Kate back on for the battle scene, dressed for war but acting merely as a spectator of her husband's defeat. The war scenes, despite gunpowder exploding and balls and chains being flung about, were rather subdued and the climactic duel between Hal and Hotspur was utterly unheroic. After the alarums and excursions of the swirling battle, the stage cleared, the movable set was pushed well back and the two men appeared engulfed in a *big* space which served to emphasize their littleness. Both men were totally exhausted; they kept sprawling and staggering, dropping their swords, depleted of energy. Finally they collapsed into an exhausted embrace, like a pair of punchy boxers in a clinch; Hal produced a dagger and stabbed Hotspur in the gut. Realistic death-shakes further reduced Hotspur, and 'Harry thou hast robbed me of my youth' was desperately screamed. There was not a jot of true heroism on either side.

This was an extremely negative version of a scene that is almost always played with some sense of heroic triumph. The purpose of the scene is to establish Hal's validity as a prince and a warrior. In defeating the strongest and most respected knight in the land, Hal absorbs some of Hotspur's power and solidifies the reconciliation with his father that has been building since the middle of the play. Nunn's reading of the scene shows how the balance of this particular play can be immoderately tipped in the interest of linking it with a darker *Part 2*.

In accordance with his overall interpretation, Nunn suppressed the various moments in this play when father and son show signs of reconciling, preferring to wait till late in *Part 2* for a climactic embrace. In *Part 1* they never touched each other. But again this seemed to be pushing a reading too far. Both on the battlefield, and earlier, during their heart-to-heart talk in III.ii, Henry and Hal, despite their differences, do come to some kind of understanding of each other. On this score, Terry Hands' production was much more successful. Most critics saw in that version a positive if uncertain Hal well on his way to kingship, practising different roles but never merely calculating or manipulative. Henry, by contrast, was neurotic and mean; his attack on his son in III.ii, where he scolds him for his prodigal ways, was hard, desperate and unsympathetic. The meeting of two such different men could hardly breed more than a very fragile peace. (The volatility of the scene is nicely registered by a note in the promptbook after l. 29: 'from here on, anything can happen!'⁹) But Hal's gracious excusing of his intemperance and his promise to redeem it all on Percy's head eventually led to a grasped hand and a hesitant embrace, which was broken by Blunt's entrance. At that point, according to the promptbook, 'Hal escapes from Kg. Henry'; the word 'escapes' suggests his reluctance and the uncertainty of the reconciliation.

Playing the scene to capture the nuances – that is what's essential. Different notions of kingship are at stake, but these are embedded in character, and in the father–son conflict. As an audience we aren't exactly asked to judge, but, rather, to understand, and we are given a broad context in which to do so. We have just witnessed a parodic preview of this scene as staged by Falstaff and Hal in the tavern. This inevitably creates some ironic distance, but it does not block the possibility of pathos as well. The double feeling is engendered by the delicate juxtaposing of opposites that is such an important feature of this play.

We end with another clever political move on Hal's part, which again might be attributed to honourable generosity, or to an astute eye for his future advantage – or both. He frees his former enemy, Douglas, thus putting the Scottish chieftain in his debt and ensuring his friendship. Again here, Nunn went too far in an anti-heroic direction: the Prince's decision was received by the other nobles with shrugs and veiled contempt. The point is that such an act is native to Hal – he is always looking for the right move, but this doesn't prevent him from being honourable at the same time. A full conception not only of Hal, but of all the major characters, involves a multiple viewpoint, one which will make the folly or blindness or shadiness of the character *and* his power to engage us equally visible. We are led to see too that the darker and lighter sides of the

characters arise from the same personal sources. The fineness of
Henry IV, Part 1 is that it can, and does, achieve a rich, multivalent
balance; but what can emerge when the play is accompanied by its
partners in the tetralogy is that the balance is delicate, and can easily
be tipped.

8
Henry IV, Part 2

Unlike the other three plays in the tetralogy, *Henry IV, Part 2* is rarely performed alone. Almost always it is seen in conjunction with *Part 1*, and often with *Richard II* and *Henry V* as well. This tends to restrict it to festivals and repertory performance and gives it a peculiar status as an only partially independent play. Furthermore, its relation to *Part 1* is problematic – in some respects it continues the action of the first play, and in others it replays that action in a minor key. With regard to the development and eventual crushing of rebellion and the emergence of Prince Hal as king, the action moves forward from *Part 1*; but, with regard to Hal's relationship with Falstaff and to his father, and the puzzling business of his reform, *Part 2* seems to forget what has happened in the earlier play. Thus the question of Hal's wastrel life, his dependence on Falstaff and the other denizens of Eastcheap, and the fears for the kind of king he will make, all come back up and are re-presented in a darker tone.

Uncertainty about the play's status is probably one of the reasons for its rather meagre stage history. It was presented once or twice in the early part of the eighteenth century, but after that it was rarely seen until this century, though the remarkable Samuel Phelps revived it in the 1840s and in doing so pulled off a noteworthy bit of bravura doubling, playing both Shallow and King Henry.[1] Even in the twentieth century, the play has not been frequently performed, although there has been a significant rise in its popularity since the sixties.

In fact, critics and directors nowadays are likely to prefer *Part 2* to *Part 1*, and for precisely those reasons that made it unpopular in earlier times: its uncertainty, its sombre tonality, its atmosphere of malaise, its distrust of the motives behind political and social behaviour, its cynicism about ideal values. The world it presents is one in which anxiety, suspicion, avarice, deceit, decay, old age, sickness and death all hold sway. And the accession of Prince Hal to glorious kingship is rendered suspect not only by the atmosphere in which it takes place but also by the distasteful rejection of Falstaff that accompanies it.

103

Not that Falstaff here is nearly so delightful nor so undeserving of banishment as he was in *Part 1*. To compare the two Falstaffs is indeed one of the best ways of measuring the difference between the two plays and of accounting for the second's unsettling theatrical effect. In a word, Falstaff has become mean. His exploits may seem similar but there is a new tone – he is more grasping, calculating and self-serving than he was. He lacks the comic largesse. He has, too, become self-conscious, aware of himself as a kind of institution; his wit reveals itself more in monologue than in repartee. His huge stomach is still his trademark, but he seems to have grown older and fallen into decay.

If we look for a minute at ii.iv, the parallel scene in this play to the great tavern scene in *Part 1*, we can see immediately that the comic inventiveness and exuberant energy of the earlier play are lessened. Perhaps Shakespeare's own powers were flagging – that explanation has sometimes been offered. But directors and critics today will normally take a different view, seeing the very lack of energy, the relative weakness of Hal's trick on Falstaff, and the subdued, valedictory close of the scene as signs of a new and deliberate tone. They will link these features with the general darkening of Falstaff's character and the simultaneous flattening of Hal's.

Hal, in fact, occupies a much less significant place in *Part 2* than in *Part 1*. He appears only twice before iv.v, the first time in a rather lifeless scene with Poins in which he complains of his vile position and his desire for small beer, the second time in ii.iv when he and Poins pretend to be drawers and overhear Falstaff's dispraise of them. He appears bored and preoccupied, concerned with his reputation but doing little about enhancing it. His tavern-hopping in *Part 1* had a verve and purpose which now are missing. Like so many of the other characters, he seems weary and depleted. In iv.v, the sight of the crown energizes him, and in the two scenes in which he appears as king he has achieved an appropriate dignity and grace. But the feeling of malaise lingers.

ii.iv, to stay with that scene a little longer, presents us with two new characters who, to a limited extent, make up for the weariness of the principals. Pistol bursts into the tavern with the explosiveness that his name implies, and a moment later is unceremoniously beaten out again, at the behest of the furious Doll Tearsheet. Pistol is a comic braggart, what the Elizabethans called a 'swaggerer', and his exact type is difficult to get across to a modern audience. He speaks grandiloquent nonsense in imitation of the exaggerated theatrical language of the time, which Shakespeare has great fun mocking. (An equivalent character today might borrow his language exclusively from the *Star Wars* saga or television soap operas.) But his language has a serious side also – its essential hollowness parallels that beneath the fancy speechifying of many of his betters. In Trevor Nunn's 1982 production,[2] Pistol was a shaking, shivering hipster who drew big laughs from the audience but seemed out of place in a predominantly Elizabethan setting. The conception was probably an attempt to find a modern equivalent for what Pistol may have meant to Shakespeare's audience. His quarrel with Falstaff and Doll was wildly raucous, in contrast to Hal's drabness and the ordinariness of his joke on Falstaff. But it didn't quite work – the scene lost its unity and became too disjointed.

Doll is a more subtly shaded figure than Pistol. Played too often as simply a buxom whore with a low-cut gown and a sexy swagger, she is actually a character of complex feeling. I have seen one brilliant performance that convinced me of this. The occasion was a rather workaday production of the play at Stratford Ontario that was suddenly illuminated by Martha Henry's appearance as Doll. Dressed in gaudy red, her hair orange and thinning under the increasing onslaught of what looked like syphilis, her body too an emblem of the decay that pervades the play, she played the scene with a terrifying and mercurial intensity. Her changes of mood were startling and abrupt – but convincing. Most actresses play the insults against Falstaff in a teasing, flirtatious way, but Henry was ferocious and bitter, and then suddenly soft and poignant in shifts such as 'Come, I'll be friends with thee, Jack. Thou art going to the wars, and whether I shall ever see thee again or no, there is nobody cares' (II.iv.65–7). Her feelings for Falstaff were a mixture of harsh, edgy sexuality, tender love and rampaging anger, with little of the usual seductive teasing. Her savage animosity against Pistol thus fitted into the general frame of the character, and her part in the Prince's little trick was wary and ambiguous. The ending of the scene, so evocative in its combination of sadness, hope, humour and tenderness, was particularly moving. Slumped and weary after taking leave of Falstaff, Doll and the Hostess were suddenly roused into fluttery activity by Bardolph's reiterated cries from within: 'Bid Mistress Tearsheet come to my master.' Like a virgin with her chaperone, this Doll was excited and hesitant, all that tired

experience of the world momentarily lightened, as Mistress Quickly
urged her to 'run, Doll, run'. 'She comes blubber'd', called the
Hostess. Doll left, puzzled, reluctant, eager, uncertain. This I
thought was both subtler and truer to the text than Nunn's version,
where the end of the scene was up-tempo: Falstaff made an
unscripted re-entry, stripped, and threw himself on a bed;
meanwhile Doll rushed down and mounted him as the lights
dimmed and a crescendo of music blared. By contrast, the combined
feelings and the overall sense of valediction in Martha Henry's
performance captured the rich, mingled tonality of the play as a
whole.

It is precisely such feelings that *Henry IV, Part 2* has to offer. It
won't do to treat it as an unsuccessful repeat of *Part 1*, a kind of
unfortunate sequel. Its strengths are darker and more hidden. Most
current productions acknowledge and try to exploit this, and many
will include a distinct anti-establishment slant as well. As in *Part 1*
only more so, it is possible to discredit the Prince almost entirely,
casting a shadow over his motivations and making his coming to
power at the end a mockery. Shakespeare has, as I have mentioned,
gone a long way towards this himself, eliminating a good deal of
Hal's charm, reducing his scenes with Falstaff, and letting his desire
for the crown ambiguously balance his sorrow for his father's
illness. It is not at all hard to tip the scales a little and have the Prince
emerge as a schemer, Machiavellian to his fingertips, with none of
the redeeming features he displays in *Part 1*. In fact it might be
difficult to avoid this picture, although in the scene with the Lord
Chief Justice, near the end, Hal shows himself to be thoughtful and
gracious, and in the final scene the rejection of Falstaff has been
successfully played as both just and inevitable.

The heaviness that pervades the play finds its single most
powerful emblem in the sickness of the titular character, the ageing
King Henry. He appears only twice: the first time wakeful and
troubled and calling eloquently on sleep to come to his aid (III.i); the
second, sick almost unto death, anxious about his son and the future
of his kingdom and guilty about the past (IV.iv–v). In the BBC
Television Shakespeare version, the King's disease was graphically
portrayed, his skin a mass of boils and scales, his weakness almost
total, which rather too obviously underlined the symbolic point.
Patrick Stewart, in the 1982 RSC version, incorporated his sickness
almost as part of the character. He carried always a pristine white
handkerchief with which he wiped his hands, lips, brow. He played

down the illness, talking of it matter-of-factly, as he in general eschewed all big effects. He threw away the speech about sleep, with all its opportunites for grandiloquence (exploited magnificently by Gielgud in Orson Welles' film). As in *Part 1*, he was contained, hard to reach, even harsh, but at the same time curiously admirable. Though he tried to keep his illness out of the way, it at last caught up with him just as he was hearing the good news of victory over the rebels. Straining to rise from his chair in triumph, he suddenly and convulsively pitched forward in a rigid fit. It was an arresting moment that bespoke not only the fate of this difficult man, but also the fragility of royal power itself.

With such a King, and a rather weak and whiny Hal, what emerged from this production was the banal point that the Prince's life was driven by his desire to please his father, something that he is quite unable to do. His father distrusted and was wary of him, as he made clear in his mocking comments about Hal before the renewed attack of his illness. But the following scene, when Henry lies near death and Hal enters to him and his crown, signalled a crucial change. The key thing is that at the peak of Henry's illness comes the reconciliation with his son. He dies happy, although we ourselves may feel more doubtful about his son's integrity than he does. We can hardly question, however, Hal's possession of the political skill necessary to become a successful king. In Nunn's interpretation, the conflict between father and son was deliberately built through both parts of the play toward this death-bed resolution. Finally Hal was able to please his implacable father, who, for the first time, showed strong feeling for his son. There was an embrace, and Henry actually put the crown back on Hal's head after the latter's tearful apology.

That is one way to do this teasingly ambiguous scene. But it downplays the discrepancies between Hal's apologetic description of what he has done and what we have actually seen him do. When Hal sits by his sleeping father at the outset of the scene, his eye is drawn to the crown resting on the pillow; he upbraids it for the trouble it has caused so many English kings. But a minute later, thinking his father has just died, he doesn't hesitate to take up the crown and put it on his own head: 'Lo, where it sits, / Which God shall guard'. He leaves, and his father wakes to find the crown gone and Hal with it. Warwick, sent to look for him, returns with a gracious description of a mourning Hal, 'washing with kindly tears his gentle cheeks'. A minute later Hal enters (in tears?), listens meekly to a long tirade on his father's part, and then apologizes. He says that he first picked up the crown,

> To try with it, as with an enemy
> That had before my face murdered my father
> . . .
> But if it did infect my blood with joy,
> Or swell my thoughts to any strain of pride
> . . .
> Let God for ever keep it from my head. . . .
> (IV.v.166–74)

But this is not strictly true, since pride, and perhaps joy too, *did* swell his thoughts when he said earlier,

> and put the world's whole strength
> Into one giant arm, it shall not force
> This lineal honour from me.
> (ll. 43–5)

The scene clearly provides the actor a lot of scope for interpretation. I remember one Warwick that treated his little speech as a way of softening the blow and protecting the dying king, rather than as an exact description of what he has seen Hal doing in the next room. With Hal, the key thing is what goes on in his mind and heart. He may genuinely be pained by his father's death, as he was in Nunn's production, and may even take up the crown in a haze of mourning. That would be the most positive interpretation, taking his later words of apology as the cue. But the text does not fully support it. The discrepancy between what he does and what he then says he has done is too great. Even his emotions at his father's death seem strangely distant:

> Thy due from me
> Is tears and heavy sorrows of the blood,
> Which nature, love, and filial tenderness
> Shall, O dear father, pay thee plenteously.
> (ll. 36–9)

Instead of expressing grief directly, he talks of what is due from him, what he will *pay* in the future. His language recalls the speech he had made as a fledgling prince, back at the beginning of *Part 1*, when he first develops his plan to 'pay the debt I never promised'.

Hal is thus still politic, still able to handle people, including his father, though not necessarily grasping or nakedly ambitious. He is touched by grief *and* anxious to prove himself in the role for which he has long been preparing. Perhaps this is why Alan Howard (RSC, 1975) chose, in the words of one critic, to play the scene 'questioningly', without ambition.[3] Hal is still unfinished, still learning.

The final scene, when Hal repudiates Falstaff, is the crux of the play, and has been a source of endless discussion among critics, actors, and theatre-goers. In mid-coronation, Hal rejects Falstaff: 'I know thee not, old man. Fall to thy prayers. . . .' Why the public renunciation, people ask, why the priggish, supercilious tone, why the blame cast on Falstaff as 'The tutor and feeder of my riots' when Hal has clearly chosen his own course and is responsible for it? Has he not made of Falstaff a convenient scapegoat, a necessary element in the theatrical ploy that he had planned way back at the beginning of *Part 1*? Does this not make him cold and calculating? Does it not darken in retrospect his entire relation with Falstaff? If directors and actors take this kind of line on the final scene, they are likely to prepare for it by undermining, or at least questioning, Hal throughout the play, especially in the scene with King Henry just discussed. Hal's hard shrewdness will thus fall into line with the machinations that have established and maintained his power – his father's original usurpation, and more recently, his brother John's deceitful and dishonourable tricking of the rebels (iv.ii).

This latter scene definitely leaves a bad taste in the mouth. It is the prime example of the anti-heroic strain in the play. Prince John, after promising to redress the grievances of the gullible rebel leaders (only the cautious Mowbray is suspicious) and inducing them to dismiss their army, promptly has them arrested for capital treason. When the Archbishop, who should be played as honourable and just, objects, 'Will you thus break your faith?', John replies,

> I pawn'd thee none.
> I promis'd you redress of these same grievances
> Whereof you did complain, which, by mine honor,
> I will perform with a most Christian care.
>
> (iv.ii.112–15)

Now this is a bare-faced lie, since the rebels' demands included acquittal 'by a true substantial form' of 'all members of our cause' (IV.i.171–3). One may therefore question whether John has any honour left to swear by! No wonder then that, when he says smugly at the end of the scene, 'God, and not we, hath safely fought today', his words usually move the audience to cynical laughter.

Although Hal is not directly involved with this, the sneakiest manoeuvre in the play, neither can he be entirely dissociated from it, since it is the means by which he retains his position. If it is true that the play finally asserts Hal's legitimacy and his worth, it does so in a distinctly interrogative context. For directors who want to discredit him in the final scene, the necessary foundation is there. But what I think will work best will be a rejection of Falstaff that takes into account our misgivings about Hal's behaviour and the questionable status of his power, while at the same time convincing us that his actions are purposeful, inevitable and personally painful. The end of Terry Hands' production (RSC, 1975) sparked lively critical disagreement, but seemed to be trying for a subtle mix, even if it was not fully successful in achieving it. Here is what he did: a white sheet was spread across the stage covering the autumn of Shallow's orchard with more than a hint of winter. The Prince, dressed all in gold, with only a small procession, entered to Falstaff and the rest, his movements deliberate and almost machine-like. For some critics, he was a robot in golden robes on a wintry stage. His lack of feeling was emblematized by the cold, rigid encasement. Furthermore, certain palliatives which Shakespeare has presumably put into the text to soften the blow – the promise of a pension for Falstaff and his followers, and the Lord Chief Justice's quiet assurance to Falstaff, 'I cannot now speak. I will hear you soon' – were cut.[4] There were perceptive critics who rejected this reading as far too one-sided. But others read it differently. Michael Billington saw the golden armour as an image of the king's essential apartness and thus as a sign of the struggle between public figure and private man that characterizes the whole tetralogy, while Irving Wardle noted that the new king 'covered his face in agony' when Falstaff confronted him, appearing to see the necessary rebuff as a 'wretched duty'. The play ended with Falstaff standing alone under a leafless tree with a raven croaking above.[5]

Since this production of the play was conceived as part of a tetralogy that focused on Falstaff and included *The Merry Wives of Windsor*, the final emphasis may have fallen too much on the fat knight; and the view of Hal was conditioned by the fact that the direction of the historical series was towards *Henry V* and took its cue from that. Hal was variously seen as detached and distant, or admirably intent on his own education. At the same time, Falstaff was given more dignity, and seemed more at home in Shallow's country estate than in Eastcheap. He was more deferent with Hal, and somewhat isolated from his cronies in the tavern. This created an inconsistency, since it seemed to indicate that it was hardly necessary to reject him at all. Hal's own feelings were clearly ambivalent. This was indicated in *Henry V* as well, when the King himself was given the task of sentencing Bardolph to be hanged, and the scene re-enacted the complex feelings of the rejection of Falstaff. There is of course a logic and a pay-off in taking such a long view, but it is well to remember that among the chief pleasures of *Henry IV, Part 2* are its breadth of characterization and the meandering, episodic quality of its plot. It abounds in great scenes that are fun in themselves and that are not particularly well served by a fixed ideological stance.

Probably the most common way of dealing with the last scene is to play it straight, letting the momentum of the action carry the audience through it. There is a double movement in the last part of the play, one that establishes the legitimacy and worthiness of the new king, and another that sets up the comic downfall of the figures from outside the court. In v.ii, the young King Henry V adopts the Lord Chief Justice as 'a father to my youth', exchanging, as it were, one surrogate father for another, after the death of his real father. Even in this scene, Hal's ability as a theatrical manipulator is in evidence: he sets the Lord Chief Justice up to expect a reprimand and/or dismissal, playing along with the expectations of the court. Then he skilfully reverses his position, declaring his intention 'to frustrate prophecies', and embraces his former opponent. Once again his awareness of theatrical effect helps him to convince his audience of the value of his emerging self. In a production that wishes to question or undermine Hal's motives, this scene would have to be played with a hard edge, the new king gaining control of his court through sharp manipulation. In a 'straight' production, the audience in the theatre will succumb to Hal's controlling charm and the sincerity of his declarations, as easily as the court audience does. The emotional momentum of this scene will then carry over into the final one, where once again Hal's theatrical acumen serves his intention of appearing, and being, a wise and humane ruler.

This is the approach taken by the 1979 Stratford Ontario production mentioned earlier, and it is essentially that adopted by John Barton in his 1966 RSC production. For Barton, the ending is not only inevitable, but just and humane. His rehearsal notes for the actors suggest that it is not the repudiation of Falstaff that is surprising, but rather the 'moderation of the sentence'.[6] The Stratford Ontario version tried to capitalize on the charm of the main actor and the positive effect established in the scene with the Lord Chief Justice. It banked too on the full panoply of a coronation scene with rich Plantagenet costumes and pennons flying. The sense of Hal's legitimacy was strong, and there was little feeling of loss at Falstaff's defeat, partly because the role was downplayed from the start, the actor competent but not outstanding. Somehow, though, the overall impression was disappointing. It lacked the disturbing edge of ambiguity, some of the scepticism about power that Hands' production seemed to imply.

Falstaff, of course, is riding for a fall. It would be wrong to sentimentalize him, to see him as a kind of oversized Winnie the Pooh unceremoniously consigned to the rubbish heap. He is, as I said earlier, mean. He has a streak of calculation at least as deep as Hal's, combined with a deviousness and avarice that lead him into duping the simple Hostess with false promises and manipulating the wealthy Shallow – all in a bid for money. His consuming interest in money runs throughout the play (in *Part 1* he robs as much for the joy of it as for the money). He has the audacity in his first scene to ask the Lord Chief Justice, with whom he has just had a witty but losing exchange, for a loan of a thousand pounds. By the end he has managed to pry the thousand pounds out of the tight Justice Shallow, who, after Falstaff's disgrace, asks timidly for half of his thousand back. We can see that, despite Falstaff's promise ('Sir, I will be as good as my word'), Shallow has little hope. We mustn't feel too sorry for old Shallow, though – he too has a shrewd interest in money, of which he has made quite a bundle. Even in the midst of his old-man's doctored memories and his reminiscences of now-dead friends, he has an eye for the price of bullocks and ewes at Stamford fair. In lending money to Falstaff, Shallow has his own interests in mind – he's making an investment and expects a good return after the death of the old king, when Falstaff rises to power.

It is precisely that assumption that makes Shallow's, and also Falstaff's, downfall a theatrical inevitability. In the delightful drinking-scene that comes between Hal's reconciliation with the

Lord Chief Justice and his rejection of Falstaff, we see the latter's arrogance flying high. Pistol's absurdly rhetorical announcement of the old king's death meets with grand promises: 'Master Robert Shallow, choose what office thou wilt in the land, 'tis thine.' Old Silence, meanwhile, quietly passes out. 'Let us take any man's horses', exults Falstaff; 'the laws of England are at my commandment. Blessed are they that have been my friends, and woe to my Lord Chief Justice' (v.iii.124–40). Since we have just witnessed Hal's adoption of the Lord Chief Justice, we can hardly not look forward, with cruel pleasure, to the unavoidable reversal of all these expectations.

There are thus two important currents joining in the final scene. The first is a conviction, created by both the theatrical structuring and by the gathering arrogance of those involved, of the rightness of the impending rejection. The other is a sense that Falstaff is being treated far more shabbily than he deserves, by a prince whose motives and methods are open to serious question. Ideally some mixture of the two, avoiding oversimplification or ideological distortion, would seem the most desirable course. This is what Terry Hands seemed to be after, even if he and his company were not wholly successful.

The new king's actual speech of disapproval sounds like a sermon, but has in it the apparent seeds of a joke:

> Make less thy body hence, and more thy grace;
> Leave gormandizing. Know the grave doth gape
> For thee thrice wider than for other men.
>
> (v.v.52–4)

Ralph Richardson's Falstaff responded brilliantly to these oddly incongruous lines: he looked on with 'puzzled half-appreciation', thinking that perhaps Hal was only kidding after all. A jest began to form on his lips, a wave of confident relief rising from the depths, only to be squelched by the King's 'Reply not to me with a fool-born jest.' At this, 'the spark died, and Falstaff faded into a man tired and old'.[7] *Is* the King joking with these lines? Does he have a bit of the old glint in his eye? If so, this might, if the actor wants to pursue it, make him all the crueller, since again he is setting up expectations, only to dash them the next moment. He may, of course, be simply oblivious to the possible humour in the lines, and, if the actor takes it that way, he may well appear somewhat priggish (as Hals are often inclined to be). Overall, the important thing is that we somehow feel sorry for Falstaff even as we recognize the necessity, and the justice, of King Henry's action. As at the end of the tavern scene, there is a sense of valediction and loss (we mustn't forget that in the penultimate scene Doll has been arrested in connection with a murder); but that feeling is mingled with the impressive ceremony of the coronation procession, the humour of Shallow's predicament, and doubt about Hal's methods. If Falstaff and his cronies appear too strongly as comic dupes or sentimentalized victims, the tone can lose its subtle shading.

It is precisely such shadows that make this play fascinating, just as it is the poignant mingling of feelings which give it a special tone. But there are also obstacles in the way of its enjoyment by a modern audience. I remember hearing lots of muttering during the intermission of one festival performance, protests against long-windedness and incomprehensibility. There is no doubt that the play is a very 'talky' one – everyone, including Falstaff, having picked up the vice of wordiness. And, compared with *Part 1*, there is hardly any action – nothing to correspond to the robbery, to Hotspur's fiery activity, to the singing of Lady Mortimer, and, climactically, no battle. Instead there is only a devious political manoeuvre. Pistol, the windy braggart who *does* nothing, is thus an apt addition to this play, as is the old, garrulous Shallow. The rebels, so impressive in *Part 1*, are here vacillating, weak and featureless. Shakespeare, in writing for an audience that knew the story and could easily identify the various participants, did not concern himself with the difficulties an uninitiated audience might have. Audiences will simply have to adapt – get to know the play and listen hard. This may mean that the play will remain less popular than it should be, which is too bad. For the sceptical ironies and interrogative humour of *Henry IV, Part 2* make it very much a play that can speak to us now.

9

Henry V

Henry V used to be thought of primarily as a pageant play, an excuse for patriotic panoply and English self-glorification. Trevor Nunn once called it 'the national anthem in five acts'.[1] Times, however, have changed. What used to be simple is now perceived as complex, what was clear is now ambiguous. The change begins and ends with the perception of the hero. None of the other plays in the tetralogy so single-mindedly revolves around one central figure. In *Richard II* Bolingbroke and Richard form the poles; in the *Henry IV* plays Henry IV, Hal, Hotspur and Falstaff vie for centre-stage. But in this play, despite the variety of character and the breadth of the canvas, Prince Hal, now King Henry, dominates the dramatic landscape. The simpler vision of the play used to regard Harry exactly as the eloquent Chorus does, a perfect man and warrior king whose 'liberal eye doth give to everyone' a 'largess universal' and whose modest soul is 'free from vainness and self-glorious pride'. More recently, however, a close scrutiny of the text and a sceptical attitude toward the glories of war have combined to cast a shadow on the monumental figure at the centre. His very human doubts, his thoughtful, almost analytic, cast of mind, his tendency to seek a moral rationale for what his will desires, even his habit of turning almost obsessively to God for justification at critical moments – such features have shaded and complicated the old emblematic portrait.

In the nineteenth century, the play was mounted with extraordinary spectacle, in an attempt, it would seem, to belie the Chorus's apology for the inadequacies of stage representation. Audiences were treated to the delights of huge dioramas with richly painted scenes, such as the departure of the English fleet from Southampton, minutely reconstructed castles, interpolated tableaux and ballets, and, in Charles Kean's production, the insertion of 'An Historical Episode: Old London Bridge, from the Surrey Side of the River', which was set up to illustrate and accompany the Chorus's fifth-act speech depicting Harry's triumphant homecoming. The Chorus himself (or, more precisely, herself) was presented as Clio, muse of history, and the scene

115

included not only the bridge and the Tower of London, but masses of welcomers headed by 'angels [and] prophets of a venerable hoariness, dressed in golden coats and singing in sweet harmony' as well as a mayor, aldermen and a 'chorus of most beautiful virgin girls, elegantly attired in white'.[2] In such a world, Henry could hardly be more than an emblazoned cipher, with neither subtlety of mind nor emotional density.

In the early part of this century, the emphasis began to change. Frank Benson, for example, who rethought so many of Shakespeare's characters, presented Henry as more serious and thoughtful than was traditional, although he was guilty too of beginning the dubious trend of representing the French King as a babbling half-wit. In 1937 at the Old Vic, Olivier and Tyrone Guthrie chiselled away at the dead wood of tradition, presenting the audience with an intellectual, sharply questioning Harry, and a deliberately unheroic, almost 'pacifist', reading of the text.[3] This may well have suited the spirit of pre-war Britain, but, when Olivier came to do his famous film of *Henry V* a few years later, Britain was in the thick of war and in no mood for pacifism. As so often during the history of this play's production, the spirit of patriotism and its tunes of glory sounded throughout the interpretation. And, since no other version has been so widely seen or so deeply imprinted in public consciousness, Olivier's glorious Harry is the one we all remember. For many years, perhaps even up to the present, no subsequent production of the play could fail to acknowledge the precedence of that wonderful but one-sided film. And it was one-sided. Fully half the lines were cut, including almost every reference to dissension in the kingdom, and all kinds of doubt, aggression, cruelty or even sharpness in the main character.

Terry Hands, who directed *Henry V* along with the two *Henry IV* plays for the RSC in 1975, has remarked on the imaginative dominance of Olivier's interpretation. In his introduction to the prompt-text, Hands invokes the ghost of the film, concentrating on the ideal of national unity that its emphasis on the ' "patriotic" element in the play' served. To facilitate this emphasis, 'all doubt and uncertainty were removed' from the character of Henry. Hands sees his production as readmitting the doubts and uncertainties 'inherent' in the role of Henry in order to work toward a more problematic kind of unity, involving both the assertion and abdication of human individuality – a 'final non-hierarchic interdependence – a real brotherhood'.[4] Accordingly, he chose Alan

1. *A Midsummer Night's Dream* (1970): Bottom (David Waller) in Titania's (Sara Kestelman) bower, with Oberon (Alan Howard) and Puck (John Kane) overseeing their delights.

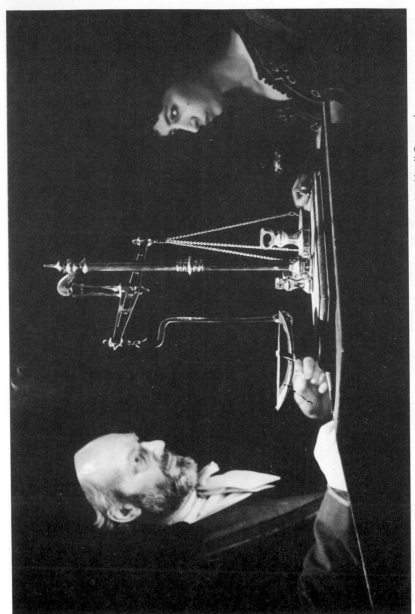

2. *The Merchant of Venice* (1978): Shylock (Patrick Stewart) in his office with Jessica (Avril Carson).

3. *Twelfth Night* (1969): midnight antics at Olivia's house, interrupted by Malvolio (Malvolio: Donald Sinden; Maria: Brenda Bruce; Feste: Emrys James; Sir Andrew: Barrie Ingham).

4. *Measure for Measure* (1950): the Duke (Harry Andrews) brings light to the darkened prison.

5. *Richard II* (1973): Richard (Richard Pasco) upon his fateful return to England, his 'horse' in the background.

6. *Henry IV, Pt 1* (1975): Falstaff (Brewster Mason) plays the mock-king, as Hal (Alan Howard) gets ready to unseat him.

7. *Henry V* (1975): the King (Alan Howard) responds with pain as he surveys the massacre in the English camp.

8. *Hamlet* (1965): David Warner's wistful Prince, scarf in hand, surrounded by Establishment gloss.

9. *Hamlet* (1976): pin-striped Claudius (George Baker) confronts a resilient Hamlet (Ben Kingsley).

10. *Othello* (1964): early in the play, Olivier's exotic dynamism.

11. *Othello* (1964): later, Othello reduced to despair and powerlessness (with Frank Finlay as Iago)

12. *King Lear* (1962): Lear (Paul Scofield) enthroned in power, demanding tribute from an uneasy Cordelia (Diana Rigg).

13. *King Lear* (1962): the Fool (Alec McCowen) parodying his master, entertaining Lear and his rowdy knights.

14. *Macbeth* (1955): 'Give *me* the daggers' (Vivien Leigh and Laurence Olivier).

15. *Coriolanus* (1959): Olivier hanging upside down in spectacular defeat and Aufidius (Anthony Nicholls) in ignominious triumph.

16. *The Winter's Tale* (1978): Hermione (Margot Dionne) returns to life (with Brian Bedford as Leontes, Martha Henry as Paulina, and Marti Maraden as Perdita).

17. *The Tempest* (1976): Prospero (William Hutt) lords it over a submissive Ariel (Nicholas Pennell).

Howard for the lead role, an actor particularly adept at projecting doubt and uneasy self-awareness, with an engaging but not a glorious stage presence. The important thing, however, is not so much the specific ideology of the later production, as the need to place it in the context and tradition that Olivier's film had set.

To get a clearer idea of what Hands had in mind, we might choose one of the high points of Olivier's version and see what Hands did with it. The famous Crispin's Day speech (iv.iii) was built by Olivier into a traditional, stirring oration (the 'grandest battlecry in literature' declared one critic[5]), delivered from a haycart to his gathered troops. As he spoke, the camera pulled back from him, including more and more of the 'band of brothers' with the yet-unarmoured King a mighty voice in their midst. James Agee saw it as more than 'just a brilliant bugle-blat'; for him, it was 'the calculated yet self-exceeding improvisation, at once self-enjoying and selfless, of a young and sleepless leader, rising to a situation wholly dangerous and glamorous, and wholly new to him'.[6] When Alan Howard came to do the same speech, he had, first of all, established his Henry as far less self-confident – no born leader, but a qualmish, fearful and reluctant hero.[7] The production as a whole was severely pared down, with no extras and several of the named characters conflated into one or two. Thus Henry had a diminished army and a distinctly nervous self.

But Hands wanted to depict the speech as a turning-point, the moment in the play which 'finally unites the English'.[8] The speech therefore began 'almost casually as the King lined up with the soldiers for his mugful of water from a keg'. It moved not to a rousing battle-cry but a 'simple gaiety'[9] which bespoke, perhaps, some new self-unity. Only after it did Howard raise himself to what he saw as 'the one rallying call of the scene', the line 'All things are ready, if our minds be so.' No longer are these men, Hands commented, 'linked merely by . . . external things . . . their unity and determination have become "interior", a state of mind and perhaps heart'.[10] This was both the ideological core of the scene and the feature that most specifically distinguished Hands' reading of the scene from Olivier's. The attempt was to make that self-enjoying and momentous lift in Olivier's film an inner and much less tangible shift.

All this seems highly interpretative and cerebral, and perhaps difficult to indicate theatrically, but in the long challenge to the French herald that follows ('I pray thee bear my former answer back . . .'), the company found an intriguing way to make the statement they wanted. They underlined a bit of the King's proverbial wisdom by playing it out in comic music-hall fashion. In his speech, Henry hurls in the face of the arrogant French the old adage, 'The man that once did sell the lion's skin / While the beast liv'd, was kill'd with hunting him.' The soldiers heard the beginning of the phrase and then completed it together with their leader as if it were a vaudeville 'number'. It was a moment they all shared, and the King, picking up their mood, delivered the rest of the speech as a 'rousing, blackly funny parody of confident kingship', rather than as a straight declaration of English glory. It was a game, but one that covered 'real brotherhood felt for the first time'.[11] Henry, in nervous but gay self-mockery, had at last found his authentic place, not above but among his men. And so, though he was criticized for speaking French too well in his wooing colloquy with the Princess at the end of the play, the point was aptly made; he had become adept at learning languages, at turning roles into inward realities – a process in which he had been involved throughout all three plays.

This then was one way of seeking to deepen and complicate a traditional image, without jettisoning it altogether. In fact, it was an attempt not to debunk heroism, but to redefine and democratize it, and thereby make it more palatable to a modern audience likely to distrust the grand gesture (so long, that is, as patriotic feeling is not running high – the Falklands crisis might have occasioned very different feelings). Some modern productions of the play have gone considerably further, deliberately undermining Henry's heroic claims and highlighting his political manipulativeness or aggressive wilfulness. To go that far, however, flattens the play in an analogous but opposite way to nineteenth-century pageantry.

The play begins with an apology and a reminder. The Chorus reminds us that we are watching a play and apologizes for the obvious inadequacies of stage representation – 'Can this cockpit hold / The vasty fields of France?' But at the same time he poses a challenge to the imagination of the audience to piece out the actors' imperfections with our thoughts, to see 'within the girdle of these walls . . . two mighty monarchies, / Whose high upreared and abutting fronts / The perilous narrow ocean parts asunder'. To emphasize the point, the Chorus has frequently appeared in modern dress, casual and matter-of-fact, moving the audience slowly into the artifice. Of course he can as easily be ceremonial or flamboyant, suiting his style to his language, impressing or exhorting his audience rather than simply addressing them. The important thing is that he introduces the idea of role-playing and theatrical reality, a theme of all four Lancastrian plays, and one marked in Olivier's film by the choice to begin with a model of an Elizabethan stage where we were at first ushered backstage and then shown the Chorus emerging to speak to an exuberant audience. As the film progressed, the scene was gradually expanded beyond the Globe's 'wooden O' so that, by the climactic battle scenes in Acts III and IV, no trace of the original theatre setting was left and we were in the 'authentic' world of cinematic *verité*. By the end, however, the theatre world had almost unnoticeably slipped back and we were dismissed by the Chorus to trundle home, like the motley Elizabethans with whom we had shared the imaginative excursion. Hands, again adapting Olivier's techniques for his own purposes, chose to begin with not only the Chorus but all the actors in rehearsal dress, making the gradual costuming of the actors (which began in I.ii with the entrance of the French ambassador in full regalia) a mark of what for him was the main theme: the search in theatrical terms for a persona and an identity.

However it is handled, the Chorus's ornate opening speech leads us into a decidedly less heroic world than the one the speech envisions. The first scene presents two wealthy and clever (perhaps even conniving) churchmen, worried about a bill that would result in the loss of half their lands, and concerned with protecting their interests by winning over the young King, who is, they say, 'a true lover of the holy Church'. The fact that the proposed bill would, among other things, provide for the establishment of 'a hundred almshouses' does little to affect their zealous resistance to it. Instead, heartened by what they see as young Harry's reformation, they have offered a bribe, 'a greater sum / Than ever at one time the clergy yet / Did to his predecessors part withal'. Their policy is essentially to divert Henry's attention to his claims in France and provide him with money for a military campaign, spending what for them is a small sum to protect a larger. Some directors who seek to emphasize the traditional glory of the play have cut this scene altogether (as at Stratford Connecticut in 1981). But the twists of economics and politics do curl around the young King, establishing an ambiguous context early on.

The scene that follows, in which Henry questions the Archbishop about his lineal right to the French throne, is notorious for its prolixity. Canterbury has one speech of over sixty lines describing in minute and confusing detail the hereditary complexity of the French monarchy, and then follows that with another twenty-line speech after a brief interruption from the King. Even to an audience for whom the claims of lineage were far more important and interesting than they are today, such a full exposition might well have seemed tedious. However, it is a cheap trick to make comic game out of the whole matter, as was done for example in the film, where the Archbishop fumbled and shuffled papers, slapped his confederate Ely's wrist for handing him the wrong scroll, stumbled over his explanation and in general made a fool of himself as the audience within the film hooted. The case is clearly a serious one, and the job of the director is to figure out why Shakespeare, who by this time in his career was clearly in control of his dramaturgy, wrote it as he did. One plausible interpretation would view the Archbishop's long-winded speeches as a ploy, a way of covering a dubious claim with elaborate legal justification, or, equally, a way of assuring that Henry's eye is turned toward the fields of France rather than the more lucrative and less costly forests of the English Church. On the other hand, it is not impossible that Shakespeare is treating the Archbishop straightforwardly and means his explanation to be full and convincing. (Hands confesses to never having finally decided between these two approaches,[12] though if I were doing the play I'd opt for the former.)

When Henry butts into the middle of the Archbishop's disquisition with the apparently impatient 'May I with right and conscience make this claim?' he seems to have been either not listening or not understanding, though Olivier made it a high comic moment. He is clearly less interested in history than in his present position and what it means for the future. He wants a firm sense of how to proceed. The Archbishop never unambiguously answers the question, but goes on in a high patriotic vein to exhort his prince to action. The assembled lords and prelates all join in and once again Henry is mostly silent, interrupting only with a strategic reminder of the dangers posed to England by the Scots if he were to lead a major expedition into France. Just how keen on war is he? Productions that want to give us either a glorious or a war-mongering Harry are likely, though for different reasons, to show him straining to get started. The ideal of honour will dominate the former interpretation, while a more cynical motivation, based perhaps on his father's death-bed advice in *Henry IV, Part 2* ('Be it thy course to busy giddy minds / With foreign quarrels'), will inform the latter. It is also possible to portray Harry as isolated from the others, more hesitant about war and worried about its consequences (as Hands and Howard did). But it seems from his ready acceptance of the court's not very strong arguments that Harry has already made up his mind before coming in. Although he shrewdly pretends to the French ambassador (whom Hands made a bishop to further the irony) that the Dauphin's insult has driven him to prove himself against France, the decision has in fact already been made before the ambassador's entrance.

A curious feature of this whole scene, and indeed of Henry's rhetoric in general, is the number of appeals he makes to God and God's will. God seems constantly in his mouth, and once again it is difficult to decide whether this is meant to display piety or policy. (Hands eliminated the problem by cutting many of the references.) At times, his use of the epithet is slightly shocking, at least to modern sensibilities:

> Now we are well resolv'd; and, by God's help,
> And yours, the noble sinews of our power,
> France being ours, we'll bend it to our awe,
> Or break it all to pieces.
>
> (I.ii.222–5)

Exactly what God's role will be in the smashing of France is unclear, but the brutal arrogance of this uneasily balances its resolute nobility.

Overall, then, Harry is a more ambiguous character than the Chorus would have us believe, and contemporary productions will often note this by underlining an ironic disjunction between the Chorus's descriptions and Henry's more pragmatic reality. In what was perhaps the keynote modern production of the play, Peter Hall's Stratford version in 1964 (marking Shakespeare's four-hundredth birthday), the distance between the Chorus's vision and what the audience saw was dramatically emphasized. The Chorus appeared in gorgeous Elizabethan finery and gave the lines their full rhetorical splendour. In contrast, the production itself was decidedly anti-romantic, its hero tired and workmanlike, but tenacious and 'stubbornly determined' as well.[13] As the play progresses, Harry's attractiveness (whether of the glorious or dogged variety) grows, and directors have occasionally looked rather too hard for undercutting elements, when the play seems to demand a gradual surrender to the appeal of his bluff and mischievous kingliness. Some directors, including Hands, have made much of the moment when Bardolph, Hal's old crony from his Eastcheap days, is executed for robbing a church. The text merely mentions the incident, to which Henry gives his approval ('We would have all such offenders so cut off' – III.vi.112). But various ways of highlighting it have served to make Henry seem repressive, or reluctantly re-enacting his rejection of Falstaff. Alan Howard, in Hands' production, had to give the signal himself, a duty he carried out with clenched teeth and deep misgivings. The moment was climactic, and clearly set up as parallel to the end of *Henry IV, Part 2*.[14] At both times, Howard's Henry was struggling against old patterns and loyalties in an attempt to assert a new, and ultimately more humane code. Thus Henry's pious lines against pillage and cruelty were presented as new rules, which his soldiers only grudgingly accepted. In a somewhat harsher vein, the Stratford Ontario production of 1966 had Bardolph's body 'dumped at the king's feet, his throat bloodied by the hangman's rope'.[15] The emphasis there, as also at Stratford in 1964, was on the guilt and blood of war.

Two other episodes on the battlefield have well served directors who seek to liberate what playwright John Arden has called the 'secret play within the official one',[16] although both have as easily been integrated into the traditional reading. One is Henry's decision to kill all the French prisoners (expediently left out of the film), and the other is his disguised sojourn among his army the night before Agincourt. This latter episode, when Henry in disguise debates the ethics of his position with the common soldiers Williams, Bates and Court, is an elusive one. The Chorus, in a memorable line, speaks of 'A little touch of Harry in the night', but modern critics and producers have often taken a less romantic, more sceptical view. Looking closely at what is actually said in the dialogue with the soldiers, they have noticed Henry's tendency to avoid Williams' main argument ('But if [the King's] cause be not good, the King himself hath a heavy reckoning to make'), and some have detected arrogance and self-delusion in the soliloquy that follows immediately. Its final lines hardly seem to embody that spirit of democratic camaraderie that the scene as a whole would exploit:

The slave, a member of the country's peace,
Enjoys it; but in gross brain little wots
What watch the king keeps to maintain the peace,
Whose hours the peasant best advantages.
(IV.i.278–81)

The quarrel that erupts with Williams at the end of their conversation also seems a bit mean-spirited, though it is possible to see it as arising from the mischievous trickery with which it is concluded. The scene as a whole raises ethical problems about the motivations and justifications for war which go back to the outset and which the play never adequately answers.

The other uneasy battlefield incident, and a much harsher one, is Henry's command to slay all the French prisoners (IV.vi.37–8). Although productions have frequently tried to suggest that his order proceeds from just indignation over French atrocities, he in fact gives the word *before* he learns of the enemy's slaughter of the boys in the English camp. To soften the effect of this, directors have sometimes inserted an interpolated scene (first used in the 1950s and seen again at Stratford Connecticut in 1981[17]), showing the attack on the unarmed boys and capped by the later appearance before the King of Fluellen carrying the dead page. A version of this strategy was presented in Michael Langham's suggestively anti-war production at Stratford Ontario in 1966, which featured a bloody rendition of *both* French and English killings.[18] Tough-minded realism was the hallmark of that production, with no attempt either to glamorize or undermine the main character. Langham's approach makes sense, although, given the climate of the time, he may understandably have underscored his point too heavily – Vietnam asserting its presence in the programme as on-stage. In fact, the text makes it clear that Henry's decision to kill the French prisoners is a purely pragmatic one, stemming from the intelligence that the French are regrouping for another main attack, and, presumably, the fact that there are no spare English to guard the captured.[19]

Hands' production went to considerable and instructive lengths to try to deal with these incidents, contriving to put the King in the best possible light without minimizing the horrors of war.[20] At the end of the amusing scene with Pistol and the captured French soldier (IV.iv), the Boy has a short, ironic soliloquy and then announces his own and his companions' vulnerability: 'The French might have a good prey of us, if he knew of it, for there is none to guard [the camp] but boys.' As he finished, three French soldiers entered, plundered and toppled the cart that had accompanied the English war scenes, and then, in silhouette, slew the Boy. The French noblemen who, in the text, enter upon the Boy's exit, were here outraged witnesses of his dishonourable murder, which was thus made a part of their motivation for renewing the attack with honour as a way of compensating for the shame that their soldiers had inflicted on the French cause. From that point, Hands radically rearranged the text. He skipped over IV.vi to a snippet of Fluellen and Gower's discussion of the killing of the boys (IV.vii.1–5), which was transformed into an announcement to the King (though he isn't meant even to be on-stage at this point) that 'there's not a boy left alive'. There was another jump to the end of IV.vii for the King's response: 'I was not angry since I came to France / Until this instant', a statement which has no single clear motivation in the text but which was here made to refer explicitly to the killing of the boys. Only then did this version jump back to IV.vi for the telling command, 'Then every soldier kill his prisoners, / Give the word through.' This clearly softens the harshness of the order, and rationalizes the text's ambiguities. But, so as to maintain a balance of ironies, and to keep before us the deadliness of the war games being played out, no sooner had Henry given the command than Pistol, on-stage with his French prisoner (in another unscripted appearance) unceremoniously cut the throat of his endearing captive. The seeming atrocity of murdering the prisoners can thus admit of many treatments: it can be cut, as in the film, softened by linking it to a justified revenge (Hands), left as a sign of the bloody horrors of war (Langham, and in a modified way, Hands), or, but this is rare, turned into a mark of the aggressive cruelty manifested earlier in the threatening speech before Harfleur.

It is to the credit of many modern productions that they have raised difficult questions without seeking to discredit Henry himself. More and more the effort has been to stress the importance of the King's *education*. Unlike Olivier's Henry, who was born glorious, many recent Henries have had to achieve glory by having it thrust upon them; they have frequently had to feel and stumble their way through hard times in order to reach some tentative liaison between public and private self. This concentration on the King's education squares neatly with the modern tendency to present the play in context, together with the other plays in the tetralogy, or at least the two parts of *Henry IV*. (One critic has aptly noted that the 'traditional version of *Henry V* stands up better if the play is detached from the other histories and produced in isolation'.[21]) Hal is thus seen to grow through all three plays, so that his coronation at the end of *Henry IV, Part 2* is viewed not as the end of a process, but more realistically as simply a stage from which he must develop further. *Henry V* ends with a charming scene in which Harry, the victorious general, successful ruler and budding statesman, has to learn to cope with a new role: that of awkward and hopeful wooer. It is a typically Shakespearean gesture that the scene in which Henry achieves the diplomatic consolidation of his power over France should include that delightfully frustrating but promising courtship. The process of his education is even now incomplete.

If Henry has in general been presented more in the round over the past twenty years or so, so too have his enemies. It used to be common, for example, to portray the French King as little more than a drivelling idiot, the Dauphin as a gilded butterfly, and the rest of the French nobility (with the exception of Montjoy and perhaps the Constable) as emblematic figures from illuminated manuscripts, gorgeous but ineffectual. Hands kept this last feature, but not chauvinistically to mock the French – rather, he wanted to show that they are 'a remnant of the age of chivalry . . . frozen in an era that has already passed'.[22] His English were blunter, muddier and much more accessible – which went along with his effort to democratize the hierarchy and stress comradeship. Obviously, any production will seek a contrast between the two nations and how they are presented (as with Rome and Egypt in *Antony and Cleopatra* or Greece and Troy in *Troilus and Cressida*). The point, however, is to avoid caricature, and to make the opposition telling; and a prevalent way of doing that has been to contrast the English 'realistic' view of war with the French 'romantic' view of it.[23]

The English, of course, are represented not only by their sinewy aristocrats and their perceptive, hard-headed, but loyal soldiery, but also by a smattering of Celtic captains and a disreputable gaggle of underworld hangers-on. We are deliberately given a much wider-angled view of them than of the French, of whom we see only aristocrats, and rather effete ones at that (except the women, who are much more attractive – the charming princess, her pert handmaiden and her impressive mother). The range of the British *dramatis personae* has often helped to underpin the jingoistic approach to the play: all Britons united under a beloved monarch. Even Pistol, the most dishonest and unreliable of the lot, declares,

'The King's a bawcock, and a heart of gold'. Warring and violent Celts, represented by the pedantic Welshman Fluellen, the dour Scot Jamy and the choleric Irishman Macmorris, show themselves tame and domesticated, comic in fact, as though emerging from the mythology of a thousand old jokes. Their vaudeville routine in III.ii, accompanied by the English straight-man Gower, is a traditionally uproarious interlude which Hands, while retaining the humour, tried to transform into a serious and threatening quarrel, breaking with the simplistic ideology of chummy British unity.

Of the captains, Fluellen is certainly the most important, linked as he is with the King at the top and Pistol at the bottom. He is of course partly a comic character with his stage accent, his bookish preoccupation with the ancient disciplines of the wars, his tendency to self-righteousness and his inability to see himself as others see him. But he is just as clearly an honest soldier, the salt of the earth. How volatile or even violent the actor wants to play him is a matter of choice, though I remember myself being taken critically to task for making him too violent in an undergraduate production years ago. What the critic couldn't have known was that the reason behind my violent cudgelling of the amazed Pistol was that I had temporarily forgotten my lines! The only real pitfall to be avoided is the temptation to make him silly, the butt of mocking laughter rather than amused sympathy. And on that point it is worth quoting Trevor Peacock, who played the part under Terry Hands: 'If you try to be funny you're finished. I knew that if I made Fluellen real then he would be funny.'[24]

In comparison with the *Henry IV* plays, the low-life scenes are rather thin, missing the central figure of Falstaff. Bardolph, his hellfire face all whelks and carbuncles, is back, but subdued; Nym, a new character, is almost as wordless as a parrot, his speech confined mostly to growls and clichés; Mistress Quickly and Pistol reappear, but now, surprisingly, joined in the holy state of matrimony, much to Nym's chagrin. Finally there is the Boy, presumably Falstaff's page from the previous play, though modern companies, unlike Shakespeare's, often have trouble filling the role with an actual boy. His quick wit, sharp perception and honest heart find expression in two delightful monologues describing the cowardice and thievery of his companions. A clear advantage of inserting the scene in which Fluellen carries in the dead Boy after the massacre is that we are movingly reminded of the stilling of that shrewd and observant voice. By the time of Agincourt, Nym and Bardolph are also dead, but ignominiously – both hanged for stealing; and Mistress Quickly, it would seem, has succumbed to the 'malady of France', though the text is obscure on this point (v.i.81–2).[25] Only Pistol, the swelling braggart with 'a killing tongue and a quiet sword', is left; and even he is diminished from what he was in *Henry IV, Part 2*. His almost heroic bombast recurs here in a minor key, while his fierce gestures are reduced to an absurd quarrel with Nym over the hand of the Hostess, and finally to futile grovelling before Fluellen's indignant chastisement. But he survives, unregenerate. For him, as for Parolles in *All's Well*, exposure is an inconvenience, but hardly a spur to reform:

> Old do I wax, and from my weary limbs
> Honor is cudgel'd. Well, bawd I'll turn,
> And something lean to cutpurse of quick hand.
> (v.i.82–4)

An elegiac tone is struck here, as it was earlier for Falstaff in Mistress Quickly's sad and funny description of his final moments. There may even be a wavering note of sympathy for the now solitary Pistol. The sadness cuts across the glory at both points in the text – the King, we are told near the beginning, has killed Falstaff's heart, and Pistol's resolution at the end darkens our perception of Henry's own resolution in regard to marriage and the future.

These characters, then, keep before us some sense of the loss involved in the King's progress, and thus are not only comic, though they often make us laugh. Seeing the play in the context of the other history plays makes us more aware not only of the education of Henry, but also of the narrowing of focus that such an emphasis involves. Hence the mystery of Falstaff's non-appearance after the promise in the epilogue to *Henry IV, Part 2* can perhaps best be explained on the grounds of dramatic necessity, rather than by reference either to protests from the descendants of Sir John Oldcastle (presumably the 'model' for Falstaff) or to personnel problems within Shakespeare's company. Keeping Falstaff out of the play and reducing the force of the world he embodied may be viewed as a loss necessarily accompanying the gain in stature and confidence that Henry enjoys. But it is a loss that in the person of Pistol, clinging tenaciously to a despised life, refuses to be absolute. For Hal to get bigger, Falstaff and the others had to get smaller; but, since that was impossible for the fat knight, he had to disappear altogether. What is crucial in performance, however, at least if one wants to avoid a single-minded reading of the play, is to keep that sense of loss before the audience and hence temper Henry V's famous victories. The text itself in the final chorus reminds us of the temporariness of Henry's gain and the imminent loss of France and bleeding of England under his son, Henry VI. The play then ends with a deliberate undoing of its own final stasis and achievement, and this is consonant with the tonal complexity noticeable throughout and amply registered in modern productions.

10

Romeo and Juliet

Is there any other play of Shakespeare so well known or so well loved as *Romeo and Juliet*? Certainly none of the other plays has inspired so many and varied adaptations – operas, oratorios, ballets, musicals. None has quite caught the imaginations or the heartstrings of so many generations, and probably only one play, *Hamlet*, has been so often quoted. Since the eighteenth century, when it was played in Garrick's sentimentalized version (complete with a *Liebstod* colloquy between the lovers in the tomb), *Romeo and Juliet* has never been long absent from the stage.

At the same time it has usually been recognized as one of the master's lesser works, challenging neither actors nor audience as the great tragedies do. For this reason, some of the finest Shakespearean actors have avoided it. Even now, producers are likely to regard it primarily as a 'popular' play. It is true that it lacks the complexity, the depth of insight and the poetic richness of the greater, more mature plays. It is, after all, a quite early work, written around 1595, five to ten years before the other tragedies. Its appeal is a youthful, energetic one, springing with vitality, dash and passion. And it will usually repay a production that approaches it on that level.

But just because it is so popular, and so relatively simple, it poses a problem to the would-be producer: it is too *familiar*. Now, the familiarity of *Hamlet* or *Macbeth* or *Twelfth Night* causes much less difficulty, because those plays are rich enough, various enough, to sustain a seemingly endless string of revivals. But *Romeo and Juliet* seems more easily exhausted. And this leads to a serious temptation: find a gimmick, a way of freshening what you think has gone stale. This saves you the trouble of having to think the whole play through for yourself. Have Romeo and Juliet appear nude in the dawn scene, for example, or turn the Prince into a mechanical doll; overstress the sexual element (one production had Mercutio making love to a bench during the Queen Mab speech[1]); make the group of boys into a teenage gang devoted to sex and violence – these are some of the ways in which the old story has been jazzed up. But a saner policy might be to let the familiarity of the play become an asset, its fire and high-spiritedness, its loveliness, sadness and sense of waste, all falling into place like the cadences of a Mozart symphony. As always, to trust the text is the first requirement.

There is another problem with the play, however – a more serious one since it arises out of the text itself. Robert Speaight, reviewing an RSC production of 1976, comments that he left the theatre more convinced than ever that, after Romeo has been banished, the 'spontaneity of the first half is fatally lost'.[2] Other critics disagreed about that particular production, but few would deny that the second half of the play is harder to keep going than the first. The mechanics of the plot are more strongly felt, there is less of the lively vitality that informs the first part, and there is a stronger sense of the role of bad luck in bringing about the catastrophe. Mercutio, the spirited voice of the earlier scenes, is dead, and the Nurse more subdued, less comically inventive; her role is reduced as Juliet becomes more isolated. There is, of course, good reason for this, as there is for many of the other differences between the halves. But the fact remains that, from the point of view of an audience, the second half is likely to be less delightful and less moving, at least until the final scene in the tomb. To offset this liability, pace is clearly important – a quickening towards the culmination, with appropriate moments of slowness and deliberation. We want to feel the grip of inevitability. This requires some strong playing from secondary characters such as Capulet, with his sudden irrational desire to hurry his daughter's marriage, and Paris, whose smooth, bland politeness should cover a fervent desire. The Friar too, whose complicated machinations bring such bright things to confusion, must be strong and convincing if we are to be carried along, rather than irritated, by his meddlesomeness.

In general, it is the older characters who will make the most difference to the second half. In the 1976 Stratford production, directed by Trevor Nunn, John Woodvine's violent Capulet helped bring off what one critic (in opposition to Speaight) felt was a 'miracle' – the second half went better than the first. Capulet was played as the 'source and fountain of the hate and violence that runs through the play'. When Juliet declared her refusal to marry Paris, he hurled her to the floor; unheedful of decorum, he kicked Romeo's corpse in the family vault and brandished a dagger at the bumbling Friar. The reconciliation that followed was hard-won, but perhaps for that reason more real, and helped to overcome any sense of contrivance.[3] Capulet's brutal treatment of his daughter (as well as of others in his circle) helped to show that the lovers, 'however steadfast, are no match for the casual passion of the surrounding world'. The accidents that plague them thus came to be seen less as a dramatic convenience and more a proof that accident is 'an inescapable part of life'.[4]

The Friar has too often been played as a dithering meddler, thus neglecting the strengths of the character. 'He should twist that dagger out of Romeo's hand with the hard sinews begotten of hard living', said Bridges-Adams.[5] In that same 1976 production, David Waller's performance was described as 'vigorously earthy', an approach that helped give his viewpoint a good deal more weight than it would have in a more conventional interpretation, without cheapening that of the lovers.[6] This is important because it keeps the latter's haste and fire in context by contrasting them with the deliberate slowness and caution of Friar Laurence. 'These violent delights have violent ends / And in their triumph die' is advice that Romeo doesn't want to hear, but our attentiveness to it provides a valuable corrective. And we are more likely to take such a view seriously if the actor has taken the character seriously. Like Capulet, who wants to marry his daughter to the Prince's kinsman, and the Nurse, who advises Juliet to bigamy, the Friar also has his cunning, self-interested side. He wants to bring about an alliance that will turn the warring 'households' rancor to pure love' (ii.iii.92). He sees himself bringing off something of a diplomatic triumph. When everything goes wrong he quite naturally falls into despair, but he has enough shrewdness left to justify himself with a long explanatory speech, although this is often cut as anti climactic.

None of the older characters is as lively or as vivid as Juliet's Nurse, who has become almost a figure of folklore. She is the perfect foil for her young charge. Her inimitable speech, marked by leaps of unexpected association and sly sexual reference, catches her spirit exactly. She teases, she bullies, she butts in, she tells naughty stories, she stands momentarily in awe before the spiritual wisdom of the Friar ('O Lord I could have stayed here all the night to hear good counsel'); even her mourning is loquacious. She loves Juliet, but her affection is tragically shallow. She is most comfortable with what is palpably present in front of her and cannot fathom the idealism in Juliet's love. When Edith Evans played the part in the 1930s, and it was one of her great triumphs, she was, according to one critic, 'slow as a cart-horse, cunning as a badger, earthy as a potato'. 'Whenever she was onstage,' wrote another, 'reprimanding, soothing, or merely catching her breath, the lovers both seemed children.'[7] The role is a gift for the right actress, and will rarely fail to please. But there is at least one important question about it: where does her betrayal of Juliet, her total failure to understand this girl she has nursed since infancy, come from? Somewhere in the earthy garrulousness so comically endearing throughout the first half of the play, there has to be a hint of the insensitivity, the hard practicality, that emerges in III.v, hardly an hour after Romeo has left, when the Nurse advises Juliet to forget him, and commit bigamy by marrying Paris. The moment was marked in Nunn's production by a 'series of significant withdrawals' on Juliet's part so that 'from nestling in the Nurse's lap she came to be completely separated from her on an isolated stool stage-centre'. The scene was quiet and still, the Nurse's advice appearing 'more diabolical in its softness'.[8] The phrase 'cunning as a badger' catches the necessary hardness in Dame Edith's performance; something similar will be required of any actress. There is nothing the least bit sentimental about the Nurse.

All of these characters – Capulet, Nurse, Friar, even old Montague – though subject to caricature, are best played as mixed, as not purely one thing or another. Attending to the possible depth, conflicts or complexities of the older characters will lead to a better balance between their situation and the emotional charge of the young: the fieriness of Tybalt, the brilliance of Mercutio, and especially the passion of the lovers.

It is the young, however, in their impulsive, breathless haste, that give to the play its special, characteristic tone. From the opening minutes, that tone needs to be set. When Peter Brook staged *Romeo and Juliet* in 1947, he wrote that the keynote to its atmosphere is to be heard in a single line: 'For now, these hot days, is the mad blood stirring' (III.i.4). He stressed that 'it is a play of youth, of freshness, of open air, in which the sky – the great tent of Mediterranean blue – hangs over every moment . . . a play of wide spaces, in which all scenery and decoration can easily become an irrelevance' (this in the forties, when pretty realism was still very much in fashion). Accordingly, he stripped the play of much of its customary decoration, contenting himself with a few crenellated walls, and sought, in his treatment, 'to capture the violent passion of two children lost amongst the Southern fury of the warring houses'.[9]

The result was not much appreciated by critics or public at the time, but by now Brook's basic approach has taken hold and become dominant.

The old poetic–romantic tradition, against which Brook was in part reacting, was effectively done away with by Franco Zeffirelli in his famous production of 1960, which was later made into a film. Zeffirelli too emphasized youth, passion and hot blood; rowdiness among the teenagers; the sweetness, awe, and fearfulness of first love; the brilliance of the Southern sky; the heat of Verona's streets; the excitability of its people. All these were incorporated into the conception. Visually there was nothing splendid or fancy about the young men. Romeo was no gallant, but a plain and comfortably dressed, though spirited, member of a gang. He and his friends 'ate apples and threw them, splashed each other with water, mocked, laughed, shouted'. High spirits were attended by moments of seriousness, wonder, strong affection. In such an atmosphere, how easy it was for a brawl to erupt and become dangerous. And, as John Russell Brown argued, the lively action was not extraneous, but tied closely to the language. For example, as the lovers left the stage with the Friar to be married, 'Romeo walked backwards so that he continued to face Juliet who was supported on the Friar's arm: Romeo was "bewitched by the charm of looks".'[10] The animation of the text and the action gave new dramatic life to the poetry, but the production had difficulties with moments of stillness, and failed to find a suitable means of representing the older, more authoritative figures.

The idea of stressing the gang of boys has been developed in several subsequent productions, and frequently darkened. Terry Hands (RSC, 1973) directed a dark, moralistic version of the play on an abstract metallic set that reminded several reviewers of a state penitentiary. (' "Yonder window" does seem to look out on Sing Sing', wrote one.[11]) Hands apparently sought to work against the text's familiarity. So the high spirits and hot blood of Brook's and Zeffirelli's conceptions were here reduced to anger, violence and sexual disgust. Mercutio, as he so often does, set the tone. He dragged after him a 'large female dummy . . . which he casually dismembered . . . in the speech about Rosaline's high forehead, fine feet and quivering thigh'.[12] The Nurse cowered from him and his gang as she might have in the world of *Clockwork Orange*. With Mercutio a 'flamboyant pervert and rival gang-leader to the sadistic, bullet-headed Tybalt', the love of Romeo and Juliet necessarily took second place; it was determined by the passionate hate around them.[13] This same idea was extended in 1980 in another RSC production, again in an abstract set – two 'tattered, plaster-exposed walls', which formed a 'faceless precinct for urban violence'. The gang-members looked like muggers, and Romeo, in black leather, hammered at his lines in what seemed 'an internal version of the violence around him'.[14]

Both of these productions, stretching to make a moral and social point, lost the warmth of the play. Both seemed to try too hard to blame the lovers and their society for their fate, and thereby lessen the sense of accident that the plot, perhaps too obviously, depends on. But precisely the emotional force of that accident, the inescapable, arbitrary cruelty of chance, and the chief characters' stance in the face of it are what give the unfolding of the play its poignancy and power.

Nunn's production in 1976 treated the group of boys more casually, downplaying the element of incipient violence. And accordingly Mercutio was conceived less as a gang-leader and more as a 'local joker' for the young bloods, witty and easy-going. He was deliberately provocative with Tybalt in the duel scene, but his actual death came apparently by accident when, the duel over, he fell back into Tybalt's arms and the blade went in. The whole approach was more 'openly theatrical' and 'extroverted' than Hands'.[15]

When Brook developed his unlocalized approach, he was looking for an approximate equivalent to the Elizabethan stage. In later years, the idea has been refined and exaggerated, leading, for example to the cold, metallic, multi-levelled set, presided over by the Apothecary as Fate that Hands used in 1973, and to an equally abstract setting for a production at the Guthrie Theatre in Minneapolis (1979), which featured an octagonal floor made of blue plexiglass, with matching backdrop and skeletal, polished steel props. One critic noted that this set 'fused unlocalized remoteness with an undisturbed intimacy',[16] though we may wonder why such remoteness is desirable. Self-consciously abstract sets (i.e. not just Shakespeare's bare stage) lose the social context, which Brook's ordinary uncluttering or Zeffirelli's Verona did not, and float the lovers in empty space.

I wonder too whether metallic remoteness in the set is conducive to the humour in the play, which is another of its important elements, especially in the earlier scenes. What would be incongruous in any other Shakespearean tragedy – beginning with an exchange of bawdy jokes – is here quite appropriate. The play continues in the same vein: Mercutio and the Nurse are full of salacious humour. Mercutio cannot even tell us the time without a double entendre: 'the bawdy hand of the dial is now upon the prick of noon' (ii.iv.110); nor the Nurse recall Juliet's age without also recalling, to our delight, her husband's sly joke about women falling on their backs. Sexual humour, though present in *Antony and Cleopatra* and occasionally in *Hamlet* (where it is tinged with bitterness), is typical more of the comedies than the tragedies. Its presence in *Romeo and Juliet* alerts us to this play's special closeness to the comedies. If, then, Mercutio is too contemptuous and disgusted, the humour is lost and the tone suffers.

The play is often funny, even in its serious moments; not many productions will have the boldness to make us laugh at Romeo in the balcony scene, but it is certainly not impossible. Our first glimpse of the hero certainly reveals him to be the butt of gentle comic mockery – he is the mooning lover, over a barrel in his pursuit of the cruelly chaste Rosaline. The lightning swiftness with which he switches mistresses is also comic, although it is expressed in a jewelled lyricism that inhibits laughter. He swears undying love in the manner of Orlando in *As You Like It*, but Juliet's quiet refusal to hear oaths rather deflates him. Both his extravagance and his crestfallenness may amuse us; as Ian McKellen played him in Nunn's version, there was both humour *and* intensity, resulting in what many reviewers saw as an exciting performance.

The emotional weight of the play clearly rests with the lovers – from the hushed moment of their first meeting, through the lyricism of the famous balcony scene, the rush of their marriage, the tangled feelings of their one night together and their parting at dawn, to, finally, the heavy sadness of their unnecessary deaths. More than anything else, it will be these moments that an audience will carry away with them.

Significantly, each goes through a change, a sudden, enforced growing-up. Romeo in Mantua, when he gets the news of Juliet's supposed death, manifests a new awareness and determination, mixed with an otherwordly compassion for the Apothecary. 'The scene should surely be directed in a way that can show how grief *and* resolution have entered deeply into Romeo's soul', commented one critic in reaction to Zeffirelli's version, which saw a merely agitated Romeo repeatedly strike and browbeat the 'caitiff wretch'.[17] Juliet has something of the comic heroine in her from the beginning –

resourceful, ardent, straightforward, witty and realistic. These characteristics undergo a rapid development under the pressure of circumstance when she suddenly finds herself utterly isolated, not only repudiated by her family but betrayed by her old confidante, the Nurse, who advises her to make the best of the situation by marrying Paris. The moment was effectively marked in Nunn's production, as mentioned above, by Juliet's movement away from the Nurse and the isolation that suggested. From this point on, Juliet, though she seeks the Friar's advice, has to act alone. Her famous speech before taking the potion (IV.iii) expresses her fear, but handled well can also express a steadiness and control that carry her through to the very end.

The lovers meet at a party given by Capulet; the scene is a crowded ballroom and Romeo, a Montague, has come with his masked friends. When he and Juliet first speak to each other, their words form a perfect sonnet; images of shrines, pilgrims and prayer predominate. The moment is a quiet eddy in the midst of a turbulent scene: Tybalt has just been ranting about the villainous presence of a Montague; Capulet is trying to shut him up and at the same time encourage the dancers; music is playing; servants are running about with trays of delicacies. Should we have the impression that Romeo and Juliet are grasping a moment out of the confusion, passionately seizing on unlooked-for joy? Or should there be a sudden hush, the other characters falling back as the lovers take the centre, giving their exchange all the solemn formality it seems to have in the text? Each approach has been tried and each can work. At one extreme, both Brook and Nunn cleared the stage completely, leaving the lovers temporarily alone, thus emphasizing the solemnity of their meeting. Terry Hands, in contrast, made the scene passionate and quick, keeping friends and relatives on stage and emphasizing the fiery haste that characterizes the progress of Romeo and Juliet's love and its explosive consequences.[18] Either way, something is left out as well. To clear the stage is to miss the social context and hence the pressures that impinge upon the lovers throughout, while to ignore the textual indications that the moment is quiet, subdued and formal is to lose that closely measured sense of pattern that accompanies the fire and passion at every stage. There are, in other words, contrasts at work, contrasts which make the play what it is but which are extremely hard to mark in a production. Formally expressed passion is not something that the twentieth century is especially attuned to. Romantic treatments of the play, and romantic adaptations of it such as that of Berlioz, have tended to stress the passion more than the formality, just as they have played down the contrast between social and private.

Such renderings have stressed the personal tragedy of the young lovers, leaving aside the social context in which it takes place. However, the play begins with an evocation of 'Two households . . . In fair Verona', only then turning to the 'pair of star-cross'd lovers'. And the social milieu is powerfully present throughout. The lovers' brief meeting in the balcony scene, for example, is crowded at one end by the bawdy shouting of Romeo's friends and at the other by the importunate calls of the Nurse. Their wedding-night is pressed to an early conclusion by Romeo's banishment and, more immediately, by Juliet's mother, who, the minute Romeo has left, enters with news of her daughter's impending marriage to Paris. Even their deaths are far from private. The corpses of Tybalt and Paris look blindly on at the ironic scene before them; the anxious Friar intrudes on Juliet as she prepares for death, and the imminent arrival of the watch hurries her on her way; no sooner is she dead than the Prince enters accompanied by most of the roused town. As if to re-emphasize the importance of the social context, the play ends not with death but with reparation, and a new bond between the warring families.

Brook, consistent with the approach he took to the sonnet scene, simply ended the play after Juliet's final words.[19] For him, as for most audiences, the emotional power of the play dies with its protagonists. Like Berlioz and Prokofiev in their versions, he focused on the youthful romantic core of the play, ignoring the question of the restitution of order in the troubled city and the reconciliation of Montague and Capulet. Zeffirelli did not go quite that far, but he cut the Friar's last entrance, thus rapidly patching up the final explanation, and he ended with an elaborate dumbshow whose solemn and lifeless formality seemed in deliberate contrast with the animation, now for ever lost, of the lovers.[20] Trevor Nunn's production followed through on the private emotion of the lovers by underlining the mischance, always a powerful element, in their death scene: just *before* Romeo took the poison, Juliet's 'arm around his neck began to move; swamped by grief he didn't notice that she was in fact alive'.[21] But, seeking as well to give full weight to the reconciliation, Nunn retained most of the lines and focused on Capulet, whose violence against Juliet and, in the last scene, against the Friar, was effectively subdued when he took Montague's hand

and called him 'brother' – much to the amazement of the onlookers.[22] The human fact of new amity thus emerged.

But of course much has been lost: not only the lives and vitality of Romeo and Juliet, but those of Tybalt, Paris and Mercutio as well – all that passionate youth. Aside from the principals, Mercutio is easily the most captivating of the young people in the play, and also the hardest to understand. What are we to make of this mercurial figure, so vibrant, brittle, gay, explosive, witty, sarcastic and high-pitched? When he leaves the stage in the arms of Benvolio, a grim joke and a curse combining on his dying lips, we lose a brightness and flash that is never replaced.

Paul Scofield, then a young, relatively unknown actor, played the part under Peter Brook in 1947. J. C. Trewin remembers his magical treatment of the Queen Mab speech: 'lying upon the stage in the torchlight, arms raised and eyes rapt . . . he let the words flower into the silence of the grotesquely-visaged masquers'.[23] The speech itself is famous, a set-piece, but it is puzzling as well. How fit it in with either character or situation? Hugh Hunt, in his 1952 Old Vic production, saw Mercutio as the 'adventurer–poet', the speech on Queen Mab part of his imaginative artillery;[24] the conception of Mercutio as a gang-leader, discussed above, fits the hard, aggressive side of the character but leaves the imaginative fantasy of the Queen Mab speech rather out in the cold, whereas to see him as a 'fantasist', an 'adored funny man in a group of . . . casual companions', as Michael Pennington did in 1976,[25] will suggest that the famous speech arises out of the expectations of his admiring audience. In the Zeffirelli film, I remember, Mercutio was a feverish, death-driven neurotic, whose vision of Queen Mab was the bizarre consequence of some obscure inner compulsion. At the Guthrie Theatre in Minneapolis in 1979, Mercutio carried on and manipulated a 'life-sized, stuffed, pink-satin, anatomically complete Dan Cupid' which could hardly not give the famous speech a Freudian coloration; the bawdy doll was then dragged along and 'hoisted aloft at the ball like a Priapean piñata'.[26] Some of these portrayals stress Mercutio's sexual alertness, tinged as it may be with either cheerfulness or bitterness; some look to his itchy belligerence as the key; still others see him as primarily the poet, the imaginative spinner. All can work, as long as one emphasis does not completely blot out the others. If there is too much sweet poet or class comedian about Mercutio, then there can easily be a blur or inconsistency in III.i when *he* challenges Tybalt to fight and not the other way round (a fact that is adroitly skimmed over by Benvolio in his subsequent explanation); thus a crucial part of the character and an important irony for the play can be lost. Similarly, Mercutio's sexual obsessiveness may be neurotic or high-spirited, but, if it tends to overbalance the delicate force of Romeo and Juliet's sexual passion, then it has outrun its purpose.

The contrasts of the play are essential – Mercutio's bawdiness and the Nurse's earthy sexual awareness contrast not only with each other, but, more fundamentally, with the lovers' central lyricism. Age confronts youth, slowness impedes haste, darkness surrounds light, the social milieu intrudes harshly into private life. The result of such contrasts is a balance of forces – we are, for example, slightly distanced from the powerful sexual current in Romeo and Juliet's love through the commentary of those around them; but, as in the comedies, a sympathetic irony is established, a multiple perspective which, far from undermining our sense of the value of the central relationship, actually adds to it.

Another crucial contrast in the play, that between comedy and tragedy, works in a similar fashion. Allusions to typical comic strategies, structures and character types dot the play. And, as with Mercutio and even more with the lovers, the tragic replays and replaces the comic in deliberately patterned ways. There is a comic tonality to the initial conception of character and situation, and a comic flair to much of the play's language, with a shift to darker tones in the second half. Many of the motifs present in the first half reappear in the second in a minor key. Shakespeare, especially in the early stages of his career, had a penchant for such formal patterning – it was part of his cultural inheritance. (This may to some extent account for the failure of spontaneity that many modern spectators have felt in the second half.) III.ii, for example, in which Juliet awaits news from the Nurse, repeats the design of II.v, which had presented in a wonderfully funny way an impatient Juliet trying to extract information from the garrulous and teasing Nurse, who wants instead to complain of her aching back and ask about her dinner. In the later scene, Juliet again has trouble prying the facts out of the Nurse, but now the news is tragic, the message one of death rather than marriage. Similarly, Romeo's exit in III.v, leaving Juliet at dawn, mirrors his exit after the orchard scene, both scenes blending expectation, longing and an ominous sense of foreboding (muted in the earlier, explicit in the later). The earlier scene looks forward to fulfilment, the later backward to it, and forward only to separation and death. The Prince, to cite a different kind of example, appears three times in three parallel scenes, at the beginning, middle and end: first to quell a primarily comic brawl, then to attempt to repair the damages of a much more violent clash, and finally to preside over the tragic *dénouement*.

Modern audiences, as indeed modern directors, may not always appreciate the studied formality of such effects; nor are they always going to be attuned to the elaborately elegant verbal byplay that characterizes much of the text. People today are frequently impatient with the kind of artifice that is tied up with highly self-conscious structure or language. They take it as an indication of insincerity. But the Elizabethans in general, and Shakespeare in particular, did not. The play begins with a neatly turned sonnet, the pattern of which is repeated not only by the second Chorus speech but by Romeo and Juliet in duet when they first meet. There are innumerable other examples of ornately fashioned speech: the strained and self-consciously clever wit of the young men as they trade 'conceits' (i.iv, ii.iv), the threnody on the word 'banished' played separately by both Romeo and Juliet in successive scenes (iii.ii, iii.iii), the sparring of Juliet and Paris in iv.i, the seemingly exaggerated mourning for Juliet in iv.v. Whether we like it or not, such language is as characteristic of the play as the bawdiness of Mercutio or the passionate lyricism of the lovers.

Modern practice has been in general to de-emphasize this formality, by, for example, cutting the most extravagant verbal bits (the 'banished' sequence, some of the mourning, the most obscure sallies of wit), or by playing down structural parallelisms. Stress has fallen instead on the less symmetrical features of the play, its fire and light, its mad blood and Mediterranean blue. In taking this line, directors have lost some vital contrasts, but at the same time they have gone after what is unique about this play, what separates it from innumerable other examples of formalized baroque art. This is not only inevitable, but, I suppose, even desirable, since it is aimed at catching that essential spirit which has held audiences for generations. But, still, I should like some time to see a production that boldly embraced the formality as well.

11

Julius Caesar

When I was an undergraduate in the early sixties, I was involved with a production of *Julius Caesar* which deliberately sought to rescue the play from the familiar dramatic-society blandness of Roman togas, declamation and statuesque postures. The play, for us, was about 'the politics of men' and hence was only superficially Roman. Accordingly, we transferred the locale to an unspecified Latin American country, and turned the assassination of Caesar into an attempted leftist coup against a strutting, militarist dictator. (At the Guthrie Theatre in Minneapolis in 1969, there was a production with a similar theme, though with an Aztec–Mayan overlay.) In our production, all references to Rome were expunged, 'Caesar' became 'César', the Capitol a colourful marketplace. We were clearly influenced by Castro's still quite recent overthrow of Baptista in Cuba in 1959; we even dressed the conspirators in army fatigues, while Caesar appeared in a crisp white uniform. Luckily, we weren't consistent enough to be bothered by the contradiction that Brutus and Cassius were wandering freely around the plaza in fatigues and rubbing shoulders with Caesar, their outfits proclaiming their intentions and political sympathies.

We also radically rearranged the text. Assuming rather smugly that, had Shakespeare known about the cinematic flashback, he would certainly have used it, we began the play with the famous quarrel between Brutus and Cassius (iv.ii–iii), which in the text modulates softly into the quiet interlude where the soldiers and the boy Lucius fall asleep in the midst of the latter's song. Brutus then reaches for a book and the ghost of Caesar appears to him. In our version, Brutus too fell asleep, and over the loudspeaker came the words he had spoken so urgently to Cassius a moment before: 'Remember March, the ides of March, remember. / Did not great Julius bleed for justice' sake?' Suddenly the stage filled up with singing and dancing citizens, and rang with the sounds of castanets and a Spanish guitar. The first three acts of the text were then presented in sequence, as Brutus's dream or remembrance, culminating in a frenzied attack on Cinna the poet and a return to

Brutus's tent at Philippi, where he was accosted by not only Caesar's ghost, but Portia's and Cinna's as well. Act v followed, complete with the rattling of submachine-guns and the overhead whine of aircraft.

What we didn't know at the time was that in several respects we were re-creating an idea that Orson Welles had developed some twenty-five years earlier, before any of us was even born. In 1937, Welles directed an extensively cut version of the play at the Mercury Theatre in New York, focusing sharply on the character of Brutus (played by Welles), the liberal bourgeois intellectual up against the menace of Caesarism, which as a force was shown to depend on the backing of the mob. The New York press, encouraged by the pressure of the times as well as the modern look of the show, was quick to label it anti-fascist, though Welles denied it.[1] The play was enormously popular – it ran for 157 performances, the longest run on record.[2] And, especially in North America, the production has proved to be enormously influential as well; by now it has moved into the realm of theatrical folklore. As students in the sixties, we didn't know we were under Welles' influence, but we probably were.

Where we were original, however, was in the unorthodox adaptation of the text, which turned out to be surprisingly successful. The idea of beginning late in the play and then flashing back was seen again in the late sixties at Wayne State University in Detroit, though there the battle scenes were played first, mainly for dramatic effect, followed by Acts i–iv, and then the battle was repeated.[3] But in general such flashbacks have not caught on, nor are they likely to. In the twentieth century, critics and directors have learned a good deal about Shakespearean dramatic structure, and wholesale rearrangement of scenes is less common than it was in the nineteenth (though many recent productions have indulged in unobtrusive tampering).

As is obvious from what I have been saying, *Julius Caesar* invites political readings, although the leftish, libertarian approach has mostly fallen out of favour at present, at least in major North American and British theatres – perhaps because of the generally conservative political climate. It would not, however, be difficult to imagine a production with a Sandinista flair, something which has probably already been done in some small college or regional theatre. More common now is the approach that equalizes the political forces in the play, emphasizing the many-sidedness of each of the major participants. This has less to do with a shift to conservative politics and more to do with an understanding of how Shakespeare's text actually works. Criticism of the play over the past few decades has increasingly revealed the gaps and inconsistencies in these men, the lack of symmetry between private feeling and public posture, the very human muddle that affects their politics. And the theatre has adopted a similar view. Caesar is unlikely to appear only as a 'comic monster or a black tyrant',[4] and Brutus will be neither the stoic idealist giving himself up for his country (as he usually was in the nineteenth century), nor the impotent bourgeois liberal helpless in the face of crushing militarism.

Shakespeare presents various perspectives, but his own politics are themselves in question. Modern productions, sensing this, work best when they resist the temptation to take sides. One of the most telling marks of the aims of a production will be its attitude toward Caesar, since he, more than any of the major characters, evokes ambivalent, even contradictory, responses. Over the years, critics and theatre-goers have often questioned the title of the play, wondering why it should be called after a character with quite a small part who dies halfway through. Eighteenth-century critics complained of the impropriety of that, as well as the historical diminishment that the character of Caesar undergoes, while actors of the time turned Caesar into a buffoon or a pompous ass. In recent years, the assumption that Shakespeare knew what he was doing has prompted a different set of questions: what was he drawing attention to in naming the play as he did, and why does he make the titular character (the mighty Julius) so apparently weak and colourless?

There are different approaches to this basic problem, but all of them put Caesar at the centre. If he appears as a powerful dictator whose public role has obliterated his private self, his centrality might be indicated, as it was in Trevor Nunn's 1972 revival, by a huge statue that was introduced at key points, including (rather incongruously) the battle scenes. Usually some form of symbolic presence will be used to suggest the continuing power Caesar has after his death. Shakespeare, of course, brings in his ghost to tell Brutus 'thou shalt see me at Philippi', and Brutus, as his cause founders on the battlefield, recognizes that power:

> O Julius Caesar, thou art mighty yet!
> Thy spirit walks abroad, and turns our swords
> In our own proper entrails.
>
> (v.iii.94–6)

The metaphor becomes literal a few moments later as Brutus falls on his sword, reiterating his awareness of Caesar's inescapable presence: 'Caesar, now be still. / I kill'd not thee with half so good a will' (v.v.50–1). Productions will frequently add to these hints – by extra appearances of the ghost, by devices such as the RSC statue, or, as was used in an important revival at Stratford-upon-Avon in 1957, by a dispassionate star twinkling in the background. 'I am constant as the northern star . . .', says Caesar, 'unassailable . . . unshak'd of motion' (iii.i.60–70), and the irony is that he is both right and not right; his words are an ironic prelude to his assassination, but his constancy remains after his death to plague the conspirators.

Caesar's weaknesses, and there are many, balance but do not cancel out his symbolic strength. He is deaf in one ear, epileptic, and, at least according to Cassius's account, feeble when it comes to physical exploits. He is vain, pompous and conceited, while at the same time he wavers fearfully in the face of his wife's doubts. On the positive side, he is affable, shrewd and loving to his friends; nor is there any evidence to suggest that he is not a just ruler. Still, his personal qualities do not match his public stature. Shakespeare, in line with his usual strategy in the play, deliberately alerts us to the gap.

A strong opening can sometimes both establish the necessary sense of power and grandeur associated with Rome and especially with Caesar, and simultaneously set up the ironic disjunctions. In the 1957 Stratford production just mentioned, the setting, dominated by huge movable slabs, suggested the continuity between city and ruler. The curtain rose to reveal a huge gold statue of Caesar at the apex of a stone triangle. During the first scene the image was disrobed by the 'envious tribunes', as critic Roy Walker described them, and then the statue 'pivoted backwards out of sight, the two walls of grey stone parted and against the blue sky at the back the living Caesar was acclaimed'. This sight, together with the majesty of actor Cyril Luckham's bearing, prompted Walker to describe Caesar as the 'incarnation of an immutable and pivotal principle of order'. Rome itself was, for him, 'visible in the massive fluted monoliths of light grey stone, ranged outward from Caesar as their personal centre in two symmetrical lines, continued in the tall stone portals flanking the fore-stage. Here was the wide perspective of Caesar's Rome with Caesar himself as the keystone.'[5] At the beginning of Nunn's 1972 revival in the same theatre, there was a trumpet call, a roll of drums, and a scarlet carpet unfurled itself from the back to the very front of the stage. There were shouts of 'Hail Caesar' as he 'entered in splendid procession [and] strode downstage . . . to stare with chilling arrogance at the audience as Brutus crowned him with laurel'.[6] Here the irony seems disproportionately heavy, though Nunn argued that 'if one *doesn't* suggest that Caesar is fast becoming a military dictator . . . if he doesn't in some way embody that military power, then . . . we get to the moment of his assassination and we just think that it's dreadfully unfair'.[7]

But perhaps the point is that it is unfair. Shakespeare gives Brutus a long soliloquy in II.i in which he concludes that Caesar must be killed not for what he *is* but for what he *might* become. Later, he admonishes the other conspirators to 'be sacrificers, but not butchers', killing Caesar 'boldly, but not wrathfully'; 'Let's', he says, 'carve him as a dish fit for the gods, / Not hew him as a carcass fit for hounds.' The image is grotesque in what is proposed as well as in what is refused. Brutus's purpose is so to appear to the common eyes that 'We shall be call'd purgers, not murderers'. Throughout the play, Brutus frequently shows his concern with his public image, with how he and his actions will be read by followers and citizens. His distinctions between sacrificer and butcher, purger and murderer, seem primarily aesthetic. Though he is concerned too with the inner attitudes provoking men to the crime, he seems oddly unaware of the personal motives behind the determination of many of the conspirators, including Cassius (or else he deludes himself about his own ability to purify such motives). He even goes along with Metellus Cimber, who suggests the recruitment of Caius Ligarius to the cause, naming a personal grudge as the motive: 'Caius Ligarius doth bear Caesar hard, / Who rated him for speaking well of Pompey.' Thus the assassination of Caesar, if it *is* fair, is not unequivocally so.

Modern productions have begun to catch up with this more ambiguous and elusive Brutus. No longer, as I said, merely the stoic idealist, Brutus's anxieties and repressions are now likely to surface, at least occasionally. John Wood's performance for the RSC (1972) was exemplary. Caesar, in line with Nunn's conception, was all public figure and emerging tyrant. Brutus, as a right-thinking liberal, felt obliged to do away with him; but at the same time, he was more than a little queasy about it. Following on a magnificent, studied entry proclaiming Caesar's power, the assassination was a scene of carnage (prompting the inference that perhaps even Nunn did not really see it as completely fair). Here is John Ripley's description of it:

> As Casca struck, the conspirators all rushed in, the blood staining their white gowns like butchers' aprons. Brutus, bent on sacrifice not bloodlust, pushed into the mêlée, grasped Caesar reluctantly, and flicked his knife against a throat artery, only to recoil in revulsion as blood spurted into his face. Meantime Cassius stabbed at the corpse with insatiable fury until Brutus dragged him off. Gradually, however, the assassins became aware of the blood on their hands and clothes. Their eyes wandered to the bleeding hulk at their feet; and they were struck dumb by their own temerity.[8]

To make it all the more difficult for Brutus, his friendship with Caesar was genuine, and his revulsion from the deed of blood produced actual nausea – but still his principles urged him on. This overlay of rationalized idealism covering violent, conflicting feelings was the key to Wood's interpretation: his tense, fastidious deportment with the conspirators led to a fit of shivering after they had gone; a moment later he burst out suddenly and impatiently at Portia and Lucius; and at the end of the quarrel in iv.iii, during which he had remained cool and prim, 'picking up the scattered papers one by one . . . condescension in every gesture', the surprising entrance of the Poet suddenly tipped him off balance. This seemingly pointless little sequence is almost always cut, but Wood made powerful use of it, slapping the hapless intruder across the face, his pent-up emotions again eluding his attempts at self-control. This led to a grief-stricken outpouring a few seconds afterwards, as he told Cassius about the death of Portia.[9] Usually played with resigned stoicism, this moment showed poignantly the power and depth of Brutus's feelings.

For all the major parts, the key is not to neglect the nuances and inconsistencies of character, the intrusion of personality into public action, the ability or inability of a man to cash in on opportunity. Cassius and Antony, even more than Brutus or Caesar, can be, and often have been, treated as clichés. But to do so falsifies both text and character. In the nineteenth century, Cassius was frequently played as the man of emotion, a foil to the reasonable Brutus; in the twentieth, this same general view has continued, although he has appeared as vengefully discontented or shrewdly political as well. Occasionally he has seemed the very wellspring of the action – most notably when Gielgud played the part in 1950. Neither vengeful nor mean, Gielgud's Cassius was noble as well as lean and hungry, heroic as well as driven. Some Cassiuses, in the opening scene with Brutus (i.ii), are deliberately detached and manipulative, taking their cue from the closing soliloquy:

> Well, Brutus, thou art noble. Yet I see
> Thy honorable metal may be wrought
> From that it is dispos'd. . . .
> For who so firm that cannot be seduc'd?
> (ll. 308–12)

A tone of mocking superiority (itself perhaps a result of a frustrated sense of inferiority) can easily slip into such lines, and often has. Gielgud capitalized on the frustration, but showed it to be the source of passionate conviction rather than bitter alienation. He appeared as a 'fanatical crusader against totalitarianism, burningly sincere and driven by a torrent of energy'.[10] But his tactical intelligence was powerful enough to remain untouched by the fervour of his convictions – so that when it came to the showdown during the quarrel between them, Gielgud as Cassius was perfectly aware of Brutus's mistakes; yet, 'secretly a little in awe of Brutus's moral ascendancy', he open-heartedly 'sacrificed strategic judgement to noble impulse, and sealed the tragic outcome of the action'.[11] This was a complex portrait of a figure too often reduced to either glowing feeling or cool, hard opportunism. Brutus, played by Harry Andrews, was a perfect foil to Gielgud's fervid brilliance; he was gentle, mild, quiet – almost immobile in both the opening scene with Cassius and the quarrel. But he had authority and integrity, and hence the power, to outlast his more dynamic partner. As in this production, so in any effective one, some balance between these two major figures must be struck. Each has power, but each is hamstrung in his effort to utilize that power by inner, private needs. Shakespeare's awareness of how personal necessity can tip public action shapes the tragedy.

Antony too is more complex than he is often made to be. In John Philip Kemble's classical 'Roman' production of 1812, which set the style for many later nineteenth-century productions, Antony (played by Charles Kemble, brother to the great actor, who played

Brutus) was Caesar's dear friend, and was thus motivated by a just desire for revenge. Conceived as a noble athlete, his cruel calculating side was expunged, most tellingly in the elimination of iv.i (the 'proscription scene'), where he coolly fingers his political foes for liquidation. Conversely, this latter side has often been overemphasized in this century, the noble athlete turned now into a cynical manipulator. One director went so far as to set the proscription scene in 'a grove hung with dangling corpses',[12] a decision that makes the point a wee bit too obvious. Even Antony's physical prowess has been whittled down in recent years, his athletic grace redefined as mere sensuality.

The actor who plays Antony has to contend with what looks like an abrupt shift in the character from voluptuary to ambitious political realist. He has very little to do before Act iii, appearing in Act i only long enough to be identified as one of the runners in the 'holy chase' and to give Caesar some not very shrewd advice ('Fear not Cassius'); and in Act ii he shows up as a late-night reveller come betimes to accompany Caesar to the Senate house. For the assassination itself he is lured away by Trebonius, and so it is only after the deed, when he confronts the conspirators, that we can take his measure. One way to get a grip on Antony is to see him as a man who reacts to the world directly, without ideology, moral scruple or terribly deep feeling. This gives him an advantage over the scrupulous Brutus and the divided Cassius. He may also appear as someone who discovers his own skills in the course of exercising them. This was how Richard Johnson played him in a memorable performance in Glen Byam Shaw's important 1957 revival at the Old Vic. Johnson's Antony was passionate and magnetic, his grief at Caesar's death genuine; during the funeral oration, it was his 'sincerity, rather than his tactics, which moved the mob. But once aware of his gifts as a spellbinder, latent vanity, ambition and ruthlessness rapidly surfaced.'[13] From then on he was ruled by his own self-interest. Perhaps most effective is an Antony who is both passionate and careful, aware of his effects even as he is carried away by feeling. Circumspect and acute, he never completely drops his ironic guard and thus makes his passion count. This is made sharply manifest in the scene (iii.i) where he grips the bloody hands of each of the conspirators in turn, naming each as he does so, and coming at last, but 'not least in love', to 'good Trebonius', the man who had lured him out of the way. 'Gentlemen all –', he concludes with disarming candour and just enough venom to keep the conspirators alert, 'alas, what shall I say?' They are uncertain of his attitude, he is busy assessing them and calculating his chances; even when he is drawn into grief by looking down at Caesar, he can recall himself with irony and he quickly sees his opening in the possibility of a funeral oration. His request granted, and Brutus's conditions accepted, he responds simply, 'Be it so; / I do desire no more.' A docile answer, but, as Granville-Barker remarks, 'if ever a smile could sharpen words, it could give a grim edge to these'.[14]

The Forum scene (III.ii), in which Mark Antony delivers his sweeping incendiary oration to the Roman citizens, is undoubtedly the most famous in the play. It culminates in the mob's frenzied murder of Cinna the poet, an incident that before Orson Welles had almost always been left out as unseemly or unnecessary. Welles made it the keystone of his version – mob violence ruling in the wake of ineffectual liberal action. Since then audiences have usually witnessed the nightmarish attack, which many recent productions have underscored by bringing in the intermission immediately afterward.

Antony's handling of the speeches can range from the most sincere to the most ironic: from Richard Johnson's moving his hearers by the genuineness of his own grief to Charles Thomas, in an RSC revival in 1968, whose 'harangue resembled nothing so much as a vicious puppet show, with a malicious puppeteer savouring his own cynicism throughout'.[15] The strangest I ever saw was at Stratford Ontario, where the whole scene, indeed the whole play, was done without the citizens. Antony harangued an empty stage, speaking to the audience as if we were the Roman people. But, since we had no lines to throw back at him and were prevented by the etiquette of theatre-going from becoming directly involved (although more than once I wanted to hiss), the actor had nothing to play off; the overall effect was both ludicrous and boring.[16] Taking away the *people* from the play – one is tempted to call it the most unkindest cut of all – steals an important political dimension from it, and seriously reduces its dramatic impact. An additional absurdity in that production emerged when Antony produced Caesar's bloody and torn mantle as evidence of the conspirators' butchery ('See what a rent the envious Casca made; / Through this the well-beloved Brutus stabb'd . . .'). The mantle was convincingly mangled – the only trouble was that the assassination had been presented as a ritual mime, without daggers and without blood. So when Antony raised the grisly evidence, there was a dissonant clash of realistic and ritualistic conventions.

To over-ritualize the assassination is a mistake, since it takes Brutus too much at his word ('We must be sacrificers but not butchers') when the point is the discrepancy between Brutus's idealistic intentions and the ugly reality to which he descends. Equally, to present Antony's oration as sheer cynical manipulation is too one-sided for this ambivalent play. What Shakespeare gives with one hand he takes away with the other. Thus Antony really does love Caesar and his grief is genuine, but his ability to *use* that love and grief in the interests of both himself and his faction is not hampered by the strength of his feelings; rather, it is enhanced. We are drawn to his passion even as we recognize his skill and his irony. Similarly, we approve of Brutus, though we can clearly see his folly. The play never allows us a single comfortable point of view, and neither should a production.

After the blood of the assassination and the fire of the orations, the last segment of *Julius Caesar* too often brings with it a sense of anti-climax. This is especially true of the battle scenes in Act v, where we see the relentless logic of event overtake the conspirators. There is little fighting and a good deal of confusion. But once again Shakespeare is more interested in the inner life of his protagonists, their fumblings, misconstruals and inconsistencies, than he is in their glorious triumph or defeat. Cassius tells us, in a reminiscent mood, that it is his birthday; he and Brutus hedge about their philosophical convictions; then they put their differences aside to share a moment of tenderness and farewell. As the battle intensifies, Cassius's weak eyesight, combined with his tendency to jump to conclusions and assume the worst, leads to his death. Brutus enters with a weary, defeated band, just moments ahead of Antony's clean-up operation; one man sleeps through Brutus's elegiac reminiscences, but wakes in time to be the instrument of his suicide. And finally a victorious Antony enters to deliver an ambiguous eulogy over the body of 'the noblest Roman of them all', while Octavius, hovering shrewdly at the edge, echoes him even more ambiguously. Octavius is the young man on the rise and on the make, whose cool presence at the end frequently provides an ironic forecast of the role he will play in Antony's downfall and the power he will eventually wield (something that Shakespeare will dramatize in *Antony and Cleopatra*). Most actors have him standing aloof and unmoved during Antony's valediction. But in one production he stepped forward with 'a frigid smile' and kicked aside the sword Brutus had used to stab himself, moving in on Antony with the words, 'Within *my* tent his bones tonight shall lie'.[17]

Throughout this final section, each character plays himself to the limit, and in the case of Brutus and Cassius, this leads to the fatal *dénouement*. 'Our enemies', says Brutus, 'have beat us to the pit. / It is more worthy to leap in ourselves / Than tarry till they push us' (v.v.23–5). And both men are unrelentingly aware of that crucial deed, of which all that has followed is the tragic consequence: 'Caesar, thou art reveng'd, / Even with the sword that kill'd thee', says Cassius (v.iii.45–6); and Brutus, 'Caesar, now be still. / I killed not thee with half so good a will' (v.v.50–1). The dying words of the one echo those of the other, keeping before us the central image of Caesar's power.

My point is simply that there is no need for a production to founder into anti-climax in the final act. If it has been true to the subtleties of the play earlier on, then interest in the fates of these complex men should not flag. From the moment of the quarrel between Brutus and Cassius right through to the end, there is a single overarching movement, punctuated by personal episodes that deepen our perception of the characters involved. The battle itself is less important and less interesting than the rests between skirmishes. Any fine production must create a sense of strong movement and inevitability, while at the same time making us savour those quieter moments when the politics and personalities of the various leaders emerge most fully.

12

Hamlet

A German version of *Hamlet* in 1979 treated its audience to electronic multiplication of everything that happened on-stage, by attaching a row of TV monitors to a safety curtain and providing the actors with a video camera which they trained on themselves and others. The resulting fragmentation underscored the point of the production, and was enhanced by the splitting of the main part, which was played by two separate actors. One of these, a physical and mental wreck lost in crude sexual fantasies, remained on-stage, more or less speechless; the other spoke the classic lines of Schlegel's translation as richly and sonorously as possible, but never left the auditorium. At the end, with corpses laid out like stiffs in a morgue, the stage was covered by a hundred tables with as many TV sets on them, all displaying the current news, while the beautiful Ophelia, dressed like a racing-driver, emerged from a blazing sun to take over Denmark.[1] Such extravagance can be taken as an emblem of how far directors may be willing to go in search of an original slant on this most famous and familiar of plays. But despite its radical commentary on the alienating effect of contemporary media and the corruption of politics both ancient and modern, this production seems not to have got any closer to the fascinating and enigmatic centre of *Hamlet* than many more conventional attempts.

It is precisely because it is an enigma that *Hamlet* is so famous and so challenging. It shows a new face to every generation – indeed, in our speeded-up times, to every decade. It is the ultimate test for almost any actor, and a strange mirror for almost any audience. The central character absorbs the life of the actor who plays him and poses unanswerable questions about his motivation, his sanity, his desires – questions, that is, that cannot be answered definitively. There is so much uncertainty about character and situation that interpretation becomes inescapable. The play *imposes* a diversity of readings in a way that no other Shakespeare play does. For one thing, the text itself is Shakespeare's longest, and, since it is almost always cut for production, the cutting itself is an act of interpretation. There is no way of fully encompassing the range of

the play's possibilities. However much this may be true of other
Shakespeare plays, it is more true of *Hamlet*. Hence all versions are
bound to fall short, and thus simplify the play, lighting it from one
particular perspective, which will be more or less illuminating
according to the skills of director and cast. This diversity, of course,
accounts for the play's continuing, culturally central fascination, as
well as for its popularity with producers.

Hamlet himself can be gloomy and melancholic, violent and
active, confused and rebellious, poetic and tender, lonely and
disillusioned, hysterical and impulsive, extravagant and witty,
rational and decisive, or some complex mixture of several of these
plus other ingredients. Back in the eighteenth century, Garrick
played the part as an active, energetic, passionate prince, but in
1783, when John Philip Kemble first took it on, he changed the
character to a philosopher, thoughtful and deliberate: 'the beauty of
his . . . Hamlet was its retrospective air – its intensity and
abstraction'.[2] In the early nineteenth century, with Kean, Hamlet
became a romantic: violent and gentle by turns, spasmodic and
emotional. In our own century, Gielgud in 1930 as well as in various
later revivals was lonely, desperately frustrated and at odds with
himself, though at length he managed to resolve his problem and
accept his destiny. Also in the thirties, Alec Guinness played the
part with dreaminess and sadness, and was extremely gentle with
Ophelia, a mood first adopted by Kean though he used it as a
contrast to his dynamism elsewhere in the play. Guinness's Hamlet
was closely followed by Olivier's, whose emotional, even hysterical,
power was the dominant characteristic; directed by Tyrone Guthrie,
Olivier was forceful and driving, fired by only partially hidden
Oedipal conflicts. Michael Redgrave, in the thirties and again in the
fifties, was quiet and intellectual, charming, without violent
emotion in the nunnery or closet scenes.[3] And so it has gone from
period to period, each interpretation of Hamlet embodying
something of the age that enjoyed it, and something of the actor that
played the part. Since the early sixties, we have had, among others,
David Warner's forlorn and apathetic student (1965), Ben Kingsley's
tough, competent and completely sane man of action (1975) and
Michael Pennington's gentle, gracious and wry prince (1980),
somewhat in the Guinness mode but with the added feature of
bewilderment, uncertainty about whether what he is asked to do is
'real or shadow'.[4]

Trying to bring some order into this array of particularities may seem hopeless, but perhaps we can distinguish a few basic approaches to the role. Coleridge introduced the idea that Hamlet is a contemplative, a thinker not a doer, who, because he sees the complexity of his situation, finds himself in a quandary about it. Coleridge was probably describing himself as much as Hamlet, but his attitude has been picked up by actors and critics ever since. It has resulted in perhaps the most familiar Hamlet, the indecisive melancholic, gloomily contemplating a skull or castigating himself for his own failings. At the beginning of Olivier's well-known film, a voice cuts through the Danish mists with the announcement, 'This is the story of a man who could not make up his mind', although Olivier's portrayal itself gave us a caged and vigorous melancholic rather than a contemplative one (several of the soliloquies were cut). The opposite approach to the Coleridgean sees Hamlet as active and authoritative, energetic and perhaps even violent. If this Hamlet verges on madness, it will not be depression and suicidal musings that mark the character, but a manic drive, amounting sometimes to frenzy. Nicol Williamson, in Tony Richardson's film, tumbled over himself, barely able to contain the energy that engulfed him. Such a character, like Richard Burton's portrayal as well, has no trouble making up *his* mind; his is more likely to be a problem of focus, of grounding his perception and assessment of the world.

Other Hamlets may fit somewhere between these extremes. One is the poetic, tender and vulnerable young gentleman, typified by the 'sweet-voiced' Forbes-Robertson at the turn of the century, and later by Guinness and Paul Scofield. This Hamlet is far from pathology of any kind, though some of his characteristics could easily be allied with those of the melancholic. Another is the mixed up adolescent in inchoate rebellion against the establishment, a view that came into prominence in the 1960s (not surprisingly) in an epoch-making production at Stratford with David Warner. Director Peter Hall saw young Hamlet as 'trembling on the point of full maturity . . . about to jell'.[5] Wrestling with his sense of the moral corruption of his elders, trapped in a 'hive of bustling militarism and courtly display',[6] and bewildered by his own inability to do anything, Warner's was a Hamlet who was half flower-child and half neurotic intellectual. In an 'existentialist panic' in the early stages of the play, he came to a sense of liberation at the end – not, however, in the Gielgud style of resigned acceptance; rather, Warner's was a 'dazed triumph' which came from having fulfilled the Ghost's command 'without having taken any decision of his own'.[7] The production photos reveal a sad, lost face, wistful and out of place; Hamlet, his neck and shoulders draped by a long, knitted, reddish scarf, appears soft, anguished and a bit sensual, not made for the shiny parquet, the jet platforms, the polished inlaid tables and the black formica walls that surround him (see Plate 8).

The youth of the time loved it. Warner became an idol. Critics sometimes grumbled, but teenagers queued up for two days and nights to get tickets. And they kept coming back. Hall's claim that 'for our decade . . . the play will be about the disillusionment which produces an apathy of the will so deep that commitment is impossible' obviously struck a resonant chord, although the young audience was anything but apathetic. Once again, Hamlet proved his age-old power to elicit identification. The youth of the sixties were doing no more than Coleridge had done 150 years before: seeing themselves in Shakespeare's most elusive character.

This interest in the youth of the character, though there is good evidence in the play that Hamlet is pushing thirty, can take a different turn. Hamlet can be immature and impulsive without being particularly lost or neurotic. An actor might emphasize his wit and dash, his extravagant flair for language, his shifts of mood and persona, his love of the *theatrical*, which can be so important for some conceptions of the play. Alternatively, the moral and political idealism of youth might be stressed, or dreamy adolescent charm, as in a performance such as Guinness's.

Hovering around the enigma of Hamlet's character is the question of his 'madness'. Is he really mad, mad but 'north north west', or is he, indeed, not mad at all? One notable production at the RSC's Other Place in 1975 (directed by Buzz Goodbody) gave us a Hamlet who was normal, rational and practical, never mad or mysterious. Ben Kingsley played the part with a 'hard competence' and an agile comic control that distinguished him as much from the vulnerable poetic Hamlets of previous versions as from the bewildered neurotics. According to Richard David, this may have removed the extra dimension, the suggestiveness of the whole play, but at the same time it brought out the play's effectiveness as a piece of theatre.[8] In contrast, some directors and actors have been fascinated by what Trevor Nunn has called the 'shift between real madness and performed madness unknown to the person in the middle of it all'.[9] Thus Alan Howard, in Nunn's 1970 production, seemed more burdened by, and concerned with, his own mental disorder than by the charge to kill Claudius. The players, who epitomize the split between the feigned and the real that pervades the play, will obviously loom large in such a Hamlet's consciousness. And thus will emerge some clarity about his excitement at the players' arrival, his eagerness to use them, his hysteria at his own failure to generate emotion as they do, and his exact concern for their handling of the illusion that mirrors his reality. Inconsistencies, such as Hamlet's meditating suicide in the 'To be or not to be' speech a few minutes after his apparently clear formulation of a plan – 'The play's the thing / Wherein I'll catch the conscience of the King' – will pose less of a problem for such a Hamlet than for Kingsley's, and seriously dangerous actions, such as Howard's 'frenzied stabbing'[10] of Polonius will form part of the pattern. In the last act, after the sea voyage, Howard's tone was considerably lightened – he emerged as clear and strong, no longer so vulnerable to his own thoughts; the religious atmosphere that had been toyed with throughout seemed to emerge from the played to the real in this final emphasis on Christian acceptance. But precisely the drive and effect of the Goodbody–Kingsley reading were less evident in Nunn's more intellectually conceived version.

To start with an idea about the play's meaning rather than a sense of the main character, as Nunn apparently did, yields an approach that will give less weight to the style and personality of the leading actor. John Barton's interest in the 'play-image' at the heart of the text, for example, clearly informed his 1980 revival with Michael Pennington in the central role. Hamlet's line 'These are actions that a man might play' was used as an epigraph in the programme, which featured as well a short essay by Anne Barton, the director's wife and a distinguished literary critic, focusing on the theatrical self-reference of the play. She concentrated on Hamlet's 'understanding of how art may acquire a temporary and unpredictable dominion over life', using as an instance the player's speech describing Pyrrhus' killing of Priam and the grief of Priam's wife, Hecuba. The speech partially mirrors Hamlet's own situation and his mother's. He has therefore, it seems, deliberately chosen it for the player to recite and even quotes a few lines to get him started; in the production, when the player reached the passage depicting Pyrrhus' hesitation, Hamlet was clearly affected and he echoed the climactic phrase, 'Did nothing', fulfilling Barton's point exactly. The theatre has thus become for Hamlet, as he chooses to use the play to catch the conscience of the King, a paradoxical means 'of deciphering a treacherous world'.[11]

The production insisted on the stage metaphor throughout, using rehearsal clothes, a prop basket, a bare wooden platform on the forestage for much of the action, benches for 'off-stage' actors at the side, and other devices that highlighted the presentation itself, the idea being that we remain all the time in the world of impersonation. The set, the portrayal of the main character, and much of the detail combined to stress the fact that the line between is and is not, is and seems, is finely and ambiguously drawn.[12] Critics praised the coherence of the production and its dominant idea, but at the same time many objected to the loss of the actualities of palace life and the feeling for a real social environment that the play also and unmistakably elicits.[13]

When Sir John Gielgud directed his famous production, with Richard Burton in the title role, he too elected to do the play in rehearsal clothes, but with a very different aim. He wanted to avoid the trappings of scenery, lighting and costumes, which all too frequently 'cramp the imagination and the poetry' that the actors can bring to a final run-through without technical support. 'Often, in rehearsal,' Gielgud told his actors at their first meeting, 'one sees an actor pick up a piece of material for a cloak, as it were, and fling it over his shoulder convincingly, and he seems to believe it more than when he has the final costume. Actors seize on things they need.'[14] Gielgud sought a calculated semblance of that spontaneity, with an emphasis on both the actors' and the audience's belief. In his case, then, unlike Barton's, the rehearsal atmosphere was used not to detach spectators by reminding them that they were witnessing only a play, but to encourage them to imagine their way *past* the mere theatrical externals.

Gielgud's conception was clearly helped along by Burton's driving and athletic style of acting and his sense of the character as impulsive, mercurial and active, verging even on schizophrenia. Analogously, Michael Pennington fit his approach to John Barton's overall interpretation, presenting Hamlet as gentle and uncertain. Bewildered by the Ghost, unsure whether what he was asked to do was reality or appearance, he seemed to have difficulty sorting out action from 'acting'. In the short soliloquy 'Now could I drink hot blood . . .' he started big but then checked himself, aware of his 'melodramatic excess'.[15] Neither he nor anyone else seemed clear about whether he was really losing his reason.[16] The textual ambiguity of Hamlet's madness was thus externalized by stressing its doubly theatrical character – as an 'act' of Hamlet's and as a performance of the actor's. His most intense moment came in the last soliloquy, on 'I do not know / Why yet I live to say this thing's to do, / Sith I have cause and will and strength and means / To do't.' Interestingly, this was also a key line for David Warner's adolescent Hamlet years before, but the latter had spoken it slowly, with 'arms outflung' and a dazed and bewildered mind.[17] Pennington was pitched and wild here, tormented by the very theatrical uncertainty that characterized the production as a whole.

Hamlet is a play that emphasizes loss, mourning and remembrance. Its most famous image, the dark prince in the graveyard holding in his hand the quizzical skull of the jester, Yorick, epitomizes these motifs. The fool is dead but is mourned by Hamlet, who speaks his remembrance not only in the famous words to his companion, 'Alas, poor Yorick! I knew him, Horatio . . .', but also in the very posture he, Hamlet, has adopted in the face of the court: the antic disposition that he has chosen as strategic disguise and vehicle for satire. Ophelia giving out flowers, the Ghost instructing Hamlet to remember, Hamlet's dying injunction to Horatio to live on and tell his story, Fortinbras's retrospective epitaph ('Bear Hamlet like a soldier to the stage, / For he was likely, had he been put on, / To have prov'd most royal') – all these insist on loss and the value of remembering. This recurrent sense of lost possibility colours the world of the play, accounting for the domination of black, not only in Hamlet's clothing, but in the setting and costumes of most productions.

Loss is personal, existential, and is felt and expressed that way in the play. But it is also political, or has important political overtones. The German production mentioned at the beginning tried a flippant way of alluding to the multiple sense of loss, including the political, that the play registers. Nevertheless, its insistence on fragmentation and alienation in place of wholeness made a telling point – a point that Hamlet himself makes over and over. His feelings for his father, his idealization of the marriage of his father and mother, his nostalgia about his own love for Ophelia, his inability to hold on to an optimistic view of man and nature ('What a piece of work is a man . . .'), and, finally, his yearning for a simpler political system where heroic action can outdo intrigue and treachery (focused on his father once again and underlying his admiration for Fortinbras) all are expressions of his overwhelming sense of isolation and decay.

But the play does not belong only to Hamlet. This is one of the lessons to be learned from recent productions;[18] in the theatrical world of the late twentieth century, the star system is not nearly as dominant as it was in earlier years, the director and the company having taken on equal importance. This means that we no longer get seventy-year-old Hamlets, as in the days of Betterton (in the early eighteenth century), or even fifty-year-olds, as with Redgrave in the 1950s. Hamlet is now part of an ensemble, and must fit into a conception. When Robin Phillips directed the play at Stratford Ontario in 1976, he chose two actors to alternate the main part (each with his own Gertrude, the rest of the cast remaining the same), something that would have been inconceivable with Gielgud or Olivier. One reviewer commented that the 'revelation was not by how much but by how little the characteristics of the one or the other [actor], their individual ways of playing the part, determined the impact of the tragedy',[19] even though each oriented the part in his own way and neither tried to imitate the other.

On the changing status of Hamlet in relation to the subsidiary characters, we may make an instructive contrast between the Warner–Hall *Hamlet* of 1965, and the BBC Television Shakespeare version with Derek Jacobi. In the former, the effort was deliberately to put Hamlet in conflict with the repressive and bureaucratic 'Establishment' around him. Hamlet himself was a scruffy undergraduate, testing his parents and refusing to behave in decorous, princely fashion. He was decidely anti-heroic, but this paradoxically is what made him a hero for contemporary audiences. A fine image for his alienation from, and entrapment by, his elders was in his very first scene (I.ii), traditionally played with Hamlet at the side, brooding in black, while Claudius butters up the rest of the court. Hall placed Hamlet squarely in the centre, flanked by Gertrude and Claudius on one side, Polonius on the other, as all four sat behind a shiny, inlaid table. These four were surrounded by ambassadors and courtiers, with a row of armed soldiers at the back. Hamlet sat, bound, rigid, unwilling. His immaturity, his political and personal languor, his wistfulness, made him a sixties' flower-hero.

But the conception of Claudius and the court was equally dominant. Well-oiled bureaucratic politics were the hallmark of this regime; each minor functionary knew his place and role; the principals, such as Polonius, may have indulged in a little ironic laughter at their own foibles, but that only served to make them the more dangerous. At the top of the heap sat Claudius, a 'thoroughly competent and charming king'.[20] Hall evoked 'an enormous political machine', in which Claudius, 'the super-master politician, [was] surrounded by Polonius and all his advisers. And then Polonius had his own Secretary, and there were Councillors that had secretaries, and the secretaries had secretaries . . . .'[21] The set design by John Bury brought the point home. The basic material was shiny black formica; the shape was that of an open box with two large doors at the back – the 'design was enclosed and impervious – a huge black funnel – like the Establishment'.[22] Elsinore power politics included too a good dose of 'bustling militarism', always a serviceable medicine for a state in failing health, and the cold war with Norway was emphasized. The play opened with the lights coming up on a cannon trained directly on the audience, and the lines in the first scene about the arms build-up between Norway and Denmark, frequently cut, were retained. So this Hamlet, unlike the classic ones typified by Gielgud, was not in a state of noble, romantic isolation. He was very much *in* his world – no wonder then he felt trapped and apathetic. What could he *do*?

But, if that immobility induced sympathy and identification from the predominantly young audience, the same cannot be said for Derek Jacobi's similarly ineffectual prince of the BBC version broadcast in the early eighties. Jacobi had played the part in 1977 under director Tony Richardson and even then his tendency to break into 'falsetto hysterics' was noted by critics, though they also commented on his recuperation of the figure of the Renaissance prince.[23] In the TV version, the dominant impression was of an intelligent, skilful but exasperatingly immature young man (far too old to be acting in such a silly way), making unnecessary trouble in what looked like a smoothly functioning court. Even his mother seemed embarrassed by his antics. The result was that Claudius, rather than Hamlet, commanded the most respect. This was the only production I have ever seen in which I cared more for and about Claudius (played briskly and surely by Patrick Stewart) than for the ostensible hero. (This may be a mark of the times: one critic has suggested that as Hamlet is progressively deromanticized, Claudius becomes 'highly playable.')[24] All those flower-children of 1965 have now grown up; twenty years later their concerns are adult concerns, and the BBC *Hamlet* gave them an adult Claudius dealing with real problems. He loved Gertrude deeply and genuinely, had killed for her and wrestled with the guilt of having done so; at the same time, he was the King, and charged with the responsibility of his role. All this he took seriously and handled with dexterity and dispatch. If he was forced into hypocrisy, it seemed to go against the grain. And the last thing he needed was this goading, pestering stepson, complicating his plans and ruffling his feathers. During the play scene, for example, Hamlet wandered through the action, interrupting to make comments and getting more and more elated, almost hysterical. When Claudius eventually called for 'Lights', he did so not with fear or guilt or anger, but softly, with complete control over the situation; he took a torch, walked slowly up to Hamlet, who hid his face in his hands, and gave him a look which delivered the verdict – Hamlet had gone too far in suggesting his own murderous intentions toward his uncle (the nephew in 'The Mousetrap' murders his uncle). Only then did Claudius say, very coolly, 'Away', and turn to exit, while Hamlet laughed hysterically. The remarkable thing about this sequence is that it was very close to the Warner–Hall reading, where, in rising, Claudius registered only 'offended dignity', rebuking Hamlet for a 'social gaffe'.[25] But the effect was totally different: Jacobi's wildness, in contrast to Warner's bafflement (and given too the change in the times), tended to alienate rather than attract. Claudius's refusal to be flustered seemed the *right* response in the circumstances, rather than, as in Hall's production, a politically astute move on the part of the leader of the Establishment. In Hall's version, Claudius's response confirmed Hamlet's perceptions but made his problem all the more difficult to solve, thus underlining his morally unexceptionable helplessness; in the televised version, on the other hand, *Claudius's* behaviour seemed unexceptionable, and Hamlet's response out of touch with the facts.

These two productions were similar in that they each placed Hamlet firmly in his milieu rather than feeding a romantic sense of his isolation. This seems a mark of most recent *Hamlet*s, consistent with the importance of the ensemble and the renewed emphasis on the other characters besides the hero. On the question of Hamlet's madness, however, these two productions differed: Warner's neurosis seemed an understandable, even reasonable response to his external situation; Jacobi's skittishness and hysteria, his antic disposition, came more from within. Jacobi's 'madness' was not so much a deliberate *act*, as many Hamlets have made it, as a condition.

A Hamlet who refuses both of these patterns is today likely to seem the most admirable, if also somewhat distant. Ben Kingsley, at all times completely sane, exerted an 'agile control' over his

situation and the other players. With Polonius, Rosencrantz and
Guildenstern, and Osric, he showed his superior skill at intrigue,
even though none of them, except perhaps Osric, was presented as
a push-over. Polonius was shrewd, manipulative, and, under the
double-breasted surface, tough. Hamlet's bitter response to
Polonius's falsely sympathetic question, 'What do you read, my
lord?' – 'Words, words, words' – was characteristic; actors have
sometimes suggested nearly hysterical rage here (directed perhaps
half at himself) or self-consciously ironic wit. Richard David
describes Kingsley's treatment thus: ' "Words", curt; "Worrds" as,
seated back to the audience, he flips the pages of his book under the
old man's peering nose; a pause, and then "Words", sharp and
rudely dismissive'.[26] Claudius here was no less a mighty opposite
than in the Warner or Jacobi *Hamlet*s, but Kingsley matched him
evenly (see Plate 9). The ending of the play scene can once again
provide an example. The play-within began with the dumbshow
(frequently cut in modern productions), which was presented in
white masks – the King saw it, but sat poker-faced. (The text is
ambiguous on this point and some productions show him not
paying attention to the dumbshow so that his later reaction will be
sudden.) Again, David's description is a vivid one: Claudius

> was balanced and held by Hamlet's rigid, eager face, with nose
> jutting, on the other side of the stage. The sense of mystery and a
> horror about to be unleashed was very strong and Hamlet's
> perhaps too blatant provocations . . . increased the pressure of
> the screw. At the moment when it became intolerable Claudius
> and Hamlet both started from their seats and met in the central
> 'spot' [created by one of the players standing in the centre aisle
> with a flashlight], to glare at each other, nose to nose, over the
> body of 'Gonzago' before Claudius made his distracted exit down
> the central aisle.[27]

Here we have a hero who knows exactly what he is doing, who is
determined to reveal to the court the precise nature of Claudius's
guilt, and who has the strength to carry out his purpose. The
conception is anti-romantic, but not anti-heroic. Unlike Warner and
Jacobi, who both 'lost' at this juncture, Kingsley clearly won. And he
won on the strength of his own toughness, not because Claudius
was a slimy and tyrannical hypocrite.

The actor standing in the centre aisle with a powerful flashlight trained on the play-within-a-play is himself an emblem of how this production worked. Mounting it in Stratford's Other Place and then at the Roundhouse in London, both small flexible spaces allowing for intimate contact with the audience, director Buzz Goodbody chose to use the auditorium frequently as an adjunct to the stage. At the Other Place, itself little more than a barn with benches, lights and a playing-area, the show began in blackness; suddenly flashlights (held by the watch) snapped on, their beams scouring the auditorium before picking up the Ghost at the back of the room.[28] At the Roundhouse, the Ghost was pinpointed in the centre aisle; later it appeared to the awestruck Hamlet on a side platform, retreated 'to the back of the auditorium, and from there led Hamlet up the central gangway to the "more removed place", which was the stage itself'.[29] Use of the *whole* space continued throughout the play, forcing the audience to acknowledge their own role as spectators while paradoxically involving them the more directly. Some critics found themselves momentarily alienated by this strategy, but most nevertheless applauded the production's effectiveness and its power to hold the audience. One reason for this is that staging, costumes, text and even the size of the cast were all spare and economical; and going along with this was a deliberate effort to face and engage the audience. When, for example, the Ghost led Hamlet up to the stage, they both turned to face the audience, with Hamlet kneeling and the Ghost towering above him. Hamlet, on his knees with his arms flung above his head, remained motionless at the end of the scene as the Ghost withdrew again down the aisle. Similarly, in the closet scene, the Ghost was in the gangway and the audience received 'a front-face close-up of mother and son as they knelt together staring before them'.[30] In both cases the attention of the audience was fixed on and by the frozen figures on-stage.

Thus underlining the enacted quality of the play need not have the 'alienation effect' (to use Brecht's famous phrase) that it obviously did have in the German production mentioned at the beginning of this chapter. There the effort was indeed to put the audience off, to unsettle them and make them face the question of the meaning, or possible meaninglessness, of a 'classic' in relation to contemporary reality. Buzz Goodbody's production, on the other hand, sought to make the audience participants rather than strangers. One critic testified to that participation and its relation to the use of the theatrical space:

It was appropriate that the door through which the Ghost vanished, on which Laertes would later batter, and through which Fortinbras would make his final portentous entrance, belonged in each interval to the audience. We were sharing with the actors a neutral space whose primitive amenities became startlingly appropriate.[31]

I have been talking about the Ghost because he is clearly one of the stumbling-blocks for a modern audience and for modern producers. Some have gone in for fancy lighting-effects and amplified spooky voices, often without any material presence whatsoever. Besides going directly against the text, this approach loses an opportunity for powerful theatrical effect. Even if we no longer believe in ghosts, we do believe in them in the theatre, and that is what counts. The Goodbody–Kingsley production was strongly realistic in tone, but still the Ghost was no obstacle. And a ghost who looks like a man that you know is dead is bound to be scarier than a wraithlike apparition. In *Hamlet* the Ghost, of course, is also Hamlet's father, one of the crucial poles of his affection, and this galvanizes him emotionally, wiping out in a moment the ironic, quiescent melancholy that characterizes his first appearance. 'You can almost divide Hamlets into those who are in love with their father and those who are in love with their mother', comments Robert Speaight.[32] In recent years we have been moving away from the weak-kneed Oedipal Hamlets of earlier decades to those who, for better or worse, are more deeply connected to their father (some, such as Warner, sadly aware of the distance between themselves and that idealized figure). For such Hamlets the Ghost is clearly significant, and needs to be solid and believable.

Gertrude's place, correspondingly, is no longer as secure as it once was as the electric focus of Hamlet's ambiguous love. Gertrudes today must do what they can. More than it used to, the relationship between Claudius and Gertrude has been receiving greater attention, and, as in the TV version, a certain pathos can enter into its gradual dissolution, as the problems around Hamlet begin more and more to interfere. But, if that love affair gets emphasized, then the one between Hamlet and his mother may be reduced in significance. One mark of this is the disappearance from some recent productions of the bed that from the thirties onwards has occupied a central place in the 'closet' scene. In the 1920s a couch was introduced into the scene, but in the next decade, under the influence of Freudian readings, the bed arrived to stay, prompting – Kenneth Tynan to wonder many years later 'why there should be a bed centre stage in every production of this scene. It is never mentioned and never slept in.'[33] Of course many Hamlets, including Jacobi's, have in ambiguous fury wrestled their mothers down onto that tempting bed, but to do so seems excessive and unnecessary. A simple stool, as in Goodbody's version, will do as well.

Gertrude can be played quietly, as a woman of tough courage: at the Other Place, she stood between the furious Laertes and her cowering husband, coolly talking the rebellious young man down. But not all Gertrudes are so strong. They can be blowzy and hedonistic, weak and passive, confused and pained. The interpretative question that any actress has to face is just how guilty Gertrude really is – how much does she know? Has she been her husband's criminal partner (like Lady Macbeth)? Has she been dallying with him before her first husband's death and thus become an unknowing accomplice to what she now gradually realizes was murder? The text once again gives us no straight answer. I personally prefer a Gertrude who is not initially guilty but through her passion for Claudius has become enmeshed in a situation which she can do little to help. But this, I acknowledge, makes her weaker than many contemporary actresses will want to play her.

Like Gertrude, Ophelia can easily get lost in the shuffle. Her role is distinctly reactive, and with her, therefore, the task is to bring her up, refusing to fall prey to the tendency to make her wispy and sentimental. She needs activity – in the Goodbody production, for example, she first appeared not as the submissive younger sister meekly receiving counsel from Laertes, but was engaged with him in packing his trunk, while they traded bits of advice. Especially tempting for sentimentalizers are her mad scenes, where it used to be *de rigueur* for her to appear in white muslin and adopt pre-Raphaelite poses. 'I've a dread of those pixie Ophelias who rush around with wild flowers looking fey and pathetic', Robin Phillips declared in an interview.[34] So, in rehearsing his production, he at first tried tying her hands to a lady in waiting and then came up with the idea of fastening them to a stick set like a yoke across her shoulders. This suggested the possibility that she was dangerously lunatic, setting the flower-giving in a new perspective, and powerfully motivating Gertrude's shock and fear. As usual in modern productions, the scene's strong sexual allusions were not hidden; but, spoken as they were by this penned and distraught woman in black, they evoked a violence and anxiety that was both new and consistent with the trend in contemporary approaches to this play.

Since Ophelia dies in the fourth act, and her death is described by Gertrude in a beautiful but difficult aria, it is obviously unusual to have her appear at the very end, as she did in that outlandish German production – let alone that she was dressed like a racing-driver and poised to take over Denmark. But the outrageousness of such a conclusion is a calculated response both to the patriarchy implied by the text's treatment of Ophelia and to the real problems posed by the play's finale. Chief among these latter is what exactly happens with Hamlet. Many critics and with them many producers have taken the view that, when he returns to the play in the last act, Hamlet has grown to wisdom and resignation, made peace with himself and come prepared. Hamlets who have been torn up with doubt or gripped by hysteria frequently evince in these final scenes a calm maturity typified by the speech, 'There's a special providence in the fall of a sparrow . . . the readiness is all.' In such readings, the long tortuous apology to Laertes is frequently cut, and the opening of v.iii, in which Hamlet describes his dispatch of Rosencrantz and Guildenstern, has been similarly trimmed. But, if the reborn Hamlet has become the norm, it is not the only way to play the scene. In fact the text, taken uncut, reveals a much more interesting Hamlet, prone to violence and rashness (his own word) as well as patience, to mischief as well as resignation.

How Hamlet succeeds in achieving his long-sought revenge should, of course, cap the reading, and may also leave us wondering about the precise scope of his transformation. In Olivier's film, the star executed a breathtaking leap from a gallery to deliver the *coup de grâce* to the miserable Claudius, while in Buzz Goodbody's production Claudius emerged from a recess at the back of the stage, where he had momentarily taken refuge, to give up his life to the victorious, if dying, Hamlet. In different ways, these strategies emphasize that Hamlet has overcome his mighty opposite, that he has won at the odds, though not necessarily through the force of patience and resignation. By contrast, David Warner's Hamlet gained only a dazed victory, the final scene thus reinforcing the whole interpretation. Hamlet thrust the poisoned cup upon the King and stood laughing at the death throes. A sense of liberation had come over him from having 'fulfilled the Ghost's command without having taken any decision of his own'. As J. C. Trewin reported it, 'It is over now; he moves around with a dazed smile of triumph, relief that his task is done, that action has been forced upon him.' He sank onto a bench, dying himself but still triumphant, as he kissed his father's miniature which had hung on his neck since the beginning. This was 'the single touch of uncomplicated sentiment saved up for the last moment'.[35] In the BBC version, Hamlet seemed to achieve his revenge in spite of himself. This was driven home by the fact that, as at the Other Place, Claudius gave himself sacrificially to Hamlet, but more as a gesture of despair at his loss of Gertrude and the dissolution of his hopes than as a result of pressure from his nephew. Claudius's move seemed more a victory than a defeat, and Hamlet was left to skitter into death. All these different readings seem to me to derive consistently from different ideas about character and overall context, as well as different responses to the complexities of the last act.

We are left finally with Fortinbras, who strides in to take over Denmark. He recalls that he has 'some rights of memory in this kingdom, / Which now to claim my vantage doth invite me'. Why not grab the opportunity while he can? In the old days, the Fortinbras section was often cut entirely, the play ending with Horatio's lyrical prayer 'And flights of angels sing thee to thy rest'. But Shakespeare ends with irony, not with lyricism, as the stalwart Fortinbras, who has been Hamlet's foil all along, gets the hero's 'dying voice' even as he displaces him. Modern productions usually find some way to measure the distance between the arrogant, powerful soldier and the brilliantly perceptive, witty, erratic and tormented prince, and they are right to do so. The Goodbody production, using modern dress, found a shockingly precise contemporary image for Fortinbras, and integrated it powerfully into the spare theatrical space that the whole performance had articulated: 'With Hamlet's command that the door be locked [v.iii.300], the doors of the theatre itself were slammed shut on actors and audience alike.' The chilling silence that followed was later 'shattered by the crashing arrival of a cynical Fortinbras in the garb of a modern paratrooper'.[36] That kind of reading keeps alive the irony and underscores the loss we feel at Hamlet's death. Despite his struggles, the time is still out of joint.

13
Othello

Othello is a big play, a romantic play, its lead character a gigantic fool who, if he doesn't capture our imagination, will have a hard time moving us to anything but scorn. During the nineteenth century, *Othello* was a huge favourite, its heightened language, passionate feelings and exotic lure lending themselves admirably to the lavish and extravagant style of playing characteristic of the period. Verdi based what most critics consider his masterpiece on it, capitalizing (as Rossini had done before him) on the operatic elements already present in Shakespeare's text. In the twentieth century too, the most successful productions, of which there have been surprisingly few, have been those which have not shied away from grand effects. But this raises a problem for modern actors and audiences. We have become more used to psychological scrutiny, hesitation and irony than we are to rhetorical flourish and sheer emotional intensity. People today are likely to be as much put off by the sufferings of the Moor as nineteenth-century audiences were moved by them. I know that I frequently have to work hard to convince students that Othello has tremendous *stature*, that simply the way he speaks demands our attention and admiration:

> Keep up your bright swords, for the dew will rust them. . . .
> (I.ii.60)

> If it were now to die,
> 'Twere now to be most happy. . . .
> (II.i.187–8)

> Excellent wretch! Perdition catch my soul
> But I do love thee! And when I love thee not,
> Chaos is come again.
> (III.iii.92–4)

> Nay, had she been true,
> If heaven would make me such another world
> Of one entire and perfect chrysolite,
> I'd not have sold her for it.
>
> (v.ii.148–51)

Othello may be an egotist; he is one in fact. But his very size redeems him, and size is a feature that the acting of the part cannot afford to ignore.

At the same time, what Othello does is outrageous – even more obviously so in our time of alert feminist consciousness. There is simply no excuse for his behaviour: swallowing Iago's pernicious story without ever consulting his wife about it; leaping to preposterous conclusions because of a missing handkerchief; debasing himself into spying on Cassio and then misinterpreting what he sees; slapping Desdemona; degrading her in both public and private; and finally smothering her despite her innocent protests. Can Othello's grandeur, the appeal of his rhetoric and nobility (' 'Tis yet to know . . . I fetch my life and being from / Men of royal siege', he tells us at the very beginning), outweigh the offence we may feel at his later action? This is a key question for any producer. Another closely related question derives from the fact that modern audiences expect some kind of psychological explanation for behaviour, exactly as modern actors are trained to look for and express such motivations. How then can an actor provide that scrutiny without losing the size of the character? If we remove Othello from the tragic pedestal, can we prevent his image from being dashed to fragments and our interest scattered in the resulting dust?

The most famous recent *Othello*, first produced at the National Theatre in 1964 and subsequently filmed (so that its effects are still strongly felt), made it clear that romantic power and psychological realism could indeed coexist. Directed by John Dexter, the production featured Sir Laurence Olivier in the title role, with Frank Finlay as Iago and Maggie Smith as Desdemona. Olivier's performance is a memorable example of *tour de force* acting; every ripple of the muscular body and every trick of the rich voice were used to etch the portrait of this powerful and sensuous man. The body, catlike and athletic at first, actually mirrored the disintegration of Othello's mind, its grace and suppleness giving way to jerky, dislocated awkwardness, until the final scene, where once again it appeared controlled and composed. Vocally too, the performance was remarkable. It was said that Olivier worked for a year to lower his voice a full octave; and yet the lower register, combined with a slight West Indian accent, still allowed for an astonishing range of effects, from a self-satisfied chuckle in recounting the story of his courtship to the fury of 'Damn her, lewd minx' to the 'piercing' softness of 'But yet the pity of it, Iago! O Iago, the pity of it, Iago!' when 'he blotted himself in agony against the wall'.[1]

One eminent critic chose the last speech as an ideal image for the whole performance. Othello, clasping Desdemona's dead body to his chest, suddenly rapped out a loud and commanding 'Soft you . . .'; there was a pause before the voice continued softly, quietly, 'a word or two before you go.' And then, 'without break, continuing the impulse that had changed his voice, Othello kissed Desdemona on the neck, sensuously engrossed. The rest of the speech followed with recollected formality: 'I have done the state some service. . . .'[2] The speech ends of course with Othello's dramatic execution of himself, exacting justice for his own crime in the same vein as he had for Desdemona's supposed infidelity. Olivier made it a *coup de théâtre*: kneeling on the bed and still clutching Desdemona to him with one hand, he suddenly flicked into sight a stiletto that had been hidden in his bracelet and slashed his own throat. He thus brought to a culmination a tendency to self-dramatization in Othello that he had been building up throughout his performance. This allowed him to give the character a richly heroic stance, but at the same time subtly to undermine the heroism by emphasizing its blind spots. Thus, although Othello kills himself in the grand manner, the hovering feeling remains that he has learned nothing, that he is still acting out a role, projecting an image of himself:

> And say besides that in Aleppo once,
> Where a malignant and a turban'd Turk
> Beat a Venetian and traduc'd the state,
> I took by th' throat the circumcised dog
> And smote him thus.

The programme for the National Theatre production featured a long quotation from F. R. Leavis, the most influential British literary critic of the time. In it, Leavis stressed the danger of romanticizing

Othello, of seeing him merely as a victim of Iago's machinations. Instead, Leavis wanted to show that Othello was responsible for his own fate, precisely because of the strongly self-idealizing, self-dramatizing side to his character. He is indeed the noble and heroic man of action, but, in adopting that view of himself and playing it to the hilt, he blinds himself to Desdemona, and finally to himself as well, since he comes to believe totally in the image he has created and fails to see its fragility and inappropriateness.

Dexter and Olivier seized on this view of Othello and made it the centre of their interpretation. It allowed them the opportunity to make the character as big as possible while at the same time maintaining a sharp, modern scepticism toward such grandeur. Psychological portraiture accompanied romantic gesture. When Othello first appeared, dressed in white against his fiercely black skin, he established immediately an aura of exoticism and power: he wore a large cross around his neck, bracelets and anklets glinted on bare arms and feet, his teeth and eyes flashed, and his voice was a calm tropical sea. He held a rose in his hand and inhaled its perfumes, momentarily caught up in sensuous contemplation, but at the same time aware of the effect he was having. The image of the rose returns later in the play, in the soliloquy just before he murders Desdemona: 'When I have pluck'd the rose, / I cannot give it vital growth again, / It needs must wither. I'll smell it on the tree', and he kissed her as she slept. Again at the end, when he kissed her neck before killing himself, the same sensuousness intervened. Desdemona and the rose – the text provides the connection but here the actor had extended the symbolic overtones, establishing the link in Othello's body and mind. The beauty and sexual force of the symbol do not hide the ominous note – the role that Desdemona, as *rose*, plays in Othello's erotic imagination. She is there as adornment as well as distraction, a part of his display. Thus his sensuousness, which was real and powerful, was also something that he used to feed the exotic aura with which he surrounded himself.

I should, however, emphasize that the major effect of Olivier's virtuoso performance was to sweep the audience into the momentous current of the play. The sceptical notes were there, but they were undertones mostly, established as counterpoint to the dominant romantic melody. The performance, as John Russell Brown remarked, demonstrated the rich opportunities that this role (perhaps pre-eminently among Shakespeare's great parts) provides for an actor 'who is at once realistic and histrionic'.[3]

In the BBC Television Shakespeare *Othello*, Anthony Hopkins took a precisely opposite approach to the title role. The shadow of Olivier's great performance seemed to hang behind Hopkins' interpretation as a kind of negative influence. He deliberately eschewed histrionic effects, downplaying the grandeur and almost throwing away the big set speeches at the beginning. The account of his courtship of Desdemona was matter-of-fact, handled rapidly and almost without pause, with none of the self-amused relish, the sheer joy in the recollection and in the language, that Olivier projected. Here was a military man who, when he apologized for being 'Rude . . . in my speech / And little blest with the soft phrase of peace', was not being disingenuous, as most actors would have it, but was telling the simple truth. And so the 'disastrous chances', the 'moving accidents' and 'hair-breadth scapes in th' imminent deadly breach', the 'Anthropophagi and men whose heads / Do grow beneath their shoulders' all slid by almost unnoticed, as mere details of military history. Even at the end of the speech, when he tells of Desdemona's interest in him and her wish for a wooer with Othello's story ('Upon this hint I spake . . .'), there was barely more than a glint of satisfaction. In contrast, the same line drew from Olivier a laugh of self-delight, as he remembered the moment and savoured it. Later in the play too, Hopkins refused the largeness of the character, toning down and interiorizing the suffering as he had the grandness.

This production was, of course, conceived for television, a 'cool' medium, one in which histrionic acting can quickly degenerate into studied posing. I don't personally feel that Shakespeare works very well on television, precisely because of the kinds of reduction it imposes on text and acting-style. And certainly a great deal of *Othello* was lost in this version. But the drastic decision to play against the size of the hero and his language still produced a painful sense of loss. This was because Hopkins projected at the beginning a quiet, confident arrogance (he didn't *need* to be histrionic), which was then painfully wrenched from him till he became embarrassingly broken.

A further distinction between Olivier's and Hopkins' Othello is simple to characterize but far-reaching in its effects. Olivier was unmistakably and exotically *black*, while Hopkins was only slightly brown, the one emphasizing his difference from his Venetian surroundings, the other doing his utmost to be part of that milieu. We may surmise that Sir Laurence had read Mr Crummles' comments in *Nicholas Nickleby* and taken them to neart: 'We had a first-tragedy man in our company once, who, when he played Othello, used to black himself all over. But that's feeling a part and going into it as if you meant it; it isn't usual – more's the pity.'[4] That Olivier did go into it as if he meant it is evident from the many pictures of his partly naked body tuned with sensuous fervour or untuned by passionate upheaval (see Plates 10 and 11). Hopkins was altogether more *covered*, more 'civilized', complete with frilly shirt and ruff. If Olivier sought to capture an element of the primitive hidden under the fragile glass of Venetian fashion (at the peak of his jealousy, he ripped the cross from around his neck in a symbolic descent into barbarism), Hopkins stayed away from the primitive altogether, even moving slightly in the direction of the bureaucrat. Hopkins' performance perhaps registers a sensitivity to the problem of racism in the play, particularly as it affects the white actor. Olivier met the issue head-on; Hopkins, it seemed, was trying to skirt it. It is noteworthy that few black actors, until very recently, have played the part, although one of its most eminent exponents was Paul Robeson. Robeson underlined the racial element, bringing the exoticism home to contemporary America, while at the same time giving a 'noble plainness to the hero who was "physically powerful with the gentleness that often accompanies great strength" '.[5] The racial issue is certainly there, though, as with anti-Semitism in *The Merchant of Venice*, it exists primarily as a social fact to which various characters respond in various ways. Othello himself is acutely aware of his blackness, his foreignness, whether he tries to display it or hide it. It certainly seems appropriate to stress racial consciousness, as Robeson did; but it would be an oversimplification to make Othello merely a victim of white distrust and hostility. In fact any approach that seeks to take away Othello's own responsibility for what happens is bound to lead to sentimentality.

By emphasizing Othello's own responsibility, I do not, however, mean to diminish the importance of Iago and the role he plays in Othello's downfall. He must not and cannot be forgotten. His cool presence haunts the play, and the ironic epithet 'honest Iago' tolls through it like a bell. But, if Iago successfully works on Othello, he can only do so because the soil is fertile, the ground prepared for Iago's successful sowing. The two in a sense form a team, a deadly foil to the married couple who stand at the centre of our sympathy, a feature that was brought out strongly in the TV version. The character of Iago has been the source of much speculation: Coleridge, perhaps remembering the morality-play tradition behind the character and the insistence in the play on images of hell and devils, described him in terms of 'motiveless malignity'; but modern psychological critics have not been discouraged by this from advancing their own views about motivation. (Even devils, after all, have motives.) Jealousy – heterosexual, homosexual or professional – is often cited as one answer to the puzzle; another has been the desire to exert power over others through the exercise of mind – the revenge of the smart boy who lacks social position or finesse. The various motives knock against each other, of course, and they all need to be combined with the obvious enjoyment Iago gets from wreaking havoc, and the spontaneous attractiveness with which he can tempt an audience. What this last point reminds us of is that Iago is primarily a *theatrical* creation, his life is very much that of the stage. His strategy is to make the audience his accomplice, to test his charms on us, as it were, before displaying them before Othello or Cassio. This may explain why many readers of the play find him simply abhorrent, while playgoers, almost against their will, are frequently drawn to him even as they condemn him. He exerts a theatrical fascination which makes the role a potent one indeed; so it is no surprise that Iago has often dominated productions of the play, with Othello playing a rather poor second fiddle.

The old way of playing Iago was as a Machiavellian villain, savouring evil for its own sake. This approach has not entirely disappeared, but it is much less common now than one that would stress Iago's bluff, hearty exterior, hiding the villainy under a cloak of masculine fellowship. Even in the nineteenth century, when melodramatic villainy was at its height in the theatre, Edwin Booth cautioned actors to keep the evil inside: 'Try to impress even the *audience* with your sincerity . . . don't *act* the villain, don't *look* it or *speak* it . . . but *think* it all the time.'[6]

Booth's own performance was one of his greatest – for the most part he followed his own advice, maintaining a cool and watchful stance, though he ended with an irresistibly melodramatic touch, 'standing over Othello, pointing triumphantly at the dead body and gazing up at the gallery with a malignant smile of satisfied hate'.[7] José Ferrer, playing Iago against Robeson's powerfully noble Othello (1943), offered a similarly motiveless villain, but one very much taken with his own amoral magnetism.[8]

The Machiavellian Iago has more or less gone out of fashion;

consistent with the new stress on Othello's guilt, Iago will appear less responsible for what happens than he once did. He is likely to be an NCO of some kind, often marked by a working-class accent, a man who has come up through the ranks and who has the professional soldier's disdain for sweet-talking theorists such as Cassio. The bonds of military fellowship will frequently tie him more closely to Othello. Playing Iago as the NCO gives a socio-economic cast to his motivations – it 'places him by rank and by social type'.[9] He will be the bluff, direct soldier, substituting hatred for villainy, class-consciousness for malignancy. This seemed to be the intent of the BBC Iago, played by Bob Hoskins, whose accent and manners were a clear statement of the class difference between himself and the others. He was solicitous and helpful, even ingratiating; at the beginning of the temptation scene, he wanted, it seemed, to work with the maps and documents on his desk. It was Othello who pursued him. But this conception was oddly at variance with a strong devilish strain in the portrayal, complete with sly looks at the camera at the end of scenes, and, most tellingly, a long peal of maniacal laughter at the end, which covered an extended exit through a series of palace doors.

Frank Finlay's reading of the part, opposite Olivier, was controversial, mainly because the soldierly, non-malevolent Iago was, at that time, relatively unfamiliar. Gone were the satanic glee, the superior, calculating intellect, the inner vindictiveness. Olivier had at first resisted doing Othello, arguing that the play belonged to Iago; since he himself had played a devilish Iago to Ralph Richardson's Othello in 1938, he knew what he was talking about. 'If I take it [Othello] on,' he said, 'I don't want a witty Machiavellian Iago. I want a solid, honest-to-God NCO.'[10] And this is what he got. One critic commented that Finlay's Iago was the first he had ever seen 'who comes near to justifying the title "honest, honest" '.[11] Director John Dexter even pushed Finlay into *believing* the accusations he makes against Cassio and Desdemona, so that he almost burst into tears while recounting Cassio's supposed dream, pained by the supposed deception of his beloved general. This touched on complexities that the strictly bluff and hearty Iago might miss – especially a repressed homosexual attraction for Othello himself combined with the mean-spirited white man's sexual jealousy of the black man. (This latter attitude was noticed by several critics, among them Ronald Bryden, who pointed to the 'fanatic mule-grin of a Mississippi redneck' and the accompanying jealousy 'sliding into ambiguous fascination'.[12]) All in all, Finlay's Iago, marked by a slight deferential stoop, was definitely subordinate to the great central performance but was also a suitable complement to it (see Plate 11).

The crucial scene of temptation (III.iii), in which Iago goads and prods Othello to murderous jealousy, exemplified the approach Dexter took to the balance between the two central characters. Tynan describes its inception:

> No sooner has Iago mentioned Cassio than [Othello] takes the initiative . . . Othello determines to quiz him, in order to get a full report on Cassio's character. 'What dost thou *think*?', he asks with avuncular persistence. . . . On 'By heaven he echoes me', he is mock-severe, rebuking Iago for talking in riddles.[13]

He seems to expect some story about mere peccadilloes. Later he corners Iago, who responds with an improvisatory shot in the dark, 'O beware, my lord, of jealousy'. The point is that Othello is in control, not Iago; he is still bathed in 'supreme self-confidence', assured and powerful. Iago is on the defensive throughout the scene, most clearly on 'Villain, be sure thou prove my love a whore', when Olivier took Finlay by the throat and hurled him to the floor. But by the end of the long, harrowing duologues (separated by Othello's pained exit with Desdemona and the loss of the handkerchief), that self-assured power has turned toward destruction. Evident in the sheer breath-control of 'Like to the Pontic sea . . .', it is unleashed in fury at the end of that speech when on 'Now by yon marble heaven' he tears off his crucifix and flings it in the air; then, 'crouching forehead to ground, [he] makes his "sacred vow" in the religion which caked Benin's altars with blood'.[14] What sounds like crude racism in this last remark was in fact determined by the production itself, which understood Othello's descent as an atavistic reversion to savagery and barbarism. That this may have been deliberately discomfiting to a modern audience was surely part of its point – we were invited not to luxuriate in Othello's sufferings but to be deeply troubled and challenged by them, even as the performance compelled from us both admiration and awe.

Desdemona, the victim of Othello's rage, has also undergone a change over the years. Earlier actresses frequently found the key to the character in the pathos of the famous 'willow' scene, where she recalls the maid Barbary and her song of false love and forsaking ('An old thing 'twas, but it expressed her fortune, / And she died singing it'). One of Shakespeare's most telling atmospheric scenes, its poignant foreboding is balanced by its precisely realistic directions about unpinning, fetching nightgowns and putting sheets on the bed. How frequently Shakespeare works his pathos through and around the most ordinary actions! But if that very soft Desdemona, so innocent that she cannot imagine infidelity, has often been the key to a whole conception, the part can also be played with a harder edge. Today's actresses, influenced perhaps by feminist perceptions, are more likely to look to Desdemona's assertive opening scene as their way into the part. When she appears before the all-male council of senators and Duke, she doesn't quail or act meek, but speaks firmly and directly of the 'rites' of love, and requests permission to accompany her new husband lest she be deprived of them. From Othello's account of their courtship, it is clear too that at the beginning *she* grasped the initiative, telling him that if he had a friend that loved her he should but teach the friend his story, and that would woo her. When it comes to the reinstatement of Cassio, she again takes the lead. And though some readers are disappointed at her apparent passivity at the end when she bows to Othello's rage, the text certainly allows an actress to protest vigorously.

When, wrought to the uttermost and exhausted from an epileptic fit, Olivier's Othello struck his wife with the rolled-up proclamation in front of the Venetian delegation, Maggie Smith, whose Desdemona was no sop, did not react in the usual way by collapsing into tears. Her response was pained and embarrassed – she was ashamed both for Othello's sake and her own. 'She is outraged, but tries out of loyalty not to show it. . . . "I have not deserved this" is not an appeal for sympathy, but a protest quietly and firmly lodged.'[15] In the final scene she awoke as if from a nightmare in a paroxysm of fear, and was momentarily relieved at the sight of her husband – but the fear crept back as he began to speak so strangely. The vulnerability induced by the nightmare accounted for the subdued quality of her struggle to be free of Othello's implacable grip. The whole scene, under Dexter's direction, had returned to quiet, Olivier's maddened wrath in Act IV modulated back to dignity and (perverse) tenderness. He kissed her on 'I would not have thee linger in thy pain', even as he strangled her with his powerful male hands around her alabaster neck.

How that climactic moment was done by Shakespeare's own company we shall never know, but it is interesting that one of the very earliest pieces of Shakespearean dramatic criticism records the skill of a young actor who played Desdemona at Oxford in 1610: 'Desdemona, killed . . . by her husband, moved us especially in her death, when, as she lay on her bed, her face itself implored the pity of the audience.'[16] While telling us little of certainty about the interpretation (though it suggests a rather passive Desdemona), this description points clearly to the importance of emotional effect in the Elizabethan playhouse, and indicates how little the overall force of a scene such as this one has changed throughout the intervening years.

Olivier's sensuous kiss just before the murder signalled an important note for the play, one that was probably more difficult to sound in those early performances with all-male casts: Desdemona and Othello have a sexual relationship that is of crucial importance to both of them. Without it, sexual jealousy would be unlikely to be such a potent force. Throughout their performance, Olivier and Smith subtly registered a sexual electricity whose charge in the final scene was a deeply ironic reminder of its presence all along. Love and death, and the disturbing connections between them that interested Shakespeare in so many plays, here find their ominous consummation.

Before concluding, I should like to glance at one other production of the play, one that deliberately subverted the grandeur of the main part, not by avoiding it (as in the TV version) but by withholding it. In an interesting account of a production by the San Diego National Shakespeare Festival (directed by Dan Sullivan), critic Stephen Booth describes how the first half of the play presented its audience with a 'neutralized' and cloaked Othello. William Marshall, playing the part, gave off a definite sense that he had the power physically and/or mentally to 'overwhelm his circumstances at any time'.[17] But there was something missing, some failure to realize his power. His body, in contrast to Olivier's naked and lithe athleticism, lumbered a bit and was covered with an outsize gown, while his hands twisted and flicked in neurotic independence of the rest of his demeanour. His voice too, though strong, seemed oddly unfulfilled. Hence Iago had no trouble dominating the first half of the play – it was an unequal contest. Only in the middle of the production did it become clear that this was a deliberate, and daring, strategy, rather than simple ineptitude. For, just at the point when jealousy took serious hold of him, Marshall suddenly 'opened up and gave Othello the energy, authority and heroic clarity we had wanted'; but this came precisely at the moment when 'we could not want it any more because it was irrevocably misplaced'. The production's refusal to give its audience the grand hero from the very beginning thus denied them the 'relative comfort of watching a noble gull snared in a vicious trap'.[18] In fact, it seemed designed deliberately to make them uncomfortable. But tragedy is hardly a comfortable art form; indeed, to find a way to make an audience experience that fact should be at the basis of any production. The San Diego version did it by withholding pleasure; Olivier did it by first inducing powerful admiration and identification, and then turning it to alienation. Both versions challenged their audience, balancing catharsis and discomfort even at the end.

14

King Lear

Writing in the early nineteenth century, when Nahum Tate's bastardized version of the play still held the stage, Charles Lamb said of *King Lear* that it was too big for theatrical representation, declaring among other things that the 'contemptible machinery by which they mimic the storm' is no more adequate 'to represent the horrors of the real elements, than any actor can be to represent Lear'.[1] Since Lamb's time, and especially since the Second World War, there have been many successful, even brilliant, productions of the play, but still this view persists. Granville-Barker did what he could to banish it, not only in print but by coming out of retirement to help direct John Gielgud in a celebrated revival (1940). However, the idea that the play cannot be fully and adequately staged remains current – not just among literary scholars, but within theatrical precincts as well. J. C. Trewin, an eminent Shakespearean and noted dramatic critic, sees the play as not carrying in the theatre – it always, he argued, seems 'minimised' on the stage.[2] And Richard David writes of the storm scenes, 'It is not quite absurd to say that Shakespeare here for once overreached himself, imagining something that just cannot be staged.'[3] Such writers have some clear advantages over Lamb: they have had the opportunity to see some fine productions of the play, thanks partly to the fact that stage conventions have changed. The twentieth-century rediscovery of Elizabethan modes of production has shown that the quest for 'realistic' or illusionistic representation was misguided. Furthermore, we no longer have to contend with Tate's notorious redaction. We have thus got a lot closer to Shakespeare's original conception than anything Lamb could have seen. If, then, the sense that *King Lear* is too big for the stage is still with us, we ought, I think, to take it seriously. Perhaps it does indeed reflect a real feature of the play – a sense of sheer size, of enormous resonance, that we respond to when we read but that we are likely to be disappointed about if we see the play in the theatre.

On the other hand, of course, stage representation will reveal aspects of the play that reading simply cannot discover. So the feeling that a production may in some ways minimize *King Lear* is in no way an argument for not mounting it. The frequency of recent productions is itself an indication of the value of staging the play, and reveals as well the deep connection that the twentieth century seems to feel to its dark, painful terror.

It was not always so. I have mentioned Nahum Tate's adaptation, first produced in 1681. This version reduced the horror of the original by providing a love interest between Edgar and Cordelia, uniting them in marriage in the end, and restoring King Lear to his throne. The harsh and violent language of the play was significantly softened, the abrasive and 'indecorous' role of the Fool was completely excised, and the Gloucester plot considerably shortened. Now the remarkable thing about this adaptation was its longevity. Not until 1838 did Shakespeare's play again see the light, although Edmund Kean restored the tragic ending in 1823. So, in the entire history of the play's productions, Tate's *King Lear* has held the stage for almost the same number of years as Shakespeare's own. Samuel Johnson, the greatest critic of his age, and a friend of the greatest actor, David Garrick, wrote that the final scenes of Shakespeare's play were so painful to him that he could not bring himself to reread them until he undertook to edit Shakespeare's works. The public's preference for Tate's version was thus for Johnson an understandable and decisive one, the original being simply too cruel for eighteenth-century sensibility.

Thus Garrick, who excelled in the role of the maddened King, played in Tate's version, though he did rescue some of Shakespeare's lines. Despite Tate's appalling (for us) text, Garrick nevertheless managed to make an extraordinary impression, and initiated an approach to the role that is still to be seen today. In comparison with his predecessors, he adopted a style that was more or less naturalistic – it was said of him that his 'very stick acted'. His reading of the mad scenes was particularly subtle, without his usual 'starts'.[4] For example, the onset of Lear's madness was signalled simply by a sudden laugh 'without any connection with the soul; an involuntary emotion of the muscles'.[5] In keeping with this understated style, he presented Lear as an amiable, honest and ill-used old man, driven to madness by the cruelty of his daughters. Garrick's own diminutive size made his emphasis on age and feebleness a natural one to take – he was not suited for the titanic grandeur favoured by some later actors.

Garrick's 'very human father' set the pattern for one particular reading of the main role. There are, of course, others – critic Marvin Rosenberg has defined four major approaches which, though not exclusive, will usually underlie, either singly or in combination, a given actor's characterization. Aside from the ill-used father, there is the titanic, godlike Lear who bursts on the scene like a 'magnificent portent' (Granville-Barker's phase); there is the tough, arrogant, authoritarian King, who commits folly and invites retribution; and there is the mad, or senile, old man, mad that is from the beginning, who moves upward to sanity, not downward to madness.[6] There are dozens of variations that can be played on these four basic patterns, but most Lears will be contrived out of some combination of them.

The opening scene will provide the key. Is Lear in awe of his daughters, or *vice versa*? Does he seek somehow to insult or cow them by putting them through the ritual he has devised? Is he magnetic and forceful, or is he needy, desperate for their love and hence easily taken in by Goneril and Regan's phony declarations? Does he enjoy the theatre of his little ceremony? Is his fury with Cordelia due to her refusal to play out the ritual, or is it a defensive reaction to a real fear that she does not, cannot, love him as he desires? Is he a god, or is he all too human? Depending on the answers to these questions, he will emerge as tough and authoritarian, brittle and easily cracked, soft and vulnerable, or comically, pathetically inadequate.

Probably the most popular characterization of Lear used to be the grand titan, like Gielgud's; this required 'big' acting and magnificent speaking of the sort that has now gone somewhat out of fashion. In 1962 Paul Scofield took on the role in a revolutionary production directed by Peter Brook, a production that underlined the unremitting harshness and existential bitterness of the text. Under the influence of Brecht, Beckett and Artaud, modern prophets all, Brook forged a vision of the play that linked it to Artaud's 'theatre of cruelty' and the aimless despair of Beckett's derelicts. Scofield's reading of the main part was utterly unsentimental: arrogant and hard, he elicited no sympathy (see Plate 12). Kenneth Tynan wrote of this interpretation,

> Lay him to rest, the royal Lear with whom generations of star actors have made us reverently familiar; the majestic ancient, wronged and maddened by his vicious daughters; the felled giant. . . . Lay also to rest the archaic notion that Lear is

automatically entitled to our sympathy because he is a king who suffers.[7]

Scofield's exact approach has not found many eager imitators – neither actors nor audiences are likely to be comfortable with such unrelenting harshness. But the general tendency to reread Lear from a modern point of view, to refuse to be awed by him, has become the norm.

Besides the Brook–Scofield production, the sixties also saw the bringing to light of another important version of *King Lear*, Grigori Kozintsev's brilliant and disturbing film. Allowing for all the differences between theatrical and cinematic technique (which in general go beyond the scope of this book), the Russian film presents a fascinating reading of the text. Like Brook's, it gives us an energetic, arrogant and unsympathetic Lear (Yuri Yarvet), but here he is small, tyrannical and vibrantly on the move (the cinema clearly supports this conception); he is constantly walking, bustling, ordering, demanding, driving – very different from Scofield's rugged, towering, almost monumental, presence. Both of them give us a powerful, authoritarian King, accustomed to obedience and furious when it is held back, but in quite opposed ways. What distinguishes the Russian version most of all, however, is a definite shift away from interest in the personal plight of Lear, and a focus on the social consequences of the actions of the great. (Brook too moved away from sympathy with Lear, but turned his attention to cosmic bafflement and the indifference of the gods.)

The film begins with a great massing of peasants moving across a bleak landscape. They are gathering from every direction – to hear, we surmise, the results of Lear's plan to divide his kingdom. Who will be their new lords? They wait in silence. The scene in the palace takes place – Lear is arbitrary and whimsical (he is late for the meeting, laughing with his waiflike fool, whom he is genuinely fond of). His daughters are wary and uneasy. When the announcement is made from the battlements to the gathered, silent crowd, it is Lear himself who makes it, and what he shouts to them is the curse on Cordelia. At the end of the film, the battle leads to the burning of the city by Edmund's own men, and Lear and Cordelia are carried along in an endless stream of refugees. The reconciliation scene (IV.vii) takes place in the open air, amid the fires of battle. The final image, after the horror of Cordelia's death, hanged from a parapet, is not the dead Lear or the philosophical Edgar, but the peasants stolidly rebuilding their still-smoking town. The people triumph – or at least survive. A tough socialist optimism emerges that exactly opposes the existential pessimism of Brook's production.

If these two productions give us a different Lear from the more traditional majestic King, they retain some sense of the awe-inspiring power of that figure. They retain too the ancient-Briton costumes and an appropriate feeling of primitiveness. To this they add an extraordinarily bleak, remorseless landscape, especially strong in Kozintsev's film, but visible too in Brook's bare and primitive setting, and even more in his film, based on the stage production; the setting provokes a sense of wide, desolate spaces, a mental, cranial territory as much as a geographical one.

More recently, a different way of questioning Lear's glory seems to have crept into vogue. Less weight is put on Lear's kingliness, on his authority and power, and more on his personal whims and weaknesses. Modern distrust of the grand gesture has led to increasing emphasis on the domestic side of the play. We see Lear 'at home' as it were, where the arbitrariness of his behaviour toward his daughters is less concealed. The division of the kingdom, the initial act which sets the rest of the action going, is presented as a small family affair, rather than a large public event. As a result, its political, dynastic ramifications are somewhat scanted in favour of the familial ones. Psychology comes to the fore. The family ritual that Lear devises as part of the ceremony of division is seen as self-indulgent and self-dramatizing – and thus in keeping with his later behaviour in relation to Goneril and Regan. The evil daughters too are no longer conceived in simple terms, but given a psychology based on their father's clear preference for their sister and his genuinely improper behaviour in Goneril's palace (Brook's production initiated this tendency to partially justify Goneril's and Regan's responses to their father). In some productions this approach has been signalled by nineteenth-century costume, replacing the ancient-Briton variety that had been in favour since Garrick's time, and a series of more intimate settings than the traditional decor allows. Robin Phillips' Stratford Ontario production, for example, deliberately confined the play to the small proscenium stage of the Avon Theatre, rather than using the big, open main stage.

In general, then, what has followed on Brook's 1962 production has been a series of reduced, domesticated *Lears*. This might seem a diminution of the size of the play – there is no doubt that such an approach turns away from titanic or mad grandeur as well as from Scofield's high arrogance in the title role – but it suits our post-modern, sceptical sensibility. We might even add a fifth category to Rosenberg's four basic Lears: one that includes some of the madness, some of the arrogance, perhaps even a bit of the ill-used father, but which defines itself primarily in terms of histrionic self-indulgence; this is a scaled-down Lear, a pathetic one, but also at times a wily and comic one. It is, in a way, the traditional Lears viewed ironically.

Two productions, both set in the nineteenth century, with Lear in military uniform 'resplendent with epaulettes and medals', will illustrate this rather narrower (though perhaps also sharper) conception. In one, directed by Trevor Nunn for the RSC in 1976, Donald Sinden presented Lear as harsh and self-indulgent, something of a petty tyrant in relation to his daughters, who were clearly afraid of him.[8] The opening scene was played as a calculated device to shock and then observe the effects, a naturalistic, domestic ritual with Lear puffing impatiently on a cigar and his daughters sitting rigidly before him. In the other (Phillips' production, mentioned above), Peter Ustinov, an actor–writer known primarily for urbanity and wit, took on the main role, seeing Lear very much in the tradition of the senile old man who moves toward sanity. Playful, foxy, crumpled, lovable and slightly comic – so the critics saw him at the outset. There were stains and cigar ashes on his uniform. Ustinov seemed deliberately to create an uncertainty in the opening scene as to whether his lapses stemmed from cleverness or senility – he forgot, or pretended to forget, Cornwall's name, for example, an interesting touch not without its resonances further on. As with Sinden, the opening ritual was very much a show in which he indulged himself. But as the play progressed, 'Ustinov [began] to discover in Lear the human being under the beaten bulk.'[9] The later scenes were quiet, restrained, deliberately 'unacted' – the performance thus traced 'a movement from mannerism to the ultimate reduction of gesture'.[10] Sinden, more histrionic than Ustinov from the start, carried that quality through to the finish but turned it to different ends, re-enacting his fool's earlier 'bits' in the scene with the blinded Gloucester, for example. This gave the arbitrary self-dramatization of the earlier scenes, which he had wielded like a weapon, a new gentleness and pathos.

If the acting of a Sinden or a Ustinov lacks something of the grand style – the rhetorical sweep and majestic presence of Gielgud, for example, who played Lear several times in the thirties and forties – perhaps it offers us some compensation as well. Older theatre-goers may regret the diminution in speaking and look back nostalgically to an earlier, bigger, more rounded style of delivery; and they may be alienated by the newer emphasis on *meaning*, in all its intricacy and particularity. But that determination to track down the vagaries of meaning can pay off. In relation to the Phillips–Ustinov *Lear*, one critic wrote of the setting and conception that they evoked a sense of Property, which gave a new significance to the division of the kingdom: 'the will . . . comes over in the dry, legal, but electric atmosphere of High Property as in no other. How can a Druid make a will?'[11] In such a setting, the villain Edmund escapes being simply an embodiment of evil; instead, as Richard Monette played him, he can become the penniless young nineteenth-century man-on-the-make, a Rastignac or Julian Sorel. This makes sense of his behaviour and places him in a recognizable social setting. Even such a scene as the blinding of Gloucester, one of the harshest in all Shakespeare, can yield a new perspective: the emphasis shifts from cosmic cruelty or the utter indifference of the gods to the idea that 'barbarism exists only in relation to civilization'. Here was a moment when 'the superstructure of nineteenth century culture cracked and what emerged was unaccommodated man'.[12]

More than any others, the storm scenes are likely to suffer from the kind of approach just outlined. It is hard to fit them into a naturalistic design of whatever shape. Indeed, as I pointed out at the beginning, they are extremely difficult to carry in any mode. But certainly to let loose the vocal power of actors such as Gielgud or Scofield will help. Trevor Nunn tried 'real' stage rain as a way of injecting a note of verisimilitude, but to do so is likely to call attention to the inadequacies of stage representation, and thus distract the audience. Film has a clear advantage over the stage here, and can raise a convincing storm. Kozintsev gave us a bleak heath and a violent wind; Lear was brooding rather than passionate, and, in keeping with the director's social preoccupations, Poor Tom was not a lone beggar but one of a large group of grotesques huddled frighteningly in the hovel. This tended to reduce the metaphysical strangeness of the meeting between him and Lear.

Brook underlined the theatricality of the storm by lowering three large thundersheets (rectangular sheets of metal operated mechanically from backstage to produce the thunder), while the actors mimed their battle with the elements on the bare stage.[13] In true Brechtian style, Brook invited the audience not only to feel what was happening but also to be aware of its theatrical nature. The storm sequence leads, in a crescendo of the bizarre and the brutal, to a double culmination: first the mad 'trial' of Goneril and Regan, in which the participants are a deranged King, a court fool and a dispossessed lord masquerading as a bedlamite; and then the supposedly sane 'trial' of Gloucester, which is in reality a travesty of justice. (Brook set both scenes [III.vi and vii] in the same hovel.) The usual practice is to place the intermission after these scenes, and that is what Brook did, but with a difference:

> At the end of the first act [i.e. part] of *Lear* when Gloucester is blinded, we brought the house lights up before the last savage action was completed – so as to make the audience take stock of the scene before being engulfed in automatic applause.[14]

The scene ended with Gloucester staggering about with a cloth that a servant had given him over his head.[15] Brook cut the exchange between Cornwall's servants that ends the scene in the text and which provides some sense of human sympathy and concern in an inhuman world. He was much maligned for this cut, which critics observed tended to bolster his view of the play and his emphasis on its dark cruelties. But he did have the authority of the First Folio text behind him, which cut these and about 300 other lines of the original quarto, and which very possibly represents an early acting version of the play.

Throughout Lear's trials he is accompanied by the Fool, a character so enigmatic that Tate simply left him out. In a nineteenth-century setting he may appear as a bit of an anachronism, but he can be given an important place as an old companion of Lear. He has a mysterious relation with Cordelia, appearing in the text only when she is out of England. Many productions, trying to make something of this relationship, have brought him on in the first scene where his presence is not strictly called for (he has no lines and is not named in the stage directions). At Ashland Oregon in 1976, the director found a poignant way to suggest these linkages. In the opening scene, Cordelia had a wine-coloured handkerchief. Her final line in that scene, 'Well may you prosper', is usually an ironic dig at her sisters, but this production made it a sincere farewell to the Fool, accompanied by a gift of the handkerchief. The Fool then used it in later scenes to make animal shapes and play tricks. In IV.vi, after the

Fool's mysterious disappearance, Lear had it, and even tried, in his madness, to copy some of the Fool's tricks with it. At the beginning of the last scene Lear and Cordelia went off to prison holding the handkerchief between them, and at the end it was clearly visible around her neck ('my poor fool is hanged').[16]

Traditionally, the Fool has been a waiflike boy, half seer and half idiot. Kozintsev adopted that view, developing an extraordinary kinship between King and Fool, from their first appearance laughing and embracing. The film kept the Fool in sight during the later scenes, registering on his vulnerable body the decay of Lear's and Cordelia's fortunes. The furthest anyone has taken this line was in the RSC production of 1982, which gave us a truly grotesque and penetrating Fool in clown make-up, a tattered frockcoat and striped trousers; crippled and bent, walking on his ankles, his hair pulled up in a bizarre bun on top like a demented samurai, he alternatively croaked and chanted his lines, accompanying himself on a tiny, scratchy violin. The strangest touch came in III.vi, when, in the midst of a wild bursting of pillows and flying of feathers, Lear stabbed and killed the Fool, who was left to rot in a barrel. This seems a capricious way to account for the curious disappearance of the Fool from the text at this point.

In other productions, such as those of Nunn and Phillips discussed earlier, the Fool has been older, as old as Lear even, and closely connected to him. In both productions, there was a sense of long-established reciprocity between them, a kind of care that made Lear's sudden consideration during the storm ('how dost, my boy? Art cold? . . . Poor fool and knave, I have one part in my heart / That's sorry yet for thee') less a metaphysical realization and more a simple human gesture – an act of old friendship.

An advantage of making the Fool older and wilier is that his primary function of getting quickly and sharply under Lear's skin may be exercised more credibly than if he is a semi-retarded waif. He knows his man, and his enigmatic or allusive comments hit the target because he knows where to aim. However he is played, this bitter but therapeutic skill needs to be at the centre of the conception (see Plate 13). Without it, the part runs the risk of irrelevance or sentimentality.

The new, unawed, naturalistic approach to *King Lear* has also yielded a different view of Lear's daughters from the traditional one. I mentioned above that Brook sought to justify Goneril's and Regan's behaviour – or at least to complicate our response to it – by unleashing the full rowdiness of Lear's followers. This has been the pattern to several other revivals as well, and is often complemented by outrageous play-acting on Lear's part. In Kozintsev's film, Goneril was rigid before her father's mocking self-dramatization as they sat at dinner (I.iv), and in the Nunn–Sinden version, she reacted to his affected pretence not to recognize her ('Your name, fair gentlewoman?') with an 'hysterical outburst', and shortly thereafter was reduced to tears of exasperation. Lines that in the traditional reading signal the beginning of Lear's repentance and the cracking of his high arrogance ('O Lear, Lear, Lear! / Beat at this gate that let thy folly in / And thy dear judgement out') were here 'a piece of ham acting accompanied by a stagey laugh'.[17]

All this, of course, shifts sympathy toward Goneril. But there remains some doubt: the little scene that precedes the confrontation (I.iii) shows Goneril looking for an opportunity to slight her father and instructing her steward to neglect him. And in the course of I.iv, with Lear wildly cursing and raging, both the Fool and Albany corroborate the King's perception. Albany's view is especially significant, not only because he is a trustworthy, if weak, character, but also because he is married to Goneril.

So there is no question of making Goneril simply a poor, wronged woman. Like her sister Regan, she is hard and cruel. The scene (II.iv) where the two of them team up to reduce to naught Lear's quota of knights (and hence his sense of his own worth) makes this evident, though here too Sinden's histrionic and self-pitying Lear helped to strike a balance, as did Regan's nervous stammer in the face of her capricious father – whenever she began to stutter, Lear would impatiently stamp his foot. Scofield took a different approach to a similar end: he remained defiant and unsympathetic throughout this scene and ended it by turning his final words, 'O fool, I shall go mad', away from the usual pathos to a vengeful threat.[18]

After this scene, it is difficult to soften Goneril and Regan any more. The coolness with which, in the aftermath of one of Lear's grandest tirades, they shut their doors to both their father and the storm, is a presage of what is to come. This little exchange, which ends II.iv, can be played differently – with tense nerves and an attempt to calm down. But the bland matter-of-factness of Cornwall's 'Let us withdraw; 'twill be a storm', and the sisters' seemingly unruffled smugness on the heels of Lear's wild exit, suggest an underlying brutality that will reveal itself a few hours later in the plucking-out of Gloucester's eyes. Goneril, we should remember, first suggests this method of punishment and Regan takes an active part in it.

By that time both the sisters seem to have discovered the sexual desirability of Edmund, whose treachery is quickly raising his fortunes. Some indication of this new ingredient will be appropriate when all three appear on-stage, for the first time since i.i, at the beginning of the blinding scene. Sexual tension is in the air. Robin Phillips told his actresses to work for the impression that opening their bodices would produce steam! In the text, there is no overt mark of such feeling till the fourth act, with Goneril's unambiguously seductive farewell to Edmund, but later we are told that, while at Gloucester's castle, 'She gave strange oeillades and most speaking looks / To noble Edmund'. Regan too is interested. Kozintsev found a bold way to indicate this: with Cornwall killed in the struggle with his servants, Regan, seeing the result, rushed from the room and in the heat dashed up the stairs to Edmund's room, where she unabashedly gave herself to him. Returning quickly to her husband, now laid out on a table in a bare chamber, she kissed his still warm mouth. The effect was chilling.

Lear's third daughter, Cordelia, has of course traditionally been the antidote to her sisters' poison. And there can be no doubt that her father's original preference for her ('I lov'd her most and thought to set my rest / On her kind nursery') is based on a sound judgement which all too soon goes to pieces. Some people have looked for an explanation, and perhaps even a justification, of Goneril's and Regan's hatred in their lifelong feelings of inferiority in their father's eyes; Cordelia too must have been affected by her position of primacy – or so the argument goes. Thus in recent years we have begun to see Cordelias who are far from perfect – marked, perhaps, by a prim self-assurance, or a deliberately provocative silence. Nunn cut Cordelia's early asides in the opening scene, in which she expresses her love for her father and her misgivings at having to take part in the ritual ('What shall Cordelia speak? Love and be silent'). Her opening words were thus the bald response 'Nothing, my lord.' This necessarily makes her look harder and more obstinate than she otherwise would. Thus again the balance between her and her sisters was evened out, as it was too at the end of the scene, when Goneril's apparent attempt at friendliness met with a priggish retort.[19]

Some attempt to make Cordelia more than a cipher, or a symbolic angel, will certainly be welcome, though this need not lead to a distortion of her character. She is, or can be, headstrong and forthright, full of youthful idealism that cannot accept the deceptions of her elders. She refuses to mince her words in the exchange with her sisters, and, when her father does get her to speak in Act I, she says exactly what she thinks. Moreover, what she says makes good sense: 'Why have my sisters husbands, if they say / They love you all?' At the end of the play, the tragic pressure of circumstance forces her to go back on this perception – she dies with her father rather than live with her husband. And the tragedy is, there is really no other choice that she can make. Her death, and here is the crucial point in any conception of her, must *matter* to us, as it does to Lear. It is a black moment. As Dr Johnson recognized, no palliative can soften it.

The last part of the play, mainly through the machinations of Edgar (a peculiar character who dons an extraordinary series of disguises in the course of the action), seems to promise the relief of a happy ending, only to withdraw it again at every step. There is something inexorable about the way comic–romantic possibilities are raised (for example, in the duel between Edmund and Edgar or in the attempted reprieve of Lear and Cordelia) and then simply flattened. Ultimately, this leads to the bitter irony of the ending.

Edgar's optimistic formulation 'Ripeness is all' turns out not to be the case after all. And his leading his blind and despairing father to the brink of a non-existent cliff proves to be no solution. The strangeness of this latter scene (IV.vi) has elicited much comment, and there is no doubt that it deliberately challenges the audience's willingness to believe in what's going on. There is no way of staging it that will make it fully credible, although gymnastic Gloucesters have occasionally tumbled from considerable heights. The more common solution nowadays is to follow the Quarto and have Gloucester simply kneel on the flat stage and, at the end of his speech, fall forward. Emphasizing the theatrical, even symbolic, quality of such an event more easily fits an approach such as that of Peter Brook, but can also be accommodated into productions that lean toward realism.

In the main plot, the reconciliation between father and child (IV.vii) seems to promise new life, but, as in the Gloucester plot, what looks like an upswing proves only a temporary reprieve. Kozintsev emphasized the fragility of this moment by setting it in the very midst of battle; its delicate poignancy was evoked by Lear's wiping a tear from his daughter's eye and licking his index finger in tender astonishment ('Be your tears wet?') – a gesture not so different from Garrick's in the same scene 200 years earlier.[20] From that point on, Lear and Cordelia were carried along in a sea of humanity, refugees at the mercy of the swirling battle, till they were sent off to prison. At the end, in an image both startling and horrible, Cordelia was seen swinging lifeless from a parapet.

On the stage, there is no call for an actual battle. Shakespeare's directions require only off-stage alarums and retreats. What must not be lost here is the necessary drive of the action, despite all the eddying possibilities that interrupt the flow. During the final scene, while people dally in the aftermath of combat, while a romantic duel is fought between Edgar and Edmund (slowed down in Phillips' production by the reading of a 'Code Duello' presumably introduced to heighten the authenticity of the nineteenth-century setting), and while Goneril and Regan die by murder and suicide, we are all the time aware of the plight of Lear and Cordelia. The intervening action between their being sent off to prison and Lear's final entrance is as it were in brackets – a deliberately distracting gap, a break designed to make the final blow strike the harder. Hence the cruelty of those last moments comes over all the more forcefully. Is it any wonder that Brook conceived the play in terms of Artaud and Beckett?

One final note on those closing minutes. Lear dies, cradling the dead Cordelia in his arms. He searches her for signs of life – a mist of breath on a looking-glass, the stirring of a feather at her lips. He gives up – 'Thou'lt come no more. . . .' But at the very end he seems to find what he has sought: 'Look on her, look, her lips, / Look there, look there!' Does he die, then, exalted by a comforting delusion – or do his last words merely register an absolute finality, an awareness that she is irrevocably gone? Actors have done it both ways. The first, less bleak but more ironic in the long run, has Lear die happy; the second emphasizes the sombre inexorability of the gods' decrees. Sinden, taking the former approach, added a nice touch by making 'Pray you undo this button' refer not to his own clothing, as is usual, but to Cordelia's, a button at her neck to give her air; this then led naturally to delusion and exaltation.[21] Scofield, by contrast, ended as a frail grey spectre come to calm, his towering arrogance gone, and his full voice 'fallen to a thread'.[22]

Like the eighteenth century, with Tate's infamous redaction, our own time has sought ways to soften the pain of this terrible play.

Our way has been less to change the text than to *interpret* it, perhaps with the help of some judicious cutting. We bring it into line with some theory of the world, and we find this comforting – even if, paradoxically, that theory is itself very harsh. But the play ultimately resists even that kind of ease. Glancing at the different programmes of 1979 and 1980 for the same production of *King Lear* at Stratford Ontario yields an interesting inference. In the first one, set up for the souvenir programme long before the play even went into rehearsal, the theme is 'the education of a king' and highlights several quotations which adopt this reductive and comforting point of view ('suffering ennobles', etc.). In the 1980 programme, photos from the actual 1979 production create an impression of quizzical, pained uncertainty; the comforting quotations have mostly disappeared, and the stress instead is on survival, terror and loss. Dare one infer from this that, in actually doing the play, actors and director come to recognize the falseness or oversimplicity of optimistic, ideological notions about it? The later emphasis on sheer loss perhaps represents a truer, if bleaker, response to the *experience* of this largest and darkest of Shakespeare's tragedies.

15

Macbeth

There is a superstition among theatre people that *Macbeth* is a bad-luck play. Actors are unwilling to quote it in dressing-rooms. Peter Brook refused to direct it because of the ill fate that so often attends it.[1] And directors who have taken it on have frequently run into trouble with illness, broken limbs or outright disaster. Nevertheless it is a popular, well-known play and is often produced. Perhaps superstition bows to economic exigency or artistic challenge.

Be that as it may, the evil that surrounds and pervades the action of the play is a palpable thing and the feeling that it is dangerous to toy with dark powers can easily overrun the banks of the play itself and invade performers and audience alike. Evil is certainly at the centre of the play, more so than anywhere else in Shakespeare. It is a spiritual, occult, contagious kind of evil, different from the more pragmatic Machiavellian kind typical of Shakespeare's villains – Richard III, for example, or Edmund in *King Lear* or even Iago in *Othello*.

It is hard to find a way to 'play' evil, to enact it theatrically – for evil is not the same as cruelty, or ambition, or bloodlust. The temptation with *Macbeth*, even more than with the other tragedies, is to simplify, to turn away from the complex vision that Shakespeare has given us and to substitute for it a play about ambition, or tyranny, or brutality. To do so is to relax what A. C. Bradley called 'the tension of imagination'.

The key here is the conception of the two main figures, especially Macbeth, the only Shakespearean tragic hero who might be regarded as a villain. Richard III, a possible exception, does not seem fully tragic; for one thing, he has no conscience, and that makes all the difference. The problem for the actor playing Macbeth is to make him sympathetic, admirable, even in a sense lovable, without scanting either the cruelty to which he gives way or the horror of the dark bargain he has struck. Olivier's Macbeth, it has been said, seemed to have 'enormous undeveloped capabilities, could have been a Beethoven or a Shakespeare, potentially as great a power for good as he became a power for evil.'[2] Kenneth Tynan saw Olivier's performance as an exception to his rule that 'no one has ever succeeded as Macbeth and the reason is not far to seek. Instead of growing as the play proceeds, the hero shrinks; complex and many-levelled to begin with, he ends up a cornered thug.' Olivier, in contrast made the play a 'thing of mounting . . . excitement'.[3] Indeed, if all an actor offers us in the final acts is a cornered thug, then the tragedy will be reduced to melodrama.

Shakespeare has given the actor lots of help. The verse, for one thing, even at the end, has extraordinary strength and vigour, a concentrated force unmatched in the other plays. Macbeth has a richly poetic and imaginative side, a sense almost of mystery, as well as at times a boyish naïveté. He is, too, unflinchingly self-aware. The 'horrid image' of his act is open to him, he sees it plainly from the start, and yet he does the deed. This is what accounts for the terrible ambivalence of feeling that the play engenders. We are sympathetic and horror-struck at the same time. Any good production will have to hold this balance and maintain the uncomfortable intensity created by the relentless seesawing of emotions. The fact that the play is very short, the shortest by far of the tragedies, will encourage such intensity of playing.

Much of *Macbeth* takes place in real as well as symbolic darkness. It starts with fog and filthy air, and in the course of it light thickens, sleep is murdered, the dark night strangles the travelling lamp and scarfs up the tender eye of pitiful day, ghosts roam and a troubled sleeper walks with a lone taper. The puny lights of man are hardly enough to keep at bay the gathering gloom. There is a strong sense of enclosure, of people huddled around fires or candles. To register this disturbing atmosphere, Shakespeare had little at his disposal beyond his words and a few props. Certainly none of the resources of the modern theatre were available at the Globe, where performances were held outdoors in the afternoon. Nowadays, a lot can be done with lighting, but the essential task of establishing the brooding atmosphere still rests with the actors.

The responsibility falls first on the witches. Shakespeare starts with them precisely to involve the audience in the spiritual milieu that they embody. Lately, a new tendency has arisen in order to help set the scene. A production may well begin with a symbolic dumbshow or tableau which is designed to capture audience attention and focus directorial interpretation. This device, used frequently for many plays, can be effective, but it can also be too

pointed, too overtly 'significant'. One production that I saw cut the
witches entirely and began with Macbeth thrusting a severed head
onto a pole planted downstage centre. The result was a titter in the
audience. Trevor Nunn's production for the RSC in 1976, at
Stratford's Other Place, began more solemnly, with organ music
and the witches shuffling onto the bare stage from different
directions to crouch together on one side. At the same time Duncan,
clad in white, the very symbol of goodness, was helped on stage by
his two sons and knelt to pray. His prayer was 'almost immediately
drowned by a horrible whining growl emanating from the witches
and gradually rising to an intolerable pitch'.[4] With a crash of the
thundersheet, the play began. In Peter Hall's 1967 production, there
was a white veil stretched across the proscenium and, as the play
began, the witches, barely visible, emerged from under a blood-red
shag carpet that covered the whole stage. Lightning-flashes
provided intermittent glimpses of them as they crouched behind the
veil in various 'unholy' postures. They were seen pouring blood
down a crucifix, the veil rose and the play began. During the first
scene, the ground writhed and shifted, the earth seeming to give
birth to phantasmal shapes which were gradually revealed as the
battle-weary soldiers of I.ii.[5]

Such beginnings probably stem from a desire to deepen the
significance of the witches, who do in fact pose a problem for the
modern director. Cutting them is obviously no solution. The
production that I saw which did eliminate them stands as a
monument to directorial obtuseness, since to do away with the
witches meant to push the drama entirely inside Macbeth's head,
and thus the whole implicated world, the earth and its mysteries
which surround Macbeth's action, was lost. In addition, of course,
opportunities for powerful theatrical effect were thrown away and
absurdity was introduced into the apparition scene (IV.i), since
Macbeth himself generated the images and riddles. No matter what
trouble a director may have with the weird sisters, he really cannot
do without them.

The essential thing is not a matter simply of staging. The witches
embody the dark shrouded mystery of the play's world; they
fashion the link with evil powers that Macbeth in some way seeks.
They work together, a hellish chorus. In that they must be
convincing. Never mind what rags or skins they may have for
costumes, or what ghoulish props they may toss into their cauldron;
such devices are extra. It is true that most members of a modern

audience do not believe in witchcraft and it is also true that most members of the original audience, including King James himself, did. But this does not mean that the theatrical potential of the witches or their hideous associations have diminished. The modern director's problem is to find a way to make them convincing. Elaborate staging is likely to distract from their central purpose (although there is evidence to suggest that at the Globe they were flown out on wires). The apparitions in iv.i pose the strongest temptation to today's technical wizards, but perhaps the simplest recourse there is to use dolls, puppets or emblems of some sort that the witches can easily manipulate. (The traditional method, to use actors behind gauze or screen, seems to have gone out of fashion.) In Nunn's austere production, Macbeth was given little talismans to hold, and he clutched them until the falsity of their predictions began to emerge.[6] Nunn made the show of kings strictly an inner vision, as other directors have done for all the apparitions. But the scene demands some externalization, I think. Ashland Oregon, in 1979, projected the apparitions onto the First Witch's chest, a strategy which sounds effective, but perhaps was a trifle too ingenious.[7]

How the apparitions, and the other witch scenes, are to be staged must grow out of a more general conception of the weird sisters and their world. In Nunn's version, where the keynote was stark simplicity in the staging and highly charged intensity in the acting, and where the conception of the characters and action emphasized directness and actuality rather than mystery, the witches 'were practical and down-to-earth, the first carrying a handbag and mixing her brew in an old kettle, and only the second having any obvious link with the supernatural'.[8] By compelling Macbeth to drink their brew, they brought him simply, but concretely, into their circle. In Hall's production (1967), the desecrations wrought by the witches, such as pouring blood down an upside-down crucifix and drinking it, were more spectacular, and more in keeping with the predominantly religious overtones of that interpretation, with its emphasis on the metaphysical struggle between good and evil.[9] Thus both productions sought appropriate ways to engender the essential horror that has to surround the central action.

Another crucial point is that the witches do not *cause* Macbeth to embrace evil. He is not their victim. From the late seventeenth right through to the mid-nineteenth century, the usual stage version of the play included Sir William Davenant's 'improvements', which tended to put Macbeth in the hands of a malign fate and thus to reduce the horror of his crimes. Today we are more likely to get the opposite emphasis, where not only Macbeth, but everyone else in the play, is shadowed by inescapable evil. In such a reading, Macbeth may emerge as nothing but a criminal or a vicious tyrant, a serious oversimplification, and the other characters too may seem susceptible to the general disease. What no production can afford to lose is the sense that Macbeth is responsible for his own actions, and painfully aware of what he is doing – 'O full of scorpions is my mind, dear wife.'

To say that Macbeth is in charge of his own fate is not to forget Lady Macbeth. She is an essential figure, as deeply implicated as her husband though in a different way. But, though traditional schoolboy wisdom may have it so, she does not cause Macbeth to carry out the crime, any more than the witches do. He falters at one key moment (I.vii), and her encouragement is what he then expects. It is part of their bargain, their style of working together. The best modern productions have brought out the central importance of the partnership between Macbeth and Lady Macbeth, and in doing so have added a dimension not fully recognized before. What is now generally seen is a couple whose initial relationship, whether passionate, affectionate or cool, is intrinsic to the whole portrayal. After the murder their relationship gradually disintegrates, so that their growing isolation from each other, and their final despair, bring an added poignancy to the tragic consequence.

In their first scene together (I.v), Lady Macbeth enters alone with Macbeth's letter describing his encounter with the witches. In the soliloquy that follows, she muses about Macbeth's weaknesses and calls on the spirits that tend on mortal thoughts to unsex her, to fill her topful of direst cruelty. Then Macbeth enters, and she speaks: 'Great Glamis! worthy Cawdor! / Greater than both by the all-hail hereafter!' The possibilities here are multiple. Does she stop him as he enters? Does she kneel to him, or simply stand where she is? Do they embrace or remain at a distance from one another? Is he about to speak and she overrides him? Do they seem to have a clear and immediate understanding? Is his first speech, 'My dearest love, / Duncan comes here tonight', a subtle suggestion, or a mere statement? It *seems* to show Macbeth to be as aware, as determined, and as ready as his wife. But it could be played as entirely innocent. In that case, we could get a boyish, easily led Macbeth, and a dominating Lady Macbeth. There would be little sense of an equal partnership.

The scene, in other words, can give us a Lady Macbeth who knows what she wants and is in control, and can suggest that that is the usual state of affairs. Or it can place the partners on a more or less equal level. Furthermore, it can suggest a strong sexual element in their relationship, or it can present them as rather cold and distant, joined more by ambition than love. The former course will add a tragic pathos to the ensuing breakdown; the latter will emphasize a hard fatalism in the events that follow. Already by the end of this very first scene between them, we may be able to discern hints of the coming destruction:

> LADY MACBETH. Your face, my thane, is as a book where men
>   May read strange matters.
>   . . .
>   He that's coming
>   Must be provided for; and you shall put
>   This night's great business into my dispatch
>   . . .
> MACBETH. We will speak further.
> LADY MACBETH. Only look up clear:
>   To alter favor ever is to fear.
>   Leave all the rest to me.
>
>   (I.v.62–73)

Lady Macbeth seems to have taken over. Is their relationship, even if it was presented positively at the outset of the scene, already beginning to look unbalanced? Macbeth says little – does his 'We will speak further' imply misgivings or a settled resolution? Does Lady Macbeth's rush of words stem from an awareness that Macbeth remains uncertain? Perhaps their love, under the pressure of their murderous thoughts, is already starting to wither. If so, then the progress of the scene would seem briefly to encapsulate the future course of the action. In Glen Byam Shaw's production at Stratford in 1955, Lady Macbeth (Vivien Leigh) stood on a bridge under the twisted angular arches of Inverness castle for the soliloquy. Macbeth (Olivier) entered below; she greeted him, descended; and they met and embraced lovingly centre-stage. His first line was straightforward. But almost immediately a gap began to open. He turned slightly away from her on her first suggestion ('O never/Shall sun that morrow see'), and on 'We will speak further' he again moved away. They left the stage separately, thoughtfully, as distant trumpets heralded Duncan's imminent arrival.[10] For Paul Scofield, who played Macbeth in Hall's version, the pair 'are kept from embracing by what [they] say'. She knelt to him on his entrance, halting him near the door; when he did come to her it was purposefully, at the end of the scene, when they embraced without passion, as if to hold each other up.[11] Ian McKellen and Judi Dench, in Nunn's production, met centre-stage in a passionately sexual embrace, and later Macbeth's doubts were 'as much quelled by a sexually expressed love as by a vehement protestation'.[12]

The important thing is to maintain a sense of the humanity of the characters, to avoid turning Lady Macbeth (especially) into a fiend. When she invokes the spirits to 'unsex me here / And fill me from the crown to the toe top-full / Of direst cruelty', we should not get the sense that she is calling upon spirits with whom she has a familiar relationship. Rather, this is a new, bold and horrifying departure for her. Vivien Leigh seemed to need the spirits to fortify herself because of her physical and psychological weakness; Judi Dench made the invocation seem a sacrifice, after which she 'sank to the floor and her long black skirt spread around her like a vast inkstain in the intense spotlight'.[13]

In I.vii, Macbeth falters before the thought of killing his king, and Lady Macbeth, through a combination of mockery and bravado, brings him round to it. Here we have an example of their partnership in action. A tiny but tell-tale indication of the kind of Lady Macbeth we are dealing with is provided by her answer to Macbeth's hesitant question, 'If we should fail?' Scholars disagree about whether her curt response, 'We fail', should be followed by a full stop or a question mark. The actress must choose, and if she decides on the former, and puts off Macbeth's anxiety with a dismissive shrug or a convincing show of determination, she is likely to come off stronger than if she echoes his question with her own. One critic remembered Dench's 'mixture of surprise and resolution and danger' at this moment.[14] Thus the little phrase 'We fail', like the scene as a whole, can give us a Lady Macbeth who is her husband's tough but loving partner, one who holds him in contempt, or one who is willing to dare anything with him.

The murder scene, II.ii, reveals Lady Macbeth still tougher and firmer than her husband. We never, of course, *see* the murder. First she stands waiting for him to return from the fatal chamber, and then he stands waiting for her. In between, a brief dialogue: Macbeth in torment that he could not say 'Amen'; Lady Macbeth rising to a great and famous moment – 'Give *me* the daggers' (see Plate 14). Around them the terrors of the night suggest themselves, and ordinary sounds (bell, owl, knocking) mysteriously invest the atmosphere with horror. Lady Macbeth's imperviousness to all this may seem complete, but at the beginning of the scene she has a tell-tale speech, one of the few indications early in the play of the sources of her later breakdown. Speaking of Duncan she says, 'Had he not resembled / My father as he slept, I had done 't.' How extraordinary that she should think of her father at such a time! There is a softness in Lady Macbeth which must be played. If it is not, we are likely to get the 'fiend-like queen' without the essential humanity. Building on the hint that this line provides, some actresses (beginning with the great Sarah Siddons herself) have played the ensuing dialogue with Macbeth with controlled but rising hysteria, bursting out on 'Who was it that thus cried?', and thereafter tightly reined in. The hint of future disintegration is planted.

The real break between husband and wife comes only after they have achieved their goal. This is the awful irony. 'To be thus is nothing,' says Macbeth at the beginning of Act III, 'But to be safely thus.' And Lady Macbeth in the next scene: 'Nought's had, all's spent, / Where our desire is got without content.' The withering-process has begun, and its first sign is a growing distance between the partners. Banquo occupies their thoughts but they can no longer work together. Macbeth in fact has already plotted to have Banquo murdered, but he will tell his wife nothing:

LADY MACBETH.   What's to be done?
MACBETH. Be innocent of the knowledge, dearest chuck,
   Till thou applaud the deed.

                                         (III.ii.47–9)

(The word 'deed' echoes ominously through the play.) Macbeth is keeping secrets, *protecting* his wife it seems – is he already aware of her fragility? – or simply taking over from her. Even the term of endearment, 'dearest chuck', seems to carry within it a feeling of

superiority and, perhaps, if the actor is up to it, a sense of nostalgia
for an irrecoverable past.

Lady Macbeth has one more powerful moment before her final
collapse – when she intervenes at the banquet; but it is laced with
desperation. Banquo, whose presence and absence dominate Act
III, is murdered in scene iii and appears as an unwanted guest in
scene iv, usurping Macbeth's chair and driving him to open
self-betrayal. The exact staging of this scene, long done with traps,
or with other actors masking the ghost's entrance, is less important
than its effect on Macbeth, his wife and the assembled lords.
Occasionally the scene has been played with no ghost, Macbeth
ranting at an empty chair. This, I think, is a mistake, although in one
version it led to an effective moment when Lady Macbeth
deliberately sat in the empty chair to prove Macbeth's hallucination.
Unlike the air-drawn dagger, this is no hallucination; it really is
Banquo's ghost. Macbeth at first is terrified; Lady Macbeth tries
desperately to cover up. The lords naturally are suspicious. They are
thinking, undoubtedly, of Duncan, since they know nothing of
Banquo's murder. The ghost retires but, no sooner has Macbeth
made excuses for his 'strange infirmity', than it returns again. This
time Macbeth's fear is mixed with fury. He drives the ghost out, but
by now the lords are aroused. Ross's ironically naïve question to
Macbeth's talk of sights – 'What sights, my lord?' – makes it clear to
Lady Macbeth that she has lost, and, barely maintaining control, she
sends them all home:

> I pray you, speak not . . . .
>   At once, good night.
> Stand not upon the order of your going,
> But go at once.
>
>   (III.iv.118–21)

She is abrupt and peremptory, forgetful, it seems, of her role as
gracious hostess. Lennox's polite, but possibly ironic, response,
'Good night, and better health attend his Majesty', seems to remind
her of her social duty, and her final line, 'A kind goodnight to all',
though covering a desire to get them out fast, has the required tone.
Judi Dench played it with near-hysteria, followed by a cover-up.
After the lords left, she and Macbeth sat, 'she bleakly smiling and he
waving goodbye in the aftermath of a foaming fit'.[15] The moment
was thus a transitional one, between her ordinary and reasonable

handling of her earlier scenes and her breakdown in the sleepwalking-scene.

At the end of the banquet scene there are no remonstrations and no scorn. There is simply a dreadful weariness. Their partnership broken, husband and wife retreat into their own dark shadows – his thoughts turning to more blood; hers, it seems, to despair. Lady Macbeth rouses herself to some sad concern for her husband – 'You lack the season of all natures, sleep' – but we remember that 'Macbeth hath murdered sleep.' And Macbeth's extraordinary reply as they go off together – 'Come, we'll to sleep. My strange and self-abuse / Is the initiate fear that wants hard use. / We are yet but young in deed' – only emphasizes the brooding isolation. In Byam Shaw's production, Lady Macbeth sank to her knees, leaning against the throne as her husband exited, while in Nunn's she collapsed, and he had half to drag and pull her off.

When she appears in the sleepwalking-scene (v.i), Lady Macbeth is carrying a candle. For many years, actresses carried that candle throughout the scene, and, when, toward the end of the eighteenth century, Mrs Siddons planned to put it down, her move was considered revolutionary. The playwright Sheridan, when he heard about it, went to her dressing-room to warn her of the risk of censure. But she went ahead with her plan, and when he saw the scene performed Sheridan recanted. Actresses nowadays do not have to contend with such rigid theatrical traditions – but neither can they reap the benefits of a well-chosen break with tradition. Mrs Siddon's sleepwalking-scene was the climax of one of the most remarkable performances in the history of the English stage. Asked by an actor to describe his response to it, writer Sheridan Knowles replied with a shudder, 'Well, sir, I smelt blood! I swear I smelt blood.'[16]

The scene itself is powerfully resonant, recapitulating the major themes and verbal motifs of the play in a highly concentrated form. The presence of the Doctor and Waiting-woman keeps before us the image of ordinary folk and their quite justified horror at what has come to pass. The gulf that separates Lady Macbeth from common humanity could hardly be deeper. 'Interpretation' is not the issue here. The actress bears the burden of getting the scene across, and she must simply find a way to burn her image into our memory. Judi Dench spoke the words 'as a long regret' encompassing both murderous deeds and 'a love which had disappeared'.[17]

Total isolation has by now overcome Macbeth and his wife. The final scenes emphasize this by surrounding Macbeth, who is immured in his castle, and gradually closing in on him. Trevor Nunn found a sharply theatrical way to realize this feeling. His RSC production was very sparely done on a bare stage with a black circle on it, the actors seated around the edges on beer crates when not actually 'on-stage'. For the siege Macbeth surrounded himself with these crates, gradually building up a 'castle' in the centre. To look for Birnam Wood, he piled boxes on one another and reached up to an overhead spotlight, directing it around the theatre. When he let it go, it swung wildly of its own accord. One commentator remarked that the spareness of the production made everything count, and cited this swinging electric light bulb throwing shadows on the dark stage.[18] The scenes of the English army, interspersed with the Macbeth scenes, were played at the sides, Macbeth remaining in the centre throughout, as if trapped. The same effect was sought by Robin Phillips in his 1978 production at Stratford Ontario, in which he too kept Macbeth stage centre and played the English scenes from near the entrances at the corners of the big platform stage.

The scenes of Act v alternate rapidly, but there are occasional moments of rest, maybe even of despair, where the action slows and Macbeth's imaginative and poetic side re-emerges:

> Canst thou not minister to a mind diseas'd,
> Pluck from the memory a rooted sorrow,
> Raze out the written troubles of the brain . . . ?
> (v.iii.41–3)

> Tomorrow and tomorrow and tomorrow . . . .
> (v.v.19ff.)

As the scope of the play widens to take in the English soldiers and the hope for a renewed Scotland, it also deepens, as Macbeth's tormented darkness is given expression. Yet he never flinches. In his refusal of self-pity, and in the loyalty that both he and Lady Macbeth continue to manifest toward each other as their world crumbles, there is a real magnificence. It is clear from Byam Shaw's notes that this is the effect he was seeking,[19] and the reviews of Olivier's performance suggest that director and actor were successful. The difficulty of the last part of the play is that Macbeth must be both criminal and noble; he is murderous but still grand, heroic and courageous. It is of course easier to play him one-sidedly, but to do so vitiates the complex balance of the ending.

As for the other characters, producers nowadays seem often to feel that, if Scotland breeds one evildoer, it must breed several, with the effect that Banquo, Ross, Malcolm and Donalbain, or some combination of them, are shown in a much more ambiguous light than they seem to be in the text. Ross is frequently presented as a time-server, and occasionally has even been implicated in the murder of Lady Macduff and her children. To play him straight may seem boring; furthermore, it is hard for an actor to think of his character as primarily functional, as Ross seems to be. Today's acting techniques encourage introspection and psychological analysis and so the actor naturally turns his attention to the multiple role that Ross does indeed have. He seems in close touch with everyone, in on their secrets. Does this make him suspect or untrustworthy? It might. Again, we are faced with how such an interpretation might fit into the overall conception. A production that seriously undermines Ross is likely to be a dark one, one that blackens not only Macbeth but almost the whole of Scotland (including, perhaps, Duncan, though not the stalwart Macduff, who keeps himself separate). Banquo will be compromised, and Malcolm will probably seem more calculating and detached. There is, I think, some justification in the text for an ambiguous Banquo. He says little; he watches carefully, he seems, as John Woodvine played him in Nunn's production, furtive and shrewd. He has his own ambitions – at the very beginning he demands a prediction from the weird sisters to match Macbeth's. On the other hand, Malcolm and Ross seem, at least in the text, more straightforward, more clearly aligned with the forces of good, as Macduff is.

Still, directors have seen them otherwise. And, if Malcolm, especially, is darkened, the ending will be significantly affected. At the end of one 'environmental' production of the play, I, along with other audience members, was rudely pushed around by roughneck soldiers, while Malcolm read his final reconciliatory speech with obvious and calculated insincerity. In several other revivals that I have seen, this speech has had a hollow ring. And at the end of Polanski's film we see Donalbain trekking up to the witches' cave, with the implication that the cycle is about to start all over again. This is a peculiarly modern twist to give to the ending, quite in keeping with our own attitudes toward politics, but out of step with what seems to be Shakespeare's implication at the end – that the political body has indeed been cleansed, its tragic, cursed head removed.

16

Coriolanus

Coriolanus is a play that does not yield its riches easily. It is more overtly political and impersonal than most of Shakespeare's work; it has a hero who is difficult to sympathize with and who is almost completely inarticulate when it comes to his own inner life; it maintains throughout a harshly ironic tone unrelieved by comedy or extravagant characterization; and it deploys a consistently cool, anti-lyrical style of verse that is brilliantly suited to the situation but unlikely to win immediate or universal admiration. It is, however, a play that rewards prolonged exposure or careful scrutiny. Politically, its analysis is sufficiently subtle and ambiguous to have been espoused by both Left and Right: the people and their tribunes have been seen as proto-democrats in search of a measure of political equality or, on the other hand, as a rowdy, stinking mob led by opportunists and bent on tearing up the social fabric. The play caused riots in Paris during the 1930s, where Left and Right clashed in the theatre and in the streets outside, and where the curtain had to be rung down some fifteen or twenty times during the first performance. Bertolt Brecht produced his own leftist version of it, and Günter Grass, the contemporary German novelist, has written an ironic play entitled *The Plebians Rehearse the Uprising* which has Brecht rehearsing his actors for his production of *Coriolanus* while a real revolution is going on outside in the streets.

As a hero, Coriolanus may lack depth, but he has magnetism and power as well as a remarkable aptitude for invective. His world is narrow; confined on the one side by his extraordinary martial skills and on the other by his unresolved love for his mother, he has little understanding of political, social or sexual life. He appears first as an arrogant patrician, insulting the common people in the grossest terms:

> What's the matter, you dissentious rogues,
> That rubbing the poor itch of your opinion,
> Make yourself scabs?
>
> (i.i.163–5)

Not a very inviting beginning for a tragic hero, but Shakespeare is true to his conception.

This opening scene will set the tone and balance of what is to come. It starts with an eruption of the mob, which most directors will choose to emphasize in some way. Peter Hall, in his 1959 production with Olivier in the central role, brought the lights down on an uncurtained stage and there followed 'a racket of bells, shouts, crowd-noises, and beating sounds working up to a climax as the mob broke through the gates on to the stage . . . "vomited, as it seemed, from the very bowels of the earth"'.[1] At Stratford Ontario in 1981, a similar effect was sought in a different way. As the houselights dimmed, electronic, percussive music began and the lights on-stage came up gradually on the balcony, where a huddled crowd slowly and rhythmically began to writhe, speeding up to a wild outburst of rebellious life. One version used a realistic, the other a ritualistic, mode to get at the same basic excitement – incipient danger and violence. But what follows this eruption is also important. The citizens pause for discussion – disorderly and inflammatory though they may be, they are willing to listen to the dissenting voice of the Second Citizen. Their leader, the rebellious, scornful and somewhat petulant First Citizen (played by the young Albert Finney in Hall's production), stops to argue. Before long Menenius enters, and again the citizens are willing to pause, to listen to 'reason'. So, we are witnessing a crowd of people willing to think about and defend what they are doing, not merely a witless mob. This is important for the political balance of the play and should temper the violence of the opening. Many, perhaps most, past productions, however, in seeking to justify Coriolanus and make him a credible tragic hero, have ignored or underplayed the basic good sense of the crowd and the political role it has. Recent productions, especially those that are alert to the ironies and seek the ambiguous balance that is the play's most important feature, have begun to restore to the citizens their rightful place. Still, it won't do to idealize them either: in their decision to direct their ire at Caius Marcius only, they are politically unsophisticated or merely vengeful – or both. In taking this course they shift away from the central issue to a symbolic target at which to aim their anti-patrician feeling, and thus weaken their position.

Dramatically, their anger at Marcius is functional, in that it leads directly to his arrogant entrance. But their bitterness is deflected temporarily by Menenius's well-timed interruption and his

humorous tale of the belly and its mutinous colleagues. Here we
have a third ingredient in the political mixture – the moderate
patrician, the peacemaker with an interest in Rome but, perhaps, a
greater stake in the interests of his own class than he is willing to
admit. He is smooth and charming, the kind of speaker who can
convince his listeners even though he has no argument, and thus
shows himself able to control and easily hoodwink the gullible
crowd. He is usually played as thoroughly amiable and rather
harmless, a man more given to wit and pleasure than politics. But
this is to underestimate him. There is, or can be, a decidedly cool,
hard edge to this grey-haired, ample-bellied old uncle. He teases the
First Citizen, calling him 'the great toe of this assembly', probably
raising a laugh from the others at their leader's expense. He may be
simply jolly, but an actor ought, I think, to treat this joke as a clever
way of driving a wedge into the opposing faction. And a minute
later he is challenging them:

> But make you ready your stiff bats and clubs.
> Rome and her rats are at the point of battle;
> The one side must have bale.
>
> (I.i.160–2)

Such lines show clearly what side he's on. And a Menenius who
emphasizes them rather than glossing them over will fit nicely into a
production that leans ideologically toward the plebeians, or one that
takes an ironic attitude toward the political machinations of all the
different groups. What is finally striking about the play is how
persuasive each point of view is shown to be on its own, and yet
how tragically incompatible they all are. Thus Menenius's charming
elitism, having its roots in his equally charming personality, has a
real dramatic power and takes its part in the complex interplay of
individual and social forces that the play depicts.

Marcius's eruption into the scene disrupts the balance achieved
by Menenius and the citizens. Olivier, in Hall's production,
suddenly appeared on the top of a large rock, 'like the apparition of
an eagle'.[2] Such an entrance would lend emphasis to his disdainful
opening lines (quoted earlier), and would as well serve to underline
the splendid isolation which is Marcius's most telling and ultimately
destructive characteristic. He is separate not only from the citizens,
who are out of his element, but even from his fellow patricians. As a
war machine, as an exile, as Revenging Death, and, finally, as a

doomed victim, he is always strangely alone, unconnected with the rest of humanity. It is, in fact, his most tragic moment when he has to admit that it is impossible to 'stand / As if a man were author of himself / And knew no other kin' (v.iii.35–7). In taking his mother by the hand, he ensures his own destruction.

Marcius's scorn for the citizens in the opening scene reaches trigger-happy proportions. He would like, he says, to use his sword to 'make a quarry / With thousands of these quarter'd slaves' (ll. 197–8), but the nobility has held him back. He is unwavering in his condemnation of the Senate's decision to grant certain rights to the citizens, most notably the appointment of tribunes to represent their interests: 'It will in time / Win upon power, and throw forth greater themes / For insurrection's arguing' (ll. 219–21). It is the beginning of the end for aristocratic power, and he is scornful of the nobility for not seeing this or, seeing it, not resisting it.

The fourth element in the political mixture – the hated tribunes – then make their appearance with the senators, thus rendering visible the very alliance that Marcius has just condemned. Left on stage after the others have gone off to prepare for the coming Volscian war, the tribunes manifest a narrowness similar to that of Marcius. Discussing the great war hero, they see only pride and a petty desire for glory, but they recognize the danger that he represents to *their* power, exactly as he had recognized the threat that their appointment posed to aristocratic hegemony. It is possible, and even common, to depict these tribunes as mean-spirited and jealous. They seem to whine and snarl like the curs for which Shakespeare shows such dislike throughout his work. And certainly a production that wants to elevate Coriolanus and present his story as the tragedy of too much nobility will benefit from a debasing of the tribunes. But to treat them in such a way is too easy. There is a political balance of power within the city that needs to be dramatically realized in some way. If the tribunes are stripped of all credibility by reason of the viciousness of their personalities, the dramatic scales will, I think, be unfavourably tipped. They, like the others, are in fact *right* in their own way, and a production can show this by taking care to give their point of view some weight.

The battle scenes come early in *Coriolanus* and thereby pose a double problem to the producer. For one thing, battles are hard for a modern audience fully to understand or appreciate, though the Elizabethans obviously enjoyed them,[3] and, for another, their coming in the first act raises the danger of anti-climax. Shakespeare clearly wants to establish the unique martial power of his hero. He wants too to set up the deadly contest between Marcius and his enemy Aufidius, which in the end is to have such devastating consequences. This is why, still in the opening scene, Marcius says of his rival, 'I sin in envying his nobility; / And, were I anything but what I am, / I would wish me only he' (ll. 230–2); and why also the second scene gives us Aufidius looking forward to meeting Marcius in the field. When they meet in the midst of battle, Marcius beats back not only his rival but certain 'officious' Volsci who come to their general's defence much against his will. The moment is climactic in terms of the immediate battle – but it also points forward, to Aufidius's shame and to his determination in the end to use less than honourable methods to get his man. So the incompleteness of the moment can be used in the rhythm of a production as a pointer, a bit of ominous unfinished business.

As for the problem of how the battle is to be handled, there seem to be two basic alternatives: a stab at realism with lots of noise, martial music, clashing of swords, smoke, dirt and blood; or some form of ritualization, in which the battle turns into a kind of savage dance. Brian Bedford's production at Stratford Ontario in 1981 opted for the second alternative, not only in the battle, but at the outset (described above) and again in the final scene. This tends to distance the action, making it more remote and even bizarre than a straight realistic depiction. I often fear, however, that directors adopt the ritualistic mode when they are not sure what else to do. It seems a popular way to load significance onto a scene without fully earning it. Still, in Bedford's production, the technique paid off in the single combat between Aufidius and Coriolanus, their bodies glistening in the half-light, twisting in an eerie, sexualized dance–wrestle. The sense of a bond between them that is so strong in the language of the play was effectively caught.

This bond is crucial. It crystallizes the male world of the play, the strange sexuality of the warrior, the glorification of the wound, the passion of rivalry. Tyrone Guthrie, in his 1963 production at Nottingham, emphasized 'the love–hate between Coriolanus and Aufidius; the hysterical and homosexual element'.[4] Typically, Guthrie is probably overstating his case, but he is thinking of moments such as Coriolanus's welcome at the house of Aufidius, after he has been banished from Rome and drawn irresistibly to the camp of his rival. Aufidius embraces him:

Let me twine
Mine arms about that body, whereagainst
My grained ash an hundred times hath broke
. . . Here I clip [embrace]
The anvil of my sword, and do contest
As hotly and as nobly with thy love
As ever in ambitious strength I did
Contend against thy valor. Know thou first,
I lov'd the maid I married . . .
But that I see thee here,
Thou noble thing, more dances my rapt heart
Than when I first my wedded mistress saw
Bestride my threshold.
(IV.v.111–23)

It is hard not to see a homoerotic element here, the flipside of the aggressive urge to wound and penetrate the other's body. The feeling, it must be emphasized, is not crassly or overtly sexual. Arising out of a male cult of rivalry, and out of an equally powerful cult of the body, it seems almost Lawrentian in character, like Birkin and Gerald's nude wrestling in front of the fire in *Women in Love* (brilliantly caught in Russell's film).

To speak so strongly of the masculine world of the play is not to forget its most formidable female character, Volumnia. With her talk of wounds and death and martial glory she is, in fact, a singular part of that male world and thereby stands in contrast to her daughter-in-law Virgilia, whose love for her husband has some deep, unarticulated source that has nothing to do with his skill in battle. Shakespeare presents them both to us in charming, even amusing contrast in the third scene of the play, a moment of quiet repose in the midst of the din of the first act. '*They set them down on two low stools, and sew*' – 'That's a friendly little opening, isn't it?' said Edith Evans in a lecture she gave on playing Volumnia. In this scene, she went on, Volumnia 'talks about Coriolanus's honour, and it is very strong meat. It's all very strong stuff – but they're *sewing!*'[5] In the production at Stratford Ontario in 1981, Volumnia unfortunately was *not* sewing and she stood during a good part of the scene, so that the contrast of which Dame Edith spoke, between the domestic ambience and the violent talk, was almost completely lost. (The text of *Coriolanus* has an unusually large number of explicit stage directions which are probably Shakespeare's own or at least represent stage practice during his time. On the whole, as with the sewing here, or '*Holds her by the hand, silent*' at the climax in Act v, a modern director would be unwise to ignore them.) An actress must find the womanliness in Volumnia as well as the bloodthirstiness, the sense of loss at the end as well as the sense of triumph at the beginning. Perhaps her tragedy is that she does not, cannot, ask her son to return to Rome with her after she wins the truce. As Edith Evans put it (and played it), 'doesn't she realize that, instead of getting him back, she has lost him a second time, almost certainly for good? He will go back to Corioli to face the music, and she will go back to Rome. No wonder she has nothing to say to the Romans when they welcome her.'[6]

Virgilia, the other woman in Coriolanus's life, offers him something very different from his mother, something he does not seem to understand or appreciate – though the question arises, and must arise for the actor when he is puzzling over the part, why did he marry her in the first place? Too many Virgilias tend to snivel, when it would seem preferable to play her with some strength, different from Volumnia's surely, but with a quiet dignity and self-awareness. She must in some way be her husband's equal. Her lines in her first scene suggest meekness, but she holds out against Volumnia's formidable will (something her husband is unable to do) when the latter, together with her friend Valeria, tries to prevail upon her to go with them. When Volumnia later accuses Virgilia of 'faint puling' (iv.ii.52), she may indeed be right; but perhaps her misunderstanding of her daughter-in-law's feelings reveals the same failure as Coriolanus has manifested to see properly who Virgilia is. At any rate, playing it like that would help to adjust the imbalance between the two women that one so often sees.

Settings for *Coriolanus* are usually massive yet simple. Sometimes, as at Stratford Ontario in 1981, just the bare stage is used, darkly lit and sombre. Or in a proscenium theatre large blocks of masonry can define the space and convey the sense of an archaic world that many directors have felt in the text. In the 1977 RSC production, directed by Terry Hands, such blocks could 'swing down to make the gates of Corioles, or [be] propelled downstage to enclose and diminish the action in the market place or the Capitol'. The costumes in the same production were of leather with lots of studs, jerkins, and a good deal of visible skin. Coriolanus himself appeared in a 'silver-studded jockstrap'.[7] (A problem with such scanty costumes, however, is that the actors playing these powerful warriors are too often physically unconvincing, with mildly ludicrous consequences.) Frequently designers seek to distinguish clearly between Roman and Volscian, conceiving the latter, in contrast to the straightforward Romans, as a *foreign* tribe, bizarrely costumed, odd, unknown and dangerous. At Stratford Ontario, for example, they wore feathery, buckskin-like jerkins and skirts, all fringed, and in battle they donned bear-masks, as of some odd cult. Again the purpose seems to have been to locate the action in archaic time, primitive and violent. This works for some aspects of the play, but the political seesawing, power struggles and incipient democracy may seem out of place. In contrast, a production in the early sixties, again at Stratford Ontario, with Paul Scofield in the leading role, set the play in Napoleonic times, the soldiers in nineteenth-century battle regalia and firing at each other with rifles. Political manocuvring might flourish in such a setting, but the sense of sheer physical strength and hand-to-hand combat, the totemic significance of wounds, and especially the one-man overthrow of a whole city, could not easily survive the relocation.

What happens in the play, as always in Shakespeare, is anchored in character, so that key decisions about setting, for example, will have ramifications for the conception of character and vice versa. In Hall's version, the scene was vertically oriented, with 'a number of perches and platforms built on a craggy, rock-like structure'. When Olivier first appeared on top of the rock, *above* the crowd, the moment was not only visually striking but was an act of characterization as well. Olivier's sense of the role revealed that 'the scorn which [Coriolanus] pours on his men is inseparable from the anger and energy which impel him in his fight against the common enemy'.[8] The strong vertical orientation of the production was a visual emblem of that domineering energy. It climaxed in Olivier's famous fall at the end, which defined the tragedy in the same basic terms as the original predominance (see Plate 15). In this connection, I once held an experiment in a course on Shakespeare, which had interesting results. I asked a few theatre students to try spontaneously to act out together, in a totally unscripted and non-verbal way, their conception of the play. The most striking feature of the short mime that ensued was its strong verticality. People kept trying to climb up onto tables and chairs, and before long a 'Coriolanus' was chosen spontaneously and hoisted aloft.

The fact that, in the little mime, Coriolanus was in a sense made and controlled by the others was also interesting, since, for all his lonely vigour, he is essentially at the mercy of others. His mother most of all, of course. But late in the play Aufidius subtly controls him, and in the middle acts the tribunes, in their canny way, manipulate him into outbursts that incriminate him. As we find out in II.iii, they have coached the citizens in advance to challenge Coriolanus's friendliness during the scene when he begs for their voices. Although the citizens are unable to do this, they recognize the scorn and arrogance behind the ambiguous words Marcius uses. And by the next scene (III.i) Marcius has been goaded into speaking his true mind directly, in a series of brilliant aristocratic speeches. In III.ii we see him under the influence of his mother, wavering but finally agreeing to act a part. And at the very end, of course, his rocklike determination is undermined for the last time, with tragic results. How easy it is to play upon the will of the man of perfect integrity!

The middle part of the play, leading up to Marcius's banishment, is its most intricate and delicate section. Here we see all the hostile factions in the class struggle deploying the tactics they think will serve them best. The tribunes are nasty and self-serving; the way they cover their tracks at the end of II.iii, by telling the citizens to blame them for the fact that Marcius has been elected ('Say you chose him . . . after our commandment'), shows them at their most crassly manipulative (if these lines [226–55] are cut, you know whose side the director is on). But at the same time they are justified in their fears about Marcius and right about his uncompromising position. The people are suspicious, gullible, easily led, but right in their instincts. Marcius is right when he argues that to create the new position of tribune and to accede to other plebeian demands is an erosion of aristocratic power. He is right too in refusing to be false to his nature. But he is also faintly absurd in this, and almost inhuman in his towering arrogance. Volumnia and the others are unscrupulous, but they too are right when they try to convince Marcius of the need to mask his true feelings for political ends. Each element is right in some sense, but these 'rights' are finally irreconcilable. In a strong production, if all are given full play, a deeply ironic sense of their incompatibility will emerge.

In III.ii, Marcius has to face his mother and his aristocratic colleagues after his intemperate outbursts and the near-riot they have caused (which Menenius has had to use all his charm to quell). He must, they say, play an appeasing part, disguise his disdain in order to gain political power. We see Coriolanus in conflict with himself, the only serious conflict that he faces before the climactic moment, again with his mother, in Act v (by contrast, his choice to join Aufidius seems to cause him no particular anxiety). The obvious way to play the scene, says Stanley Wells, would be 'with a depressed earnestness, Coriolanus grimly, even despairingly, forcing himself to behave against his nature'. Olivier, on the other hand, gave it 'a lightness of touch', an edge of humour around the fact that he was once again losing a battle of wills with his mother. His 'I will not do it' halfway through the scene was spoken not violently but quietly, 'as if with sudden acknowledgement of the truth within himself'. He listened to his mother's subsequent rebuke with mocking deference and 'his plea that he would do as he was told had the comic quality of a little boy seeking approval though he knows he has been naughty'. He agreed to speak to the people. ' "Ay but mildly", says Menenius. "Well, mildly be it then – mildly", replies Coriolanus. But instead of speaking the final word, Olivier, after a long pause, simply mouthed it.'[9] Again the humour reinforced the serious struggle and gave an extra dimension to the character.

Len Cariou, at Stratford Ontario in 1981, handled the scene quite differently. He raised a laugh with 'mildly' at the end, but otherwise his conception was more bewildered than humorous. The laugh came, in fact, from the audience's recognition of the near impossibility of this likeable overgrown boy ever managing to keep his impulsiveness in line. During the argument with Volumnia, and especially during his long silence while the others lectured him, he paced and fretted, unable to accept, or even understand, the demands being made on him. His 'What must I do?', 'Must I then do't to them?' and 'Must I go show them my unbarb'd sconce?' were spoken with more incredulity than anger. Always before, he seemed to be saying, I have been successful simply by being who I am; why am I now being told to disguise himself? His strength and absolutism were shaken. His image of himself began to crumble – how could he do these things and still retain his identity? There was then pathos in his 'I will not do it' – it was a last-ditch attempt to stave off disintegration. This meant that, in the next scene, his renewed attacks on the people and their leaders came not only from scorn, rage or arrogance, but from the irresistible need simply to be himself. There was a sense of relief that he had to play-act no longer, and the great speech 'You common cry of curs . . .' was spoken with a large, justifiable anger. Though not as powerful as Olivier's (which

Lawrence Kitchin described as having 'an impact like jagged stones parcelled together and hurled in somebody's face'[10]), it nevertheless created a strong effect. Both actors conceived the character in relation to his mother; both saw the importance of the reiteration of the word 'boy' in the final scenes. Olivier, however, had a violent energy which was appropriate to Hall's production but which might have unbalanced Bedford's more ritualized and less dynamically emotional one. Kitchin uses a vivid image to convey the pitch of Olivier's performance: 'There was', he says, 'a bizarre impression of one man lynching a crowd.'[11] Cariou was more subdued, considerably less of a virtuoso. But both performers succeeded in making Coriolanus sympathetic and interesting, without reducing his arrogance or demeaning the other political forces in the struggle.

A word on the tribunes and their role here. I said earlier that they are often presented as crafty, mean manipulators, engineering the overthrow of Coriolanus for their own advantage. And, though that is partly true, their motivation too is mixed. Oliver Ford-Davis, who played Brutus in Terry Hands' RSC production, points out that their analysis of Coriolanus is often acute, though they only understand him 'in the context of an *ordinary* political animal'. Hence some, but not all, of their distrust is justified. He makes the point too that they are swept along like the others by the current of events, and are far from actually controlling the situation. Although they first have death in mind as a punishment, they switch unaccountably to banishment (out of fear perhaps?).[12] Hands' version thus tried to show that the political situation is volatile and takes its own course – no one group is in control. This is a quite modern notion – that history has its own laws, that a struggle between classes is likely to take a particular form, leading up to an explosive moment and then retreating from it.[13] The personalities, as Shakespeare realizes, are very important, but they only contribute to, rather than direct, the general sweep of events. It thus makes sense, as Ford-Davis sought to do, to play the tribunes as themselves partly bewildered, partly carried along by the political momentum, while struggling to maintain, or manifest, some control.

After Coriolanus's banishment, the city cools off, the citizens carry their children through the streets and go on Sunday picnics. The importance of the tribunes, and of the whole political trouble, diminishes as the focus closes on Marcius and his final conflict. When he faces his mother before the gates of Rome, he cannot but succumb – especially in the kind of interpretation that Olivier and

Cariou gave the role. It would, I suppose, be possible to play Marcius as if he really were author of himself and knew no other kin, a genuine 'thing of blood' and nothing else, but then III.ii would be less subtle, and the climactic scene would seem puzzling and inconsistent. After Volumnia has finished her long plea, there is an unusually precise stage direction: *'Takes her by the hand, silent.'* True to his conception to the last, Shakespeare resists the temptation to give Coriolanus's conflict voice – it remains inward. In Bedford's Stratford Ontario production, unfortunately, this famous direction was ignored: there was little or no pause, and the two principals were separated by an expanse of stage – why I could not tell. Just as surprisingly, Aufidius's sardonic comment (he has been watching the whole time), 'I was moved withal', was dropped. So that the complex impact of the scene, with Coriolanus pulled between the two dominating figures in his life, was narrowed and flattened. This was particularly disappointing because it went against the carefully constructed picture that had been built up in the earlier acts.

After his long silence, when he speaks to his mother, Marcius manifests a new self-awareness:

> O my mother, mother! O!
> You have won a happy victory to Rome;
> But, for your son, believe it – O believe it –
> Most dangerously you have with him prevail'd,
> If not most mortal to him. But let it come.
> (v.iii.185–9)

The words may be wrung from him in desperation (as Cariou played it), or spoken softly, gently, with a new calm. I prefer the second way since it indicates that, at least for the moment, he knows that death is in store for him, even if he seems momentarily to forget it when he returns to Corioles.

Olivier made that death shocking and spectacular, an extreme image for the character and the play (see Plate 15). Kenneth Tynan describes it thus:

> Olivier is roused to suicidal frenzy by Aufidius's gibe – 'thou boy of tears!' *'Boy!'* [he] shrieks . . . and leaps up a flight of precipitous steps to vent his rage. Arrived at the top, he relents . . . throws his sword away . . . [and] allows a dozen spears to impale him. He is

poised, now, on a promontory some twelve feet above the stage,
from which he topples forward, to be caught by the ankles so that
he dangles, inverted, like the slaughtered Mussolini.[14]

It was the same promontory on which he had first appeared and
from which he had cried, 'I banish you', at the climax of the third act.
As he dangled there, Aufidius stabbed him in the belly.

In keeping with the more ritualized mode of Bedford's
production, Cariou's death was enacted within a kind of frenzied
dance. Coriolanus was above, alone on the small Stratford balcony,
as Aufidius hurled his insults of 'Traitor' and 'Boy'; the crowd was
chanting 'Kill, kill' as Aufidius went up and stabbed him slowly
from behind. Like Olivier, he toppled from above, the upward
vertical thrust of the play dramatically reversed. He was caught by
the chanting multitude, who went abruptly quiet as they lowered
Coriolanus to the stage and Aufidius descended to put his foot
triumphantly on the now-dead body. Suddenly Aufidius seemed to
recognize the enormity of what he had done, he removed his foot,
and spoke his last lines with genuine grief. At the close, the entire
Volscian citizenry, who seemed more or less equivalent to their
Roman counterparts and were played by the same actors, turned
and stared coldly at the audience for a second before the lights went
off – implicating us somehow in the catastrophe.

This desire to widen the implications of the tragedy was behind
Hands' decision, in his 1977 RSC production, to bring the Romans
back on at the end in a kind of funeral procession. The point was to
provide a follow-through on most of the major characters and to
show that each was somehow destroyed. Cominius, as well as
Menenius, was 'broken', the tribunes had lost their authority,
Aufidius and the women were all suffering in their own way.[15]
Despite Coriolanus's reckless extravagance, his loss is a
diminishment for all who knew him.

17

The Winter's Tale

When Daphne Dare, the designer of the Stratford Ontario production of *The Winter's Tale* in 1978, was working on the setting of the last scene, she asked researcher Dan Ladell to get her some photos of the shrine at Lourdes. Ladell was mystified, but complied with the request. The design that emerged featured large banks of candelabra behind the statue of Hermione which were indeed inspired by those of Lourdes (see Plate 16). The candles were lighted one by one at the beginning of the scene, creating a solemn, almost religious, atmosphere, and underlining the feeling of mystery that is unique to this play.[1] Peter Brook touches on the same feeling when he writes that 'the statue that comes to life is the truth of the play'. He continues, 'The way to understand this scene is not to discuss it, but to play it', recognizing that what he would call the play's 'holiness' can only be fully elicited on the stage.[2] And I remember a great teacher of Shakespeare, and a fine actor in his own right, Dan Seltzer, once declaring to a lecture hall crammed with Harvard undergraduates that Hermione *really* dies, and *really* comes back to life; the response to his words was a burst of spontaneous applause. In all these reactions, we can detect the strong pull of the miraculous as the play exerts it.

Not that the whole play calls for reverence and solemnity. The elements in it are very much mixed. To begin with, it has an unusual structure: two halves, divided by a gap of sixteen years, which the bearded figure of Time invites us to leap over in the course of a single speech. In the second half, there is a good deal of humour, plus a joyous, springlike celebration which leads eventually to the beautiful and mysterious ending. The ravages of Leontes' obsessive jealousy, which have been the tragic subject of the first half, are undone, and the various figures reconciled through the beneficent power of the young and the patient repentance of the old. *The Winter's Tale*, more than any other play of Shakespeare, makes manifest the formal structure of the romantic 'tragi-comedy'; the emblematic, non-rational features of that genre are exploited to the full, while at the same time they are infused with a grace, a sadness

219

and a psychological profundity that mark the play as supremely special.

We start with Leontes' jealousy. It is an odd beginning, just because of the violent implausibility of his obsession. But throughout the play Shakespeare either ignores or underlines the improbability of his story, challenging his audience to accept what is difficult to believe. In the present case, he reduces the credibility of Leontes' jealousy by stripping from him any plausible motivation; Hermione, in the eyes of everyone else, is above suspicion. Nothing that she does is in the least suggestive. This is different from the prose romance on which Shakespeare based his story, where the king is partially justified. A production that seeks to make it easier on Leontes by compromising Hermione's behaviour with Polixenes simply makes a mistake. The whole point is that Leontes' obsession comes from inside.

Still it has to be staged, to be expressed externally. And the question is, how? If the scene is Lapland, as it was for the RSC production in 1976 (directed by John Barton with Trevor Nunn), it will perhaps take place before a tent, or around a fire. If, on the other hand, it is a court somewhere in Eastern Europe near the end of the last century, the scene might be an elegant ball with uniformed gentlemen, finely arrayed ladies, and the strains of a Viennese waltz. This was how Robin Phillips chose to do it at Stratford Ontario, in the production already mentioned, and the opening effect was bright and grand. The short conversation between two seasoned courtiers that begins the play was a relaxed chat spoken at the side while dancers moved gracefully over the floor. Leontes and Hermione were downstage centre and Polixenes just behind. Gradually the stage cleared as Leontes urged Polixenes to extend his stay at the Sicilian court. By the time he turned to Hermione for help the couples were gone, leaving Hermione and Polixenes stage centre sipping wine, and Leontes lurking slightly in the background. But not suspicious, not at first. In the RSC's 1981 production, also set in the Victorian period, the opening exchange was more intimate and domestic. Hermione sat centre stage on a low stool, and Leontes lounged on the floor with his head on her lap. Here again there was little or no suspicion.

Now arises a crucial question – when does Leontes' jealousy first show itself? He is silent for a long while as his friend and wife converse, and his question when he finally does speak, 'Is he won yet?' (I.ii.86), indicates that he has not been listening. Has he been in a dark reverie, has he simply been busy with a courtier, has he been chattering with his son Mamillius (as Brian Bedford was at Stratford Ontario)? 'Is he won yet?' may be our first indication that Leontes is suspicious – it may come crafty, as one of many early hints; or it may simply be an innocent question as he turns back from whatever has engaged him. Hermione's answer, 'He'll stay, my lord', may ignite the horrible suggestion; for Leontes' half-muttered response, 'At my request he would not', may easily contain the poison that so quickly infects him. This was how Bedford played it. Innocent until 'Is he won yet?', he followed Hermione's reply with an immense pause, the ghastly idea taking hold at that moment, and then revealing itself in the petulant aside.[3] Patrick Stewart (RSC, 1981) spoke 'Is he won yet?' in a drawling, bored voice, his head still lounging in his lady's lap. He had, presumably, been thinking of something else. But in the exchange that follows 'He'll stay, my lord' Stewart introduced a dangerous boisterousness, even a touch of malice, while still remaining basically non-committal. He held off the full onset of jealousy till the last possible minute.[4] We might note in passing that it would be possible to play 'At my request he would not' in quite a jovial accent – as if to say, I knew you'd be able to convince him. Leontes' next words, 'Hermione, my dearest, thou never spok'st / To better purpose', would thus follow from what he has just said, instead of seeming like a strained cover-up. That approach, however, would lose the telling undertone that Stewart gave it.

Hermione's part in this sequence is to tease her husband, unaware of any strain he may be showing. She gets him to admit that once before she has spoken to as good purpose as she has just now:

> That was when,
> Three crabbed months had sour'd themselves to death
> Ere I could make thee open thy white hand
> And clap thyself my love. Then didst thou utter
> 'I am yours for ever.'
>
> (I.ii.101–5)

What special weight may be added to this speech, especially the last phrase, if Leontes' jealousy is beginning to fester? Stewart, for example, had been holding his wife's hands and, on 'clap thyself my love', suddenly slapped them, hard. If the air is thus supercharged,

Hermione, and perhaps Polixenes, will sense it, but they will probably be puzzled, not knowing its source.

The latest that the jealousy can strike is after Hermione's next gracious, teasing and slightly flirtatious speech (Hermione's pregnancy perhaps contributes to her sense of blithe confidence and gaiety): 'The one *for ever* earn'd a royal husband [is she answering her husband's tone by echoing his words?], / Th' other for some while a friend [does she turn from Leontes to take their friend by the hand?].' This is followed immediately by Leontes' 'Too hot, too hot . . .' and he is launched on the destructive course that will take him through the next three acts – to estrangement from his friend, the death of his son, and the presumed deaths of both his wife and daughter. Even here Stewart held back, speaking 'Too hot, too hot! / To mingle friendship far is mingling bloods' *not* as an aside, which is usual, but directly to Polixenes and Hermione as an apparent joke. Only after that, as wife and friend moved away, slightly uncomfortable, did he very suddenly change to the bitter tone he maintained throughout most of the act.

Another, different way of playing the whole scene would be to show Leontes jealous from the very beginning, though managing to restrain it until after his suspicions are 'confirmed'. His invitation to Polixenes to remain longer would thus be darkly coloured by a hidden desire to catch his friend and wife in the act, and to arrange for the former's death. This would tend to make the atmosphere uncomfortable, Polixenes sensing something unsettling in his host's manner. Thus his refusal to accede to Leontes' wishes would be clearly motivated, and both it and his subsequent surrender to Hermione's invitation would be rendered plausible and feed Leontes' suspicions. The problem with this interpretation is that it reduces the dramatic suddenness, and hence the arbitrariness, of the onset of Leontes' jealousy. It makes it more acceptable and understandable, which is precisely what the text seems to preclude.

In 1969, Trevor Nunn and the RSC set the opening scene in Mamillius's nursery, seeking an overt way to manifest Leontes' mental state. They fitted the stage with outsized nursery toys, all in white, including a hobby-horse that one critic described as 'symbolic of both innocence and lust'.[5] The emphasis was on Leontes' immaturity and his 'Peter Pan inner life',[6] and the style chosen was one in which internal events were given an external, symbolic correlative. Accordingly, there was a startling lighting-effect just at the moment when Leontes' jealousy hit; its effect was to change the colour of Polixenes' costume from brown to 'lurid red'.[7] Later, when Hermione was put in prison, a huge white doll with a black eye appeared on stage. As Robert Speaight noted, the effect of this kind of thing was to emphasize the 'old tale' quality of the play, its deliberate unreality, but for many viewers the whole thing was too pointed, too conceptual and too inflexible.[8]

What such a deliberately emblematic approach may easily miss is the other, sharply realistic, side of these scenes. Leontes' jealousy may be rooted in fantasy and erupt as in a fairy tale, but at the same time it is disturbingly real. The language he uses – the obsessiveness with which he seizes on certain words and meanings – opens up his inner life and the actor must bring that out. Words leap out at him, betraying meanings which he seeks to dodge, but which at the same time he himself is creating: 'Go, play, boy, play', he says to Mamillius; 'Thy mother plays, and I / Play too, but so disgrac'd a part, whose issue / Will hiss me to my grave' (ll. 187–9). Or take this earlier speech, also to his son:

> What, hast smutch'd thy nose?
> They say it is a copy out of mine. Come, captain,
> We must be neat; not neat, but cleanly, captain.
> And yet the steer, the heifer, and the calf
> Are all call'd neat. – Still virginalling
> Upon his palm? – How now, you wanton calf?
> Art thou my calf?
>
> (ll. 121–7)

The thought process here is complex and tortuous, as it is throughout Leontes' speeches in this section. He is tossed by violent emotion. The suspicion that Hermione's coming child is none of his turns him to examining Mamillius for signs of his paternity. He is solicitous, fatherly – 'we must be neat'. But the word 'neat' catches him – its subsidiary meaning, 'cattle', reminds him of horns, the badge of the cuckold. He seeks to suppress the suggestion, but it gets away from him. He can't resist a glance at Hermione and Polixenes on the other side of the stage. They are still talking together, animated, courtly – does she touch his hand? For Leontes, she is 'virginalling'. The word, a luminous example of Shakespeare's tendency to turn nouns into verbs, comes from 'virginals', an early keyboard instrument like the spinet; but there is a suggestion of wantonness, of playing, in the usage, ironically contrasting with the root association. The fixation on 'wanton' and on horns (neat–cattle–calf) continues to infect his language as he turns back to his son – 'How now, you wanton calf?' The 1981 RSC production gave Leontes assistance here by involving him in a tussle with his son in which Mamillius played a bull with finger-horns charging at his father. Such an overt illustration may seem unnecessary, but it can help both audience and actor through a difficult and revealing series of mental associations.

Once established, Leontes' jealousy takes its cruel course, without effective interruption. The tragic direction of the first part of the play is clearly marked, and Hermione is its central victim. Throughout her persecution, she remains astonishingly calm and dignified, a figure of wit and grace, totally free of falseness, self-pity or pomposity – though some may find her too accepting of her husband's perversity. In II.i, she undergoes a public accusation that is at least as degrading as that Othello hands out to Desdemona, and in III.ii, she withstands the injustice of a rigged trial. She is patient, but she speaks strongly in her own defence. There is nothing soppy about her.

In 1969, Judi Dench doubled the part of Hermione with that of Perdita, a feat first performed by Mary Anderson in 1887 and one not often attempted since. It offers the obvious advantage of continuity between mother and daughter, who do, in fact, share many of the same characteristics; where Hermione, however, tends toward dignity and even gravity, Perdita, fittingly, is more youthful and naïve. The problem with the doubling comes up in the final scene, when both characters have to be on-stage at the same time – a requirement that is likely to distract by the ingenuity with which it is met. In the 1969 production, Leontes fainted at the statue's likeness to his dead wife, a curtain was closed, the actual statue was removed, and Perdita, who had discreetly slipped away, became Hermione as the curtain was reopened. Meanwhile, a Perdita double slipped on, carefully masked from the audience. It was all accomplished quite unobtrusively, but still proved distracting to many viewers.[9]

To stress the connection between Hermione and Perdita by having them played by the same actress is to emphasize the symbolic side of the play – the association of both of them with spring and rebirth, for example. It makes both characters predominantly emblematic and, even in the hands of a great actress such as Dench, is likely to reduce their individual humanity. This will affect particularly the reconciliation scene, with its moving sense of a great gap being bridged. Perdita's silence in the text does not necessarily mean near-invisibility. But in Nunn's 1969 production, where the emphasis was on overt symbolism and where the *art* of the play, the fact that it is a play, was underlined (remember the hobby-horses and the doll with the black eye), such an emblematic conception of the central female role was quite consistent.

On the other hand, it would have been out of place in a production such as that of Robin Phillips at Stratford Ontario. There, the interest in psychological realism led to quite a different emphasis. Hermione, played by a relatively inexperienced but gracious actress, Margot Dionne, was overshadowed by Paulina, played by Martha Henry. The latter's scenes with Leontes, in a move that I found both surprising and rich, became the psychological centre of the play. Interest shifted away from the pastoral scenes in the fourth act, for a long time now the focus of academic and critical inquiry because of their elaboration of important themes: art and nature, springlike renewal, and so on. And Paulina, rather than either Hermione or Perdita, became the dominant female presence. Dramatically, what seemed to matter most was the creeping, destructive madness of Leontes, tight-lipped, repressed and violent, and the equally powerful, but much louder, sanity of Paulina and her intense insistence on justice. The two were sharply, evenly, matched, nowhere more so than in the scene where Paulina brings him his baby (II.iii). The very presence of the baby has a comic promise in it, which can lighten the dark intensity of the situation. And the scene itself can be quite a funny one, with its echoes of Paulina as the comic scold, Leontes as the harried male flinging out ironic comments, and Antigonus as the hen-pecked husband. But Henry's Paulina refused to fall into the caricatured mould. Leontes kept trying to see her as nothing but a 'callet', a 'hag', a 'crone', but she eluded the designations with a dignified and forceful passion. She was lyrical in her description of the baby's resemblance to her father – 'Behold, my lords, / Although the print be little, the whole matter / And copy of the father'; persuasive and bold in her insistence on justice – 'this most cruel usage of your queen, / Not able to produce more accusation / Than your own weak-hing'd fancy, something savors / Of tyranny'; and fierce in her anger – 'Let him that makes but trifles of his eyes / First hand me'. The result of having a strong Paulina was to underline the madness of Leontes' obsession, to show how totally fixed and immovable he was in his delusion. There was still humour in the scene, but it in a way glanced off the central confrontation, increasing rather than reducing the intensity. The full horror of committing an innocent baby to the fire was allowed to sink in, and, when Leontes changed his mind to order the child's banishment to a 'remote and distant place', he showed no remorse. There remained only our sense of the mysterious ways of old tales, and the announcement of the imminent arrival of the messengers from Delphos, to suggest a possible lifting of the tragic gloom.

To increase Paulina's importance does not, of course, reduce Hermione's stature, although it provokes a different emphasis. Hermione remains the embodiment of a firm, patient strength, revealed especially at her trial. Leontes' obsession leads him to repudiate the words of the oracle, but his wife is ready to withstand even that. It is only the news of Mamillius's death that breaks her spirit, causing the apparent death of the Queen, and an abrupt change of heart in Leontes. The suddenness of this reversal matches that of his shift to jealousy at the outset, though it is more obviously justified and better motivated. It is a return to sanity as swift as his departure.

The shift to the 'comic' half of the play is marked by a strange incident, the last of the tragic mishaps and one tinged with comedy despite its gruesomeness. The stage direction that announces it is justly famous: '*Exit, pursued by a bear*'; and the Clown's description of what happens to poor Antigonus when the bear finally catches up with him is humorously garbled. This bear has plagued producers of the play, who generally do not know what to do with him. The simplest, and perhaps the most common, recourse has been to cut him out, covering Antigonus's exit with a blast of thunder and lightning, or a violent roar. Productions that have brought him on – and in recent years the trend has been to do so – have tried various means.

In the nineteenth century, it was usual to depict the bear realistically – and this fitted in well with the overall style of painstaking illusionistic realism. Under Charles Kean, the bear was even described as 'zestful'. In an open-air production at Regent's Park, London, in the 1930s, reports one critic, 'we saw a very realistic bear rootling about in the bushes as a preliminary to chasing Antigonus'.[10] Such are the advantages of outdoor playing! More recently, the Stratford Ontario production discussed above, in keeping with its stress on realistic solidity, went for a large frightening bear who was seen briefly under a spot.[11] Still, the bear tended to provoke laughter and was cut back as the season went on. By contrast, in the 1981 RSC production, lightning-flashes revealed an enormous, totemic bear rearing up fully twelve feet, with Antigonus in silhouette against it. An even more overtly ritualistic approach was taken by Barton and Nunn in their Lapland version; again the choice was consistent with the overall intent. The bear was unmistakably an *actor* in a huge mask, 'guiding Antigonus off to slaughter';[12] he was conflated with the symbolic figure of Time, who begins the fourth act and the new upward movement of the plot, and in addition was connected ritualistically to Mamillius's games early on in the play, and to the folk dance at the sheep-shearing later on.[13]

The reason why a ritualistic approach such as this might work is that the bear is very much part of the trappings of romance that characterize the play. As such, he makes a fitting introduction to the section where the feeling of romance is strongest. From the dark winter of Leontes' court, we are suddenly transported, on the wings of Time, to the sunny shores of Bohemia. (That the real Bohemia has no coast is simply one of those 'facts' that intrude on the romantic verisimilitude of Shakespeare's pastoral world.) Like the bear, the hoary figure of Time belongs to the world of the old tale, and his presence at the beginning of Act IV is another indication of the radical shift in tone. The very survival of Perdita, her position as queen of the sheep-shearing festival, and the mythic allusions that associate her with springtime, natural growth and rebirth all continue the sense of symbolic significance that lights up the pastoral interlude. It is because of such associations that literary critics have tended to seize on these scenes. But, within the overall symbolic frame, there is a sure feeling for country reality as well, perhaps remembered from Shakespeare's own childhood, just as in other parts of the play domestic and psychological realism is finely balanced by emblematic import.

Various productions have sought to express this country sense and hence to balance the romantic with the realistic. The RSC in 1981 went for a nineteenth-century English setting, with shepherds out of Thomas Hardy and a somewhat caricatured Clown – a bumpkin with carrot hair. Into this world came a rather sophisticated and recognizably Victorian Autolycus, conceived of as a traditional music-hall entertainer, slinky and funny. In Robin Phillips' production at Stratford Ontario, where the stress throughout was on the realism of a late-nineteenth-century East European court, the pastoral scenes were presented in an authentically Slavic, folk milieu, with colourfully embroidered costumes and traditional dances. The contrast with the sombre, frockcoated world of Leontes' court could hardly have been more telling. In keeping with its overtly emblematic reading, the RSC under Nunn in 1969 played the shepherds as hippies and back-to-the-landers (remember, it was 1969!), a choice that according to Robert Speaight tended to oversimplify the Bohemian scenes, whitewashing the greed and duplicity that is to be found there.[14] Whatever specific setting is used, it is essential that we feel the rural reality of this pastoral world, so that its symbolic import is carried lightly, without solemnity.

As characters, Florizel and Perdita are rather thinner than their elders, neither so burdened nor so enriched by experience. Florizel in particular, like other of Shakespeare's romantic heroes, could use a bit of dazzle, or at least masculine sex appeal. He is all too likely to emerge as a bit of a wimp, which is clearly inadequate. He has more grace than, say, Romeo, but less fire. His speech to Perdita 'What you do / Still betters what is done . . .' is as lovely as any of Romeo's but in an entirely different way: for the latter's ardent image-making and impulsive intensity, it substitutes a rhythmic delicacy and measured power that reveal the subtle strength of the character. As for Perdita, as is usual in Shakespeare's comic plays, the lady is far more interesting and lively than her lover. Aside from her gaiety, she has a serious, even apprehensive side; and, to complement her natural queenliness, she is direct and down-to-earth.

When adversity threatens, however, her fearfulness quickly surfaces and she is ready to give up; as the plot thickens, she willingly lets Florizel take the lead. (Unlike the heroines of the great comedies, those of the late romances tend to be passive and submissive, impressing as much by their presence and symbolic stature as by their activity.) When Florizel and Perdita appear before Leontes and are discovered in their masquerade, Florizel appeals movingly for aid:

> Beseech you, sir,
> Remember since you ow'd no more to time
> Than I do now. With thought of such affections,
> Step forth mine advocate. At your request
> My father will grant precious things as trifles.
> (v.i.218–22)

Bedford's Leontes took a long pause before answering Florizel's request: 'I will to your father. / Your honour not o'erthrown by your desires, / I am friend to them and you.' He seemed to be struggling with the whole weight of his past, *remembering*, as Florizel had asked him to do, and, as a result of that expansive retrospection, deciding to aid the suffering youth before him. The result was a turning point of great beauty and sadness. It seemed to open the path for reunions that follow, joyous in their way but also, at least in Phillips' production, tinged with sorrow for what had been lost.

Shakespeare divides the elaborate process of recognition into two separate scenes, in the first one giving us only a report of the discovery of Perdita's true identity. As though to offset our incredulity, the gentlemen who bring the report keep comparing the news to an old tale – which by some strange chemistry only adds to the lovely, muted quality of the scene. Phillips again adopted a solemn tone here, with dark-suited gentlemen waiting in an antechamber, shadowy, still, smoking long Russian cigarettes and talking in hushed voices. Even the comic interchange between Autolycus and the Shepherd and Clown at the end of the scene was underplayed.

Shakespeare saves his theatrical magic for the second of the two recognition scenes – the discovery, indeed the resurrection, of Hermione. How to do this precious moment, as difficult as, and even more fragile than, the opening? The way to understand it, says Peter Brook, is not to discuss it but to play it. It works on stage, partly because we are all children in the theatre, ready and eager to accept the magic before us. Awkward questions, such as what was Hermione doing during those sixteen years, don't arise until afterwards, and even then they are irrelevant. The essential thing here is that we are witnessing a domestic reunion, a moment of intensity whose joy is inner, and whose tone is therefore likely to be subdued. This is certainly the trend nowadays in any case. In the RSC's Lapland version, 'Leontes and his family [touched] hands in a silent circle of reunion', creating a feeling of 'mystery and strangeness'.[15] In their later revival too (1981), the closing was 'an ecstasy of calm'.[16] At Stratford Ontario, in keeping with the tone of the previous two scenes, there was an element of profound sadness mixed with the quiet (see Plate 16). When Hermione descended from her dais, she slowly took her husband's hand, then turned away to embrace Perdita. The slightest tinge of bitterness perhaps, or a touch of shy hesitation? At any rate, the lines 'She embraces him

. . . she hangs about his neck', and the actions they imply, were cut.[17] This, perhaps illegitimately, shifts the emphasis, maintaining the sombre tone, keeping gaiety at arm's length. So too the rather hastily cooked-up marriage between Paulina and Camillo was dropped. At the close, the various figures filed slowly off toward the back, a vision in black and white, as the candles and lights were extinguished. It seemed to me a rich and moving way of doing the ending, but only one way certainly. There is room for the sheer joy of reunion to cancel out the ancient griefs. Either interpretation can sit comfortably with those evocative and retrospective closing lines:

> Lead us from hence, where we may leisurely
> Each one demand and answer to his part
> Perform'd in this wide gap of time since first
> We were dissever'd. Hastily lead away.

18
The Tempest

The Tempest presents the would-be producer with a host of problems – so many in fact that it is a wonder that it is done as often as it is. First of all there is the problem of what to do with the strange, non-human characters such as Ariel and Caliban; then there are the masque, the disappearing banquet and the storm, elaborate stage spectacles all, requiring devices that are likely to call attention either to their own self-conscious cleverness or to the sheer inadequacy of theatrical representation; finally there are some tough but interesting questions about the conception of the main character. Shakespeare originally wrote the play for performance at the court of King James and it displays some of the characteristics of the then-fashionable masque, with its reliance on spectacular and tricky effects. Whether, at that opening performance at Whitehall in 1611, Shakespeare was a little appalled at what he had wrought we shall never know, but it is certainly true that, many times since, the play has been conceived primarily as an excuse for operatic and scenic extravagance. Its literary, and especially its dramatic, values have all too often been lost in the shuffle. Peter Brook has written that, as a plot, the play is uninteresting; as a pretext for costumes and special effects, it is hardly worth reviving; and 'as a potpourri of knockabout and pretty writing it can at best please a few matinee-goers – but usually it only serves to put generations of school children off theatre for life'.[1] Brook may be exaggerating, but, when he himself worked on the play in 1968, he chose to do 'not *The Tempest* but a series of actors' exercises aimed at generating emotions required for that play and gestures to express them'.[2] He sought thereby to get in under the accretions of several centuries. Five years earlier he and Clifford Williams had collaborated on a production in which they toyed seriously with the idea of lifting the scenery at the end and putting all the characters in clown suits in order to 'underline the derisory nature of the play's "resolution" '.[3] They refrained, however.

A related problem that the producer must face is the fact that since the Second World War the play has been overloaded with allegorical

231

and symbolic meanings. Literary critics have seized on its themes of loss and restoration, estrangement and reconciliation, nature and nurture, reality and illusion, and have tended to make it into a sort of parable. This kind of thinking has crept into most general discussions of the play. Critical introductions are often pervaded with it, as the following excerpt, from one of the better modern editions, will show: 'This synthesis [between nature and civilization] suggests that the natural man within us is more contented, better understood, and more truly free when harmonized with reason.'[4] As with turning it into an opera, such allegorizing tends to reduce the play, and, worse still, runs the risk of boredom. It shouldn't surprise us that Brook's imagination leans to iconoclasm in the face of it.

But the difficulty is that the play does invite allegorical treatment; it is conceived in symbolic terms, and it features a number of specifically symbolic characters. For a production to succeed today, it needs somehow to acknowledge and accommodate that symbolic side while at the same time struggling against it.

The theatre has often reacted to too much literary allegorizing by emphasizing the falseness of the very ending that the traditional literary reading regards as constitutive. John Barton turned the ending upside-down by seeing Prospero as played out, weary and disillusioned.[5] Jonathan Miller threw his emphasis on colonization, thus calling Prospero's benevolence into question and revealing the dark side of the 'white man's burden' (both Ariel and Caliban were black).[6] For Barton's production in 1970 and again for Robin Phillips' at Stratford Ontario in 1976, the programme notes stressed the 'fundamentally enigmatic', 'baffling and elusive' quality of the play[7] – this in the teeth of virtual certainty among academics about its symbolic import. We may gather from this insistence in the modern theatre on the play's unsettling qualities that its effect can be more complex and disturbing than most literary analysts have allowed. That it presents a vision of a *kind* of perfection many commentators will still insist – but in that very idea there may lurk something perverse or frightening.

The play deals with magic; of that there can be no doubt. And magic, when it is removed from the sphere of children's entertainment, can be profoundly disturbing. It is not easy for the theatre to catch this magic, because the temptation is always to transform it into effects. And then we may be wowed by wizardry, but are left untouched at the core. This was the mistake too often made by eighteenth- and nineteenth-century productions, which featured grand spectacle, with much flying of Ariel, fantastic disappearing of banquets, miraculous rising and falling of trees, and so forth. These days, there seem to be two opposed attitudes toward the magic: either de-emphasize it as much as possible and approach the play realistically, underlining magic's ultimate inadequacy; or build an approach to the play around the centrality of the magic, but a magic that manifests itself directly and unspectacularly.

One key here is the conception of Ariel. If he is made into a 'deft, accomplished black who . . . absorbs all the techniques and skills of the white master . . . [and] who is then in a position to assume political power when the white master goes back home' (as in Miller's 1970 production),[8] then clearly the magic is being played down in the interests of a realistic, historical point about colonization. Even when Ariel is more recognizably a sprite, it is possible to keep him peripheral, an arm of Prospero's only. One tendency that has, thankfully, disappeared altogether is the Peter Pan Ariel, often played by a balletic or winged young woman. Nowadays we are more likely to get a gymnastic, dominantly physical Ariel, and concomitantly a more muscular conception of the part. Muscularity can lend itself to realism, but it can also be used to hint at an odd unreality, a paradoxical kind of anti-physics. This was the approach favoured in Phillips' production, in which Nicholas Pennell's characterization took its inspiration from the 'eldil' of C. S. Lewis' Venus trilogy – spiritual beings unbound by physical laws and appearing to humans as vibrations or shimmerings.[9] This Ariel had to seek and find a way to make himself visible: he moved on the spot and spoke as though from a distance. He was, according to one critic, the very manifestation of the magic of the island; it was as though 'a portion of the air had taken form and motion', and hence it was possible to believe that he actually was invisible (see Plate 17).[10] Thus was created an occult, non-materialist realism, centred on magic and spiritual power.

This Ariel epitomized Phillips' stylized, almost abstract, approach to the play. Everything in his production was simple and pared down. The stage was bare, dominated only by a large white disc which seemed partly a magic talisman and partly a lordly, tinted sun. Instead of a sense of the natural elements themselves, Phillips tried to give us their 'animate spirits', a 'troop of black-clad, white-faced sexless creatures' who followed Ariel around.[11] This did not always work – some critics jeered at the band of spirits in black leotards – but the point of the exercise, to express the strange otherworldliness of the genuine occult, was certainly a valid and interesting one. The idea was to find a way to place magic at the centre without descending to theatrical 'effects'.

Caliban is another key character. A production can sympathize with him in various ways, or present him as a mere beast, comic or grotesque, harmless or vicious, though a middle road is the most likely course. As with Ariel, the first decision is a physical one: what does Caliban look like? Is he clearly and recognizably a man, usually a black man, or is he in some sort a monster, a monkey, ape or 'moon-calf'? Productions that see the play in colonialist terms, and there have been several, will normally sympathize with Caliban, presenting him as the unjustly treated black, stripped of his land and traditional ways, made to learn an alien language and serve the white lords. Jonathan Miller speaks of 'the demoralized, detribalized, dispossessed shuffling field hand'.[12] David Suchet, in Clifford Williams' 1978 revival, gave Caliban dignity and beauty, but added to this an element of voodoo malice, carrying around a manikin-like model of Prospero. But, since the latter remained gracious and kind, he seemed not to deserve such ire.[13]

In the nineteenth century, it was frequently the practice of the star actor–managers to take the part of Caliban. This could lead to some sentimental sympathy for him, though there was none of the modern hint of the slave's moral superiority to his master. The motivation was mostly theatrical bravado, not political or ethical conviction. Frank Benson's 'missing-link Caliban . . . could clamber nimbly up a tree and hang head downwards from a branch, chattering with rage at Prospero'.[14] And this was when he was sixty-three years old! Beerbohm Tree's tear-jerking finale climaxed in a tableau on which the curtain rose to reveal Prospero's ship on the horizon and Caliban (played by Tree) 'stretching out his arm towards it in mute despair'.[15] No ideology of liberation there, just a bit of old-fashioned racism. The text, in fact, makes it fairly clear that Caliban will be delighted to have his island to himself again, even though he tends to fall easily into subservient postures.

If Caliban is visualized as a monster, he is likely to strike us as rather comic, even amiable, though it is certainly possible to make him hideous and frightening. Since the lovable beast does not fit in very well with modern, serious conceptions of the play, it is not much seen these days. Caliban is now usually human, but does not always inspire ideological sympathy. In Phillips' production, in keeping with the overall design, Caliban was a man, but one conceived in symbolic terms. He was bound to the earth, very much its creature; at the rehearsal stage, Phillips actually wanted to tie the actor up in order to induce in him the proper feeling.[16] In performance, Caliban appeared twisted and dirty, his face out of kilter, his body wracked.

As an earth creature, Caliban has a closer link to the island than the interlopers, and Shakespeare gives him an expressive language to describe his responses. It is speeches such as his 'Be not afeard; the isle is full of noises . . .' (iii.ii.137ff.), or 'I prithee, let me bring thee where crabs grow . . .' (ii.ii.165ff.), that have led to the recent reappraisal of him and the emphasis on his sensitivity and victimization. Such speeches, and the earnest vulnerability that seems to characterize him, do indeed prompt us to sympathy, and hence make us uneasy about his treatment at Prospero's hands. Overall, he seems to pull in two directions at once, and productions need somehow to mark that doubleness.

The central figure, however, is certainly Prospero, and other directorial decisions will follow from the initial decision about how to read the enigmatic magician. What are Prospero's motivations? What does he intend to do with Alonso and the rest? At the beginning of the last scene, prompted by Ariel, he seems to decide to forgive his enemies. But, if that is the case, what were his original intentions? Benevolence used to be Prospero's middle name, but that is true no longer. Now we are accustomed to looking askance at him, asking embarrassing questions, taking note of his tendency to quick anger, his habit of bullying people, his arbitrary moods – the arrogance, we might say, of his power. We are aware too of the limitations of the magic that he professes, its inability to touch the heart. On the other hand, he is also aware of those limitations, as he is too of the darker tendencies of humankind, which he in no way sentimentalizes. His loneliness can make him appealing, though it casts a shadow over the ending of the play. Despite his schemes of reconciliation and dynastic marriage, he remains aloof, on a pinnacle, even weary and a bit sad. With such an interpretation of Prospero, the play can become, as the *New York Times* wrote of Phillips' production, a 'masque of resignation', an approach that stresses Prospero's sadness, but is basically positive.[17] Michael Hordern's Prospero, in Williams' 1978 revival mentioned above, took a similar course, continually softening the peremptoriness of the character; he seemed, according to Irving Wardle, to be aware of greed and cold hearts, and was nevertheless kindly.[18] By contrast, presenting Prospero as primarily wilful and tyrannical yields a much less sympathetic reading, with, probably, a concomitant notion of Caliban as a victim of colonialist oppression. In Williams' production Caliban was such a victim, but, with such a kindly Prospero, several critics noted a contradiction. Miller, exploring the colonialist implications of the play, did not take the easy way out by simply devaluing Prospero. Graham Crowden projected a substantial Jacobean gentleman under the tattered magical robe, a man who had to carry, in difficulty and pain, the weight of his own authority.[19]

No matter how hard he is, Prospero seems to have at least two soft spots – one for his daughter, the other for Ariel. He treats both of them harshly at times, especially Ariel, whom he attacks for presuming to mention his master's promise of freedom. There is a charged hostility in the opening scene between them that justifies an accusation of tyranny against Prospero. But, when he says at the end that he will miss Ariel, I think he means it, not only because he will miss the power that Ariel enacts, but also because he genuinely cares for his loyal henchman. Ariel asks, 'Do you love me master? No?' Ian Richardson, in Barton's production, made it a key moment. 'Dearly, my delicate Ariel', he replied, the voice hesitating and breaking for the first time. A few minutes later, he reached for his spirit's hand and found only air.[20] That he also loves Miranda seems beyond question. Perhaps, in fact, he stages the whole elaborate show only for her benefit. It is not clear that he wants his dukedom back, but he certainly wants to place her where he thinks she belongs. If 'every third thought' will be his grave, the intervening ones will undoubtedly be turned less to matters of state and more to the couple who will unite the principalities of Milan and Naples.

Whatever Prospero's inner motions, what he actually does is to present shows, or 'revels', to an enthralled audience – whether it be composed of desperate mariners faced with a profoundly realistic (to them at least) storm, a group of guilty courtiers confronted with an enchanted banquet, or a pair of lovers rapt in wonder at the sight of a masque of spirits. Indeed, each of these spectacles within the play is like a model of the play itself, which Prospero as master of the revels presents to us. It is little wonder, then, that his farewell to his art has so often been linked with Shakespeare's own; it is undoubtedly a romantic fantasy to see the author in the magician–enchanter, but it is a very appealing one. (The fact that *The Tempest* may very well be Shakespeare's last complete play has fed the myth. But, unfortunately for romantic consistency, he seems to have collaborated on at least two other plays after this 'farewell'.)

The key problem in the presentation of the masque elements is one of style. How does one find a style that fits credibly with the overall conception, whether the emphasis is on colonialism, magic, symbolic reconciliation and renewal, or weary and resigned futility? Artifice is bound to play a role, but how to make it convincing? Some productions will seek to hide the artifice, others will frankly admit it. The latter seems the more desirable course, since it is impossible to represent the magic realistically. Provoking the audience into acknowledging and accepting the theatricality may involve them more deeply in the process that is unfolding on-stage, where the characters are continually being faced with spectacular events and encouraged to respond.

The initial stumbling-block is the storm that begins the play. It appears to be real, i.e. not a product of Prospero's magic, and then is shown later to be artificial. So one option is to try to make it look and feel real. Lightning and sound effects may help, and a director will usually throw in some swinging ropes or creaking rigging, plus maybe a gauze curtain in front to give the effect of distance and mist. Actors will shout and pitch about on the stubbornly unmoving stage-deck. The trouble is that a storm, as the example of *King Lear* makes clear, is very hard to represent adequately on stage – especially on board ship. Only one production I know of took the most extreme expedient – cutting the scene altogether and replacing it with a 'choreographed swim'.[21] Most productions unfortunately fall back on convention ('flickering spotlights and bawling sailors' in Miller's and 'sailors and passengers reeling repetitively and predictably up and down the same rope' in Barton's).[22] An alternative approach would be frankly to admit the inadequacies and use undisguised stage devices to signify the storm, although this would have to fit with the style of later scenes.

In III.iii, 'strange shapes' appear bringing in a banquet, which they invite the King and courtiers to eat; no sooner are the latter, suitably amazed, ready to set to than Ariel appears *'like a harpy; claps his wings upon the table; and, with a quaint device, the banquet vanishes'*. Exactly how the quaint device worked at Whitehall we shall never know, but it was undoubtedly ingenious and spectacular. Whether Shakespeare himself was aware of how the effect would be gained when he first imagined the scene is itself doubtful; can we detect a little of the easy arrogance of the playwright who simply scribbles 'quaint device' and throws the problem into the hands of the technicians? Again it is a matter of finding a credible way to represent the incredible. Since the banquet is part of Prospero's plan to induce amazement and, ultimately, repentance in his enemies, it needs to be convincing to *them*. Miller, perhaps wisely, threw the burden on his actors, suspending the banquet invisibly above the audience, Alonso and his court reaching for it 'with greed and fear written in their faces'.[23] Since these would-be colonialists had already faced the island with a combination of rapture and rapaciousness, the moment fitted aptly into the whole conception.

The masque which Prospero creates for the entertainment and edification of Miranda and Ferdinand (IV.i) is different from the disappearing banquet since it is presented consciously as a show, and its audience know that its actors are all spirits. They are thus in a more privileged position than the courtiers, who are being worried into repentance. The young lovers have only to watch and admire – a little like us in the wider audience. The sense of wonder that they exhibit should somehow be ours as well, though all too often the dancing nymphs and floating goddesses appear faintly absurd. Benedict Nightingale criticized Miller's production for turning the masque into a 'pastiche' featuring an Oriental, an African and a European all in flowing robes, a 'lush, sentimental tapestry brought to life', and mocked Barton's 'three nearly naked men, with what looked like long straws in their hair, crooning in the half-dark'.[24] There may be a way to bring the masque off successfully, but I must admit I have never seen one.

The masque celebrates the betrothal of the young couple, and sings eloquently of fertility and harvest. Its promise makes up for Prospero's heavy and distasteful insistence on pre-marital chastity at the beginning of the scene, a parental gravity that I should like to see undercut by a little bit of stolen passion on the part of Ferdinand and Miranda. When the former says, 'The white cold virgin snow upon my heart / Abates the ardor of my liver', must he be wholly in earnest? I should like to see a Ferdinand with more blood and more of a glinting sense of irony than that line alone might suggest. A little humour to accompany the passion, fertility and wonder may not be out of place.

Prospero abruptly breaks off the masque, aware suddenly of the 'foul conspiracy / Of the beast Caliban and his confederates'. But, before turning to that business, he takes time to deliver one of the grandest and most famous of all Shakespearean speeches: 'Our revels now are ended. . . .' It is a set-piece, of course, and hence presents a serious difficulty to actors, most of whom feel that they must struggle against its familiarity and seek new emphases and intonations. The disillusioned, weary or even bitter Prosperos will necessarily adopt a different accent from the more traditional benevolent ones. There is certainly material for the former interpretation – the idea of the insubstantiality of all human endeavour, the littleness of our sleep-rounded lives, the sense above all of an ending. 'Sir, I am vexed', says Prospero; 'my old brain is troubled'. And we ought to believe him. If the currently popular weariness, disillusion and cynicism tend sometimes to be exaggerated, the old benevolence was often sentimental.

The comics, who unwittingly interrupt Prospero's revels with their 'conspiracy', are not the funniest of Shakespeare's clowns. Thematically, Caliban's plan to have Stephano kill Prospero and then rule the island is linked to the other usurpations and attempted murders in the play: that of Antonio against Prospero many years before (which has led to the present long-delayed revenge); and that of Sebastian and Antonio against Alonso, which is plotted, rather absurdly given the circumstances, on the island itself. Hence the 'conspiracy' of the sub-plot is a comic parody of the more serious machinations in the main plot. That, plus the opportunity it affords for a bit of drunken boisterousness, and, we may hope, some deft comic business from the jester Trinculo, is the chief reason for the presence of Stephano and Trinculo on the island. Stephano can too easily be a strutting boor, but Trinculo often displays a flair for comic inventiveness. In Phillip's production, he appeared as a ventriloquist with a little doll, a nice touch which bore ironic fruit in the scene where the invisible Ariel's interruptions keep getting Trinculo into trouble (III.ii).

The ending effects a reunion of all the separated characters, including our comic friends, and confers on each an appropriate measure of justice, freedom or simple explanation. It is in a way Prospero's final, and climatic, act. It is preceded by the key scene, already mentioned, when Prospero appears to be moved to forgive his enemies. Ariel begins the process by commenting, 'your charm so strongly works 'em / That if you now beheld them, your affections / Would become tender'. 'Dost thou think so, spirit?' asks Prospero, and Ariel's reply seems to tip the balance: 'Mine would, sir, were I human' (v.i.17–20). Phillips' production gave the moment 'climactic weight', Ariel reaching out and taking his master's hand. Thus when the reply came, 'And mine shall', it marked a decisive change. Hesitation and doubt accompanied the decision to forgive.[25] The older way to do the scene is less troubled, Prospero simply confirming in his benevolent way the intention he has had all along.

A similar dual possibility runs through the famous abjuration of magic, which follows immediately, and through the elaborate show that makes up the *dénouement*. Is Prospero edgy, uncertain, or divided, or does he devote himself wholeheartedly to his 'project'? His feelings are certainly engaged, and it would be wrong, I think, to portray him as providentially above the events he so carefully choreographs. His connection to Ariel runs strongly through the scene; there too, perhaps, he has to struggle with his feelings: 'I shall miss thee; / But yet thou shalt have freedom'. It is a poignant moment when he gives him up for ever: 'My Ariel, chick, / That is thy charge. Then to the elements, / Be free, and fare thou well!' (v.ii.320–1). Ariel, however, is only delighted; any sentimentality, such as that of Charles Kean's ending in the 1840s, which had Prospero's ship sailing away in the distance and a saddened Ariel, 'alone in mid-air, watching the departure of his late master',[26] would be out of place.

About the humans whose lives he is trying to mould, Prospero also seems to have mixed feelings. Miranda's awestruck comment when she first sees all the gorgeous courtiers – 'How beauteous mankind is! O brave new world, / That has such people in 't!' – is ironically tempered by her father's more realistic reply, ' 'Tis new to thee.' But both the darkness of his feelings and the limitations of his magic are best illustrated in his confrontation with his vicious brother. Of the members of the court party, only Antonio seems untouched by the strangeness of their experience. He says nothing. But how is his silence to be interpreted? Like the silence of Isabella at the end of *Measure for Measure*, it might mean acceptance (grudging or otherwise) or rejection. A decision must be made, and directors who take a dim or ironic view of the reconciliation at the end will undoubtedly opt for the more disquieting possibility, while directors who favour Prospero's benevolence and power to transform the heart may well give us an Antonio who responds positively, if silently, to his brother's intervention. Prospero's approach is none too conciliatory:

For you, most wicked sir, whom to call brother
Would even infect my mouth, I do forgive
Thy rankest fault – all of them; and require
My dukedom of thee . . . .

(v.i.131–4)

This hardly seems designed to smooth things over. Hostility and arrogance are as much in evidence as forgiveness and forbearance. Perhaps Antonio's failure to answer signals a recognition of this; or perhaps Alonso's excited interruption, 'If thou beest Prospero . . . ' cuts Antonio off before he has a chance to speak. One recent production I saw gave Alonso's lines to Antonio, thus indicating a major conversion but at the same time erasing the subtlety of the moment.

It seems to me that Shakespeare is fully aware, and wants us also to be aware, of the boundaries of both Prospero's magic and the ephemeral magic of the theatre. There is a sharp glitter to what Prospero does, and a reconciliatory poignancy, but it is temporary and it fails, finally, to move the stubborn heart.

This, I suppose, is why so many recent directors have seen weariness, resignation or bitterness in Prospero's closing gestures, especially the nod toward his grave and the quiet surrender of the epilogue. Finally, it is Prospero who is caught ('Let me not . . . dwell / In this bare island by your spell, / But release me from my bands'). His very last word is 'free' and is part of a prayer. We are reminded of Ariel and even Caliban, who achieve a kind of liberation never granted to the Europeans; like us as we leave the theatre, Prospero and his companions must return to the fetters, golden as they may be, of ordinary life.

Notes

The first time a work is mentioned in these notes, I give the full citation. The first reference to the work in any following chapter is cited by author's name and main title, with subsequent references within chapters to author's name only. In the case of several works by the same author, short titles (or, for reviews, dates) are given whenever there might be ambiguity. I have employed the standard abbreviations for the major Shakespeare journals: *SQ* = *Shakespeare Quarterly*; *SS* = *Shakespeare Survey*.

The text of Shakespeare's works I have used is that edited by David Bevington (Glenview, Ill.: Scott, Foresman, 1980).

INTRODUCTION

1. Peter Brook, *The Empty Space* (Harmondsworth: Penguin, 1972) 18.
2. Brook 43.
3. For the first two examples, see J. C. Trewin, *Shakespeare on the English Stage 1900–1964* (London: Barrie and Rockcliff, 1964) 3, 47; for the third, J. L. Styan, *The Shakespeare Revolution: Criticism and Performance in the Twentieth Century* (Cambridge: Cambridge University Press, 1977) 26.
4. Quoted in Trewin 56.
5. Quoted in Styan 59.
6. Brook 97.
7. Harley Granville-Barker, *Prefaces to Shakespeare*, 1st ser. (London: Sidgwick and Jackson, 1927; rept. 1940) xl.
8. Quoted in Styan 82.
9. Brook 97.
10. Quoted in Styan 86.
11. F. J. Marker and L.-L. Marker, 'Craig and Appia: A Decade of Friendship and Crisis', *Essays in Theatre*, 3.2: 69–71.
12. Trewin 52.
13. William Bridges-Adams, quoted in Styan 84.
14. Trewin 172.
15. See Tyrone Guthrie, *A Life in the Theatre* (New York: McGraw-Hill, 1959) chs 13 and 21.
16. A. C. Sprague, 'Robert Atkins as a Shakespearian Director', *Deutsche Shakespeare-Gesellschaft West Jahrbuch 1973*, 19–30.
17. Robert Speaight, *Shakespeare on the Stage: An Illustrated History of Shakespearian Performance* (Boston, Mass.: Little, Brown, 1973) 163; Trewin 96–8.

18. Guthrie 190–2.
19. Tim O'Brien, 'Designing a Shakespeare Play: *Richard II'*, *Deutsche Shakespeare-Gesellschaft West Jahrbuch 1974*, 111.
20. See, for example, Stanley Wells, 'Director's Shakespeare', *Deutsche Shakespeare-Gesellschaft West Jahrbuch 1976*, 64–78; and Kenneth Muir, 'The Critic, the Director and the Liberty of Interpreting', in J. Price (ed.), *The Triple Bond: Plays, Mainly Shakespearian, in Performance* (University Park, Penn.: Pennsylvania University Press, 1975) 20–9.
21. In Toby Cole and Helen Chinoy (eds), *Directors on Directing* (Indianapolis: Bobbs-Merrill, 1963) 420
22. John Russell Brown, a prominent critic and man of the theatre, has been the most persuasive spokesman for this point of view. See his manifesto, *Free Shakespeare* (London: Heinemann, 1974).
23. Simon Callow, *Being an Actor* (Harmondsworth: Penguin, 1985) 218; and John Barton, *Playing Shakespeare* (London and New York: Methuen, 1984). See also Richard David, *Shakespeare in the Theatre* (Cambridge: Cambridge University Press, 1978) 236–7.
24. John Russell Brown, 'Three Kinds of Shakespeare', *SS*, 18 (1965) 151–2.
25. Michael Kahn, in Ralph Berry, *On Directing Shakespeare: Interviews with Contemporary Directors* (London: Croom Helm, 1977) 84.

CHAPTER 1. *A MIDSUMMER NIGHT'S DREAM*

1. Charles Marowitz, *New York Times*, 19 Mar 1978.
2. Irving Wardle, *The Times*, quoted in *RSC Yearbook 1978*. The production was directed by John Barton.
3. Quoted by John Barber, *Daily Telegraph*, 14 Sept 1970.
4. Peter Thomson, *SS*, 24 (1971) 126; also Styan, *Shakespeare Revolution*, 226.
5. Thomson 126.
6. J. C. Trewin, *Going to Shakespeare* (London: Allen and Unwin, 1978) 99.
7. Styan 97–9.
8. Quoted in Styan 99.
9. David Addenbrooke, *The Royal Shakespeare Company: The Peter Hall Years* (London: William Kimber, 1974) 166–7.
10. 'Spotlight', *Vogue Magazine*, June 1971, quoted in Addenbrooke 168.
11. Brown, *Free Shakespeare*, 45, quoting Brook himself.
12. This production was directed by Ron Daniels. I am indebted to my friend Crispin Elsted for details about it.
13. Dan Ladell, Stratford archivist.
14. Richard Eder, *New York Times*, 8 June 1977.
15. Roger Warren, *SS*, 31 (1978) 144.
16. Martin Knelman, *Saturday Night*, July 1977.

17. Quoted in A. C. Sprague, *Shakespeare and the Actors: The Stage Business in his Plays (1660–1905)* (Cambridge, Mass.: Harvard University Press, 1945) 54.
18. Trewin, *Going to Shakespeare*, 104–5.
19. Warren 142.
20. Brown seems to me right about this; see *Free Shakespeare*, 44; Styan, in *Shakespeare Revolution*, seeks to justify all Brook's decisions, but he is wrong when he claims that Shakespeare's company probably doubled these parts (228). What evidence there is points to a directly opposite conclusion. See W. A. Ringler, Jr, 'The Number of Actors in Shakespeare's Early Plays', in G. E. Bentley (ed.), *The Seventeenth Century Stage* (Chicago, 1968) 110–34.
21. Thomson 126.
22. Warren 143.
23. Styan 225, 231.
24. The production was staged in Vancouver in 1980, directed by Klaus Strassman.
25. Thomson 126.
26. *The Nation*, quoted in Styan 101.

CHAPTER 2. *THE MERCHANT OF VENICE*

1. John Russell Brown, *Shakespeare's Plays in Performance* (London: Edward Arnold, 1966) 73, quoting Kemble.
2. Gordon Crosse, *Shakespearian Playgoing 1890–1952* (London: A. R. Mowbray, 1953) 14.
3. Speaight, *Shakespeare on the Stage*, 61.
4. The term comes from critic Northrop Frye, and has been widely adopted.
5. William Hazlitt, *The Chronicle*, 4 June 1816.
6. Brown, *Free Shakespeare*, 35.
7. Ralph Berry, review of Stratford Ontario *King Lear*, *SQ*, 31 (1980) 172–3.
8. Ann Cook, *SQ*, 30 (1979) 159. (Barton directed the play twice in three years, at the Other Place in 1978 with Marjorie Bland and Patrick Stewart, and at the Royal Shakespeare Theatre in 1981 with Sinead Cusack and David Suchet.)
9. Irving Wardle, *The Times*, 23 Apr 1981.
10. Crispin Elsted, in a letter to the author. See also Michael Coveney, *Financial Times*, 23 Apr 1981.
11. Wardle.
12. Elsted (see n. 10).
13. Trewin, *Going to Shakespeare*, 109.
14. Berry, *On Directing Shakespeare*, 31.
15. Elsted (see n. 10).
16. Bernard Levin, quoted in *RSC Yearbook 1979*, 34.
17. Roger Warren, *SS*, 32 (1979) 204–5.

18. Warren 205.
19. Michael Billington, *The Guardian*, 23 Apr 1981.
20. Billington.

CHAPTER 3. *AS YOU LIKE IT*

1. David, *Shakespeare in the Theatre*, 135.
2. Roger Warren, *SS*, 33 (1980) 179.
3. Peter Thomson, *SS*, 27 (1974) 148–9.
4. Jack Jorgens, *SQ*, 24 (1973) 423.
5. Warren 179.
6. Peter Jenkins, *The Spectator*, 11 Aug 1979, 22.
7. Trewin, *Going to Shakespeare*, 141.
8. Jorgens 423.
9. Walter Kerr, *New York Times*, 8 July 1973.
10. Jorgens 424.
11. David 135–6.
12. Noel Witts, *Plays and Players*, 25.2 (Nov 1977) 23.
13. Roger Warren, *SS*, 31 (1978) 146.
14. Warren (1980) 180.
15. Ian McEwan, *New Statesman*, 10 Aug 1979, 210.
16. Warren (1980) 179.
17. See Warren (1980) 179–80; and Gordon Gow, *Plays and Players*, 26.12 (Sep 1979) 28.
18. Kerr.
19. Gow 28.
20. Thomson 149–50. All the quotations in this paragraph are from Thomson's vivid description of Pasco's performance.

CHAPTER 4. *TWELFTH NIGHT*

1. Interview in *Plays and Players*, 17.2 (Nov 1969) quoted in Stanley Wells, *Royal Shakespeare: Four Productions at Stratford-upon-Avon* (Manchester: Manchester University Press, 1977) 45.
2. Wells 53. The review quoted is from the *Glasgow Herald*, 25 Aug 1969.
3. Berry, *On Directing Shakespeare*, 60.
4. Julius Novick, *The Nation*, 16 Aug 1980, 164.
5. Styan, *Shakespeare Revolution*, 93.
6. Wells 52, 55.
7. The quotations are from, in order, *The Observer*, 11 Jan 1931; Ronald Bryden, *The Observer*, 24 Aug 1969; P. Thomson, *SS*, 28 (1975) 145; Sprague, *Shakespeare and the Actors*, 4.
8. T. J. Spencer, quoted in Brown, *Free Shakespeare*, 67.
9. Robert Speaight, *SQ*, 20 (1969) 438–9.
10. RSC 1979, directed by Terry Hands. Roger Warren, *SS*, 33 (1980) 170.

11. Hugh Hunt, *Old Vic Prefaces: Shakespeare and the Producer* (London: Routledge and Kegan Paul, 1954) 77–8.
12. Hunt 56–8.
13. *Birmingham Post*, 25 Apr 1958. Quoted in A. C. Sprague and J. C. Trewin, *Shakespeare's Plays Today: Some Customs and Conventions of the Stage* (London: Sidgwick and Jackson, 1970) 95.
14. Wells 50.
15. Quoted in Brown, *Shakespeare's Plays in Performance*, 210.

CHAPTER 5. *MEASURE FOR MEASURE*

1. Quoted in Jane Williamson, 'The Duke and Isabella on the Modern Stage', in Price (ed.), *The Triple Bond*, 168.
2. Williamson 169.
3. Herbert Whittaker, *The Globe and Mail*, 12 June 1975.
4. Berners Jackson, *Hamilton Spectator*, 5 July 1975. Additional information about this moment was supplied to the author by Dan Ladell, archivist at the Stratford Festival.
5. Craig Raine, *New Statesman*, 22 Aug 1975, 230.
6. Richard David, 'Shakespeare's Comedies and the Modern Stage', *SS*, 4 (1951) 137.
7. Brook, *The Empty Space*, 99–100.
8. See Herbert Weil, 'The Options of the Audience: Theory and Practice in Peter Brook's *Measure for Measure*', *SS*, 25 (1972) 27–35; and Williamson 152–3.
9. See Roger Warren, *SS*, 32 (1979) 206–7; and *RSC Yearbook 1979*, 24.
10. The phrase is Guthrie's own, quoted by Williamson 162. The production was staged at the Bristol Old Vic.
11. Styan, describing this scene, quotes from the promptbook, but misidentifies the scene as I.iii: *Shakespeare Revolution*, 215.
12. T. C. Worsley, in the *New Statesman*. Quoted in Styan 216.
13. Peter Thomson, *SS* 24 (1971): 125.
14. Whittaker.
15. The first phrase is Urjo Kareda's, from the *Toronto Star*, 12 June 1975; the second is Whittaker's.
16. Personal discussion with Richard Monette.
17. Williamson 151.
18. Anne Barton, in a programme note.
19. Jackson.
20. Thomson 124.
21. John Elsom, *The Listener*, 21 Aug 1975, 250.
22. David 136–7.
23. Robert Speaight, *SQ*, 21 (1970) 444.
24. The material in the previous two paragraphs has been reconstructed from reviews, from an interview with Robin Phillips in Berry, *On Directing Shakespeare*, 91–105; from

discussions with Dan Ladell, Stratford Festival archivist; and from my own examination of the promptbooks.
25. Elsom 250.

CHAPTER 6. *RICHARD II*

1. Ernst Kantorowicz has written a full account of this political theory in *The King's Two Bodies* (Princeton: Princeton University Press, 1957).
2. Anne Barton, note in programme for 1974 RSC production.
3. David, *Shakespeare in the Theatre*, 169–70.
4. Tim O'Brien, 'Designing a Shakespeare Play: *Richard II*', *Deutsche Shakespeare-Gesellschaft West Jahrbuch 1974*, 113.
5. James Stredder, 'John Barton's Production of *Richard II* at Stratford-upon-Avon', *Deutsche Shakespeare-Gesellschaft West Jahrbuch 1976*, 36.
6. O'Brien 115–16.
7. O'Brien 117, 118.
8. Stredder 42.
9. O'Brien discusses this at length, describing its use for Richard's descent from the walls of Flint Castle.
10. Trewin, *Going to Shakespeare*, 82.
11. David 164.
12. Stredder 38–9; O'Brien 118.
13. John Gielgud, *Stage Directions* (London: Heinemann, 1963) 37.
14. Trewin 88; and Sprague and Trewin, *Shakespeare's Plays Today*, 42–3.
15. David 170.

CHAPTER 7. *HENRY IV, PART 1*

1. The programme note was written by Ronald Bryden; the second quotation is from Michael Billington, *The Guardian*, 25 June 1975.
2. Irving Wardle, *The Times*, 25 Apr 1975; see also David, *Shakespeare in the Theatre*, 199–200.
3. Letter to A. C. Sprague, in Robert Speaight (ed.), *A Bridges-Adams Letter Book* (London: Society for Theatre Research, 1971) 47.
4. Peter Thomson, *SS*, 30 (1976) 154.
5. Brown, *Shakespeare's Plays in Performance*, 44.
6. Michael Billington, *The Guardian*, 25 Apr 1975. Other details about this moment have been culled from the production promptbook in the Shakespeare Memorial Library, from Wardle's review (n. 2), and from Billington's review of *Part 2*, 25 June 1975.
7. Wardle; and B. A. Young, *Financial Times*, 25 Apr 1975.
8. Trewin, *Going to Shakespeare*, 116.
9. In the Shakespeare Library (see n. 6).

CHAPTER 8. *HENRY IV, PART 2*

1. A. C. Sprague, *The Doubling of Parts in Shakespeare's Plays* (London: Society for Theatre Research, 1966) 17–18.
2. For the RSC at the Barbican Theatre.
3. Michael Billington, *The Guardian*, 25 June 1975.
4. David, *Shakespeare in the Theatre*, 205–6; see also Peter Thomson, *SS*, 29 (1976) 154–6.
5. Billington, and Irving Wardle, *The Times*, 25 June 1975.
6. Quoted in the programme for the production, which was directed by Barton, Nunn and Clifford Williams.
7. Trewin, *Going to Shakespeare*, 131.

CHAPTER 9. *HENRY V*

1. Berry, *On Directing Shakespeare*, 57.
2. Sally Beauman (ed.), *The Royal Shakespeare Company's Production of 'Henry V' for the Centenary Season at the Royal Shakespeare Theatre* (Oxford: Pergamon Press, 1976) 10–11.
3. Crosse, *Shakespearian Playgoing*, 105, uses the word 'pacifist' to describe the Guthrie production. See also Beauman 12, quoting J. C. Trewin on the dead wood of tradition.
4. Beauman 15.
5. Bosley Crowther, 'Henry V', in C. W. Eckert (ed.), *Focus on Shakespearean Films* (Englewood Cliffs, NJ: Prentice-Hall, 1972) 61.
6. James Agee, 'Henry V', in Eckert 56.
7. David, *Shakespeare in the Theatre*, 198.
8. Beauman 193.
9. David 199.
10. Beauman 192–3.
11. Beauman 193.
12. Beauman 110.
13. Ralph Berry, *Changing Styles in Shakespeare* (London: Allen and Unwin, 1981) 76, quoting G. L. Evans.
14. David 198.
15. Eliot Norton, quoted in Berry 73.
16. Quoted in Berry 77.
17. See Sprague and Trewin, *Shakespeare's Plays Today*, 52–3, and D. S. Kastan, *SQ*, 33 (1982) 214.
18. Berry 72.
19. The question is complicated, however, by Gower's later ascription of the more emotional motivation to Henry. See IV.vii.5–9.
20. Beauman 200ff.
21. Berry 74.
22. Beauman 137.
23. See John Pettigrew, *Queen's Quarterly*, 73 (1966) 395; and Berry 73.

24. Quoted in Beauman 72.
25. Pistol talks of 'Doll' rather than 'Nell', the latter being his wife, the former the disease-ridden whore from *Henry IV, Part 2*.

CHAPTER 10. *ROMEO AND JULIET*

1. Joan Hartwig, *SQ*, 30 (1979) 208.
2. Robert Speaight, *SQ*, 28 (1977) 188.
3. Michael Billington, *The Guardian*, 2 Apr 1976.
4. Irving Wardle, *The Times*, 5 Apr 1976.
5. Quoted in Trewin, *Going to Shakespeare*, 94.
6. Roger Warren, *SS*, 30 (1977) 170–1.
7. See Crosse, *Shakespearian Playgoing*, 65, and G. W. Stonier, *New Statesman and Nation*, 10 (1935) 598.
8. David, *Shakespeare in the Theatre*, 118.
9. Peter Brook, 'Style in Shakespearean Production', *Directors on Directing*, 422.
10. Both quotations from John Russell Brown, 'Zeffirelli's *Romeo and Juliet'*, *SS*, 15 (1962) 148. See also his *Shakespeare's Plays in Performance*, 167ff., for a revised version of this essay.
11. Benedict Nightingale, *New Statesman*, 6 Apr 1973, 506.
12. Nightingale.
13. Peter Thomson, *SS*, 27 (1974) 150.
14. Roger Warren, *SS*, 34 (1981) 150, 151.
15. John Elsom, *The Listener*, 8 Apr 1976, 449.
16. Thomas Clayton, *SQ*, 31 (1980) 240.
17. Brown, 'Zeffirelli's *Romeo and Juliet'*, 152–3.
18. Trewin 95; and David 28.
19. Brown, *Shakespeare's Plays in Performance*, 175.
20. Brown, 'Zeffirelli's *Romeo and Juliet'*, 152.
21. Warren (1977) 171.
22. Warren (1977) 171.
23. Trewin, *Shakespeare on the English Stage*, 206.
24. Hunt, *Old Vic Prefaces*, 134–5.
25. David 115.
26. Clayton 240.

CHAPTER 11. *JULIUS CAESAR*

1. See John Ripley, *Julius Caesar in England and America 1599–1973* (Cambridge: Cambridge University Press, 1980) 222ff. I am indebted to this fine and thorough book for many of the details cited in this chapter. For the Welles production, see also R. France, *The Theatre of Orson Welles* (Lewisburg, Pa.: Bucknell University Press, 1977) 106–23.
2. Ripley 9.

3. B. J. Field, *Shakespeare's Julius Caesar: A Production Collection* (Chicago: Nelson-Hall, 1980) 6–7.
4. David, *Shakespeare in the Theatre*, 150.
5. Roy Walker, *SS*, 11 (1958) 132.
6. Ripley 271.
7. Berry, *On Directing Shakespeare*, 65.
8. Ripley 272.
9. This description of Wood's performance is culled primarily from Ripley's account of it (272–3). The quotation is from the *New Statesman*, 11 May 1972.
10. Ripley 247.
11. Ripley 249. The quotation 'secretly . . .' is from the *Evening News*, 5 May 1950.
12. The production was directed by Minos Volanakis for the Old Vic in 1962. See Ripley 261.
13. Ripley 258.
14. Harley Granville-Barker, *Prefaces to Shakespeare*, 1st ser. (London: Sidgwick and Jackson, 1927; rept 1940) 73.
15. Ripley 268.
16. The production was directed by John Wood in 1978.
17. Trewin, *Going to Shakespeare*, 157.

CHAPTER 12. *HAMLET*

1. The production was staged in Cologne, and was directed by Hansgünther Heyne. See W. Hortmann, *SQ*, 31 (1980) 410–11.
2. *The Port Folio*, 41 (1823). Quoted in A. C. Sprague, *Shakespearian Players and Performances* (Cambridge, Mass.: Harvard University Press, 1953) 45.
3. Gielgud: Trewin, *Shakespeare on the English Stage*, 117–18; Olivier: Trewin 164; Guinness and Redgrave: Crosse, *Shakespearian Playgoing*, 124, 127.
4. G. L. Evans, *Stratford Herald*, 1 July 1980.
5. Programme notes.
6. *The Times*, 20 Aug 1965.
7. J. C. Trewin, *Birmingham Post*, 20 Aug 1965.
8. David, *Shakespeare in the Theatre*, 70–2, 75–6, 80.
9. Trevor Nunn, interview in *Plays and Players*, 17.12 (Sep 1970). Quoted in Peter Thomson, *SS*, 24 (1971) 122.
10. Thomson 122.
11. Anne Barton, programme note to 1980 RSC production, taken from her introduction to the New Penguin Shakespeare edition.
12. Evans.
13. John Fenton, *Sunday Times*, 6 July 1980.
14. R. L. Sterne, *John Gielgud Directs Richard Burton in Hamlet* (New York: Random House, 1967) 13–14.
15. Michael Billington, *Guardian*, 3 July 1980.
16. Irving Wardle, *The Times*, 3 July 1980.

17. Trewin, *Birmingham Post*.
18. Berry, *Changing Styles in Shakespeare*, 105–6.
19. Berners Jackson, *SQ*, 28 (1977) 198.
20. Addenbrooke, *The Royal Shakespeare Company*, 130.
21. John Kane, quoted in Addenbrooke 129.
22. Tony Church, quoted in Addenbrooke 130.
23. Irving Wardle, *The Times*, 31 May 1977.
24. Berry 105.
25. *The Times*, 20 Aug 1965.
26. David 70.
27. David 71.
28. Details taken from an unpublished account by Richard Knowles.
29. David 66.
30. David 67.
31. Peter Thomson, *SS*, 29 (1976) 151.
32. Robert Speaight, *SQ*, 16 (1965) 321–2.
33. Kenneth Tynan, *He that Plays the King* (London: Longman, 1950) 133.
34. Berry, *On Directing Shakespeare*, 100.
35. This account blends details taken from different reviews: *The Times*; Trewin in the *Birmingham Post* and *Illustrated London News*, 28 Aug 1965; and Speaight in *SQ*.
36. Richard Knowles (n. 28).

CHAPTER 13. *OTHELLO*

1. Robert Speaight, *SQ*, 15 (1964) 379.
2. John Russell Brown, *SS*, 18 (1965) 147.
3. Brown 155.
4. Charles Dickens, *Nicholas Nickleby* (Harmondsworth: Penguin, 1978) 724.
5. *Theatre Arts*, 27 (Dec 1943) 701. Quoted in Norman Sanders (ed.), *Othello* (Cambridge: Cambridge University Press, 1984) 47.
6. Quoted in Sprague, *Shakespearian Players and Performances*, 127.
7. R. Dickins, quoted in Sprague 129.
8. Sanders 47.
9. Ralph Berry, *SQ*, 31 (1980) 172.
10. Quoted in Kenneth Tynan (ed.), *Othello: The National Theatre Production* (London: Hart Davis, 1966) 2.
11. Bamber Gascoigne in *The Observer*. Repr. in Tynan 108.
12. Ronald Bryden in the *New Statesman*. Repr. in Tynan 106.
13. Tynan 7–8.
14. Bryden, in Tynan 106.
15. Tynan 10.
16. See Geoffrey Tillotson, *The Times Literary Supplement*, 20 July 1933, 494.
17. Stephen Booth, *SQ*, 28 (1977) 233.
18. Booth 234.

CHAPTER 14. *KING LEAR*

1. Charles Lamb, 'On the Tragedies of Shakespeare', *Works*, I, ed. T. Hutchinson (Oxford: Oxford University Press, 1908) 136.
2. Trewin, *Going to Shakespeare*, 205.
3. David, *Shakespeare in the Theatre*, 101.
4. Sprague, *Shakespeare and the Actors*, 286; and Sprague, *Shakespearian Players and Performances*, 37.
5. Aaron Hill, quoted in Speaight, *Shakespeare on the Stage*, 30; and Sprague, *Shakespearian Players*, 37.
6. See Marvin Rosenberg, *The Masks of King Lear* (Berkeley, Calif.: University of California Press, 1972), and a summary article, 'The Characterization of King Lear', *Deutsche Shakespeare-Gesellschaft West Jahrbuch 1974*, 34–47.
7. Kenneth Tynan, *A View of the English Stage 1944–63* (London: Davis-Poynter, 1975) 343.
8. The quotation is from David 97; see also G. L. Evans' review in *SQ*, 28 (1977) 192.
9. Lawrence O'Toole, *Maclean's Magazine*, 22 Oct 1979.
10. Ralph Berry, *SQ*, 31 (1980) 175.
11. Berry 174.
12. Berry 175.
13. *The Spectator*, 16 Nov 1962; Trewin, *Shakespeare on the English Stage*, 248.
14. Brook, *Empty Space*, 82.
15. Promptbook, Shakespeare Memorial Library.
16. Alan Dessen, *SQ*, 28 (1977) 249–50.
17. David 98.
18. Tynan 345.
19. David 97.
20. See Sprague, *Shakespearian Players*, 38.
21. David 104.
22. Trewin, *Shakespeare on the English Stage*, 249.

CHAPTER 15. *MACBETH*

1. Addenbrooke, *The Royal Shakespeare Company*, 149.
2. David, *Shakespeare in the Theatre*, 95.
3. Tynan, *A View of the English Stage*, 157.
4. David 91.
5. M. Rosenberg, 'Macbeth in Rehearsal', *Deutsche Shakespeare-Gesellschaft West Jahrbuch 1973*, 113–15; G. L. Evans, *SS*, 21 (1968) 119–20.
6. David 87.
7. Alan Dessen, *SQ*, 31 (1980) 279.
8. Roger Warren, *SS*, 30 (1977) 177.
9. Rosenberg 113–15.

10. Michael Mullin (ed.), *'Macbeth' Onstage: An Annotated Facsimile of Glen Byam Shaw's 1955 Promptbook* (Columbia, Mo. and London: University of Missouri Press, 1976) 65–7.
11. Rosenberg 118.
12. G. L. Evans, *SQ*, 28 (1977) 194.
13. Evans 194.
14. Evans 195.
15. Warren 178.
16. Sprague, *Shakespearian Players and Performances*, 65, 67.
17. Evans 194.
18. Warren 177; and Charles Marowitz, *New York Times*, 19 Mar 1978.
19. Mullin 219–20, 227.

CHAPTER 16. *CORIOLANUS*

1. Wells, *Royal Shakespeare*, 12, with a quotation from Frank Granville-Barker.
2. Lawrence Kitchin, *Midcentury Drama* (London: Faber, 1960) 143.
3. David, *Shakespeare in the Theatre*, 145.
4. Quoted in Trewin, *Going to Shakespeare*, 237.
5. 'A little talk' to Stratford Theatre Summer School, quoted in Wells 15–16.
6. Wells 16.
7. Nicholas de Jongh, quoted in *RSC Yearbook 1978*, 60.
8. Wells 10 and 18; Kitchin 143.
9. Wells 19–20. Kitchin (146–7) adds that Olivier 'convulsively retched', thus focusing the conflict between himself and his mother directly on the word 'mildly'.
10. Kitchin 148.
11. Kitchin 148.
12. In an interview with J. R. Mulryne, *SQ*, 29 (1978) 330–31.
13. See E. Le Roy Ladurie, *Carnival in Romans*, tr. Mary Feeney (New York: Braziller, 1979) 367ff., for a description of the various phases of protest and revolt in a traditional, hierarchical society, one that matches the action of *Coriolanus* remarkably well.
14. Tynan, *A View of the English Stage*, 264; see also Wells 21.
15. Mulryne interview 329, 332.

CHAPTER 17. *THE WINTER'S TALE*

1. Dan Ladell told me this anecdote and provided other useful information about this production.
2. Brook, *Empty Space*, 101–2.
3. B. A. Young, *Financial Times*, 7 Aug 1978.

4. For details about Stewart's performance, I am indebted to my friend Crispin Elsted.
5. Robert Speaight, *SQ*, 20 (1969) 437.
6. G. L. Evans, *SS*, 23 (1970) 134.
7. Brown, *Free Shakespeare*, 25.
8. Speaight 437; and Brown 25.
9. Speaight 437.
10. Crosse, *Shakespearian Playgoing*, 112.
11. Young.
12. Roger Warren, *SS*, 30 (1977) 174.
13. David, *Shakespeare in the Theatre*, 222–3.
14. Speaight 438.
15. Warren 174.
16. The phrase is Crispin Elsted's.
17. Ralph Berry, *SQ*, 30 (1979) 169–70.

CHAPTER 18. *THE TEMPEST*

1. Brook, *Empty Space*, 106.
2. Ronald Bryden, *The Observer*, 21 July 1968. Brook had already done a more conventional version of the play in 1957, with Gielgud as Prospero.
3. Clifford Williams, quoted in programme for 1963 production.
4. David Bevington, *The Complete Works of Shakespeare* (Glenview, Ill.: Scott, 1980) 1499.
5. Anne Barton's programme note for her husband's production speaks of Prospero's 'weariness and disillusion, coupled with a desire for rest'.
6. Berry, *On Directing Shakespeare*, 33–5.
7. The first phrase is from Anne Barton's programme note; the second, itself a quotation from Peter Brook, appears in the programme for both Phillips' and Barton's productions.
8. Berry 35.
9. This detail comes from Stratford Festival archivist Dan Ladell.
10. B. A. W. Jackson, *SQ*, 28 (1977) 201.
11. Jackson 200.
12. Berry 34–5.
13. Bernard Levin, *Sunday Times*, 7 May 1978.
14. Crosse, *Shakespearian Playgoing*, 29.
15. Sprague, *Shakespeare and the Actors*, 44.
16. Ladell (n. 9).
17. Clive Barnes, *New York Times*, 10 June 1976.
18. Irving Wardle, *The Times*, 3 May 1978.
19. Hilary Spurling, *The Spectator*, 27 June 1970, 855.
20. John Higgins, *The Times*, 17 Oct 1970.
21. William Babula, *SQ*, 28 (1977) 216.
22. Spurling, and Benedict Nightingale, *New Statesman*, 23 Oct 1970, 542.

23. Spurling.
24. Nightingale, *New Statesman*, 26 June 1970, 923, and 23 Oct 1970, 542.
25. John Pettigrew, *Journal of Canadian Studies*, 11.4, 46.
26. Sprague 44.

Index